Donation Commitment

100 percent of proceeds from the sales of *Waging Justice* will be donated to sustainable development.

Praise for Waging Justice

Waging Justice is a deeply personal story of courage and compassion with global implications. This heartfelt memoir shows how a doctor with vision can help fix what's broken in our world. Dr. Zeitz is a man of conscience who shares my commitment to bringing hope to the world's poor. Please read *Waging Justice*. You won't regret it!

—Archbishop Emeritus Desmond Tutu

I've known Paul since 2001 when we first teamed up in the global fight against HIV/AIDS, and we've worked together ever since. I'm moved by the backstory in *Waging Justice,* as Paul inspires me with his courage and tenacity. Put the biggest boulder in the path of the ambitious, stubborn, and hardworking Dr. Paul Zeitz and you can be sure he'll find a way around it. If not over it, under it, or around it, he'll grab a jackhammer and pound right through it. Paul is a driving force in ending the epidemics of AIDS, poverty, and sexual abuse that are raging through the world. Paul brings his can-do spirit to everything he does, including fighting for justice. This is a book you want to, no, you *have* to read. Dr. Zeitz's voice should be heard by everyone.

—Alicia Keys

"In a world of searing injustice and glaring inequality, Dr. Paul Zeitz is a reminder that love, truth, and compassion remain the strongest forces on earth. His story is inspiring, challenging, and hope-restoring. I hope *Waging Justice* is read widely and his example is emulated more widely still. With people like Dr. Zeitz on our side, achieving the Sustainable Development Goals (SDGs) is not just possible, it's distinctly probable."

—Dr. Tedros Adhanom Ghebreyesus, Director-General, World Health Organization

By raising his voice and standing up for what is right, Dr. Paul Zeitz's work has saved countless lives. Paul has made invaluable contributions to global health with his bold vision for addressing the AIDS crisis and his passionate advocacy in Washington and on the global stage. *Waging Justice* is a must-read for the peace and justice warriors of our time.

—U.S. Congresswoman Barbara Lee (CA-13)

Dr. Paul Zeitz's story is a combination of serving humanity according to his oath as a health professional and questioning the injustice and inequality surrounding us. He does so fearlessly, with courage and passion. *Waging Justice* is what everyone in the world who is working on sustainable development needs and a must-read for professionals and activists.

—Advocate Bience Gawanas, United Nations Under-Secretary General and Special Adviser on Africa

Waging Justice is one of those special books that shows someone to be ordinary and extraordinary at the same time. Dr. Paul Zeitz is just a regular guy but his journey so far has been nothing short of amazing. All of us have the "defiance gene," but Paul shows us that when you put your mind and heart to it, you can achieve wonderful things, whether at home or on the world stage. This book is inspiring, whether you want to be a better parent or want to end poverty around the world—or both.

—Dhananjayan Sriskandarajah, PhD, Secretary-General, CIVICUS

Waging Justice is an extraordinary testament to the courage of one man, Dr. Paul Zeitz, who fights to build a world of greater justice and equity. This is a story of a man with a vision and a mission, a man with deep determination to do as much as he can to help heal the world, and a man who finds ways to emerge from the burdens of personal trauma to be able to make a difference for others. In *Waging Justice*, Dr. Zeitz travels the world, sets up organizations, builds relationships, and speaks truth to power. Determined to wage justice, he would not let go of his vision, and as a result he has built amazing coalitions to bring health and justice to all people. Hundreds of thousands of children around the world owe their lives to his actions.

—Ruth W. Messinger, Global Ambassador, American Jewish World Service

Waging Justice is a moving story that traces the path of a life dedicated to seeking justice. Dr. Paul Zeitz takes us on a journey of global activism for equality that is forged in a very personal mission to reclaim and rediscover dignity. This memoir is a fascinating, intimate exploration of the connection between confronting personal challenges and taking effective public action. *Waging Justice* is valuable reading for anyone interested in the personal seeds of political change.

—Chris Collins, President, Friends of the Global Fight Against AIDS, Tuberculosis, and Malaria

Dr. Paul Zeitz is a passionate, articulate, and visionary change-maker—but above all he is courageous, showing us how healing oneself and healing the world are intricately connected. *Waging Justice* is truly trailblazing, a book that stands up to centuries of taboo and secrecy, and opens a door, allowing ALL of us who have experienced sexual violence to come forward. *Waging Justice* invites us to let go of the shame we often carry, and to be part of a global and inclusive healing movement.

—Daniela Ligiero, CEO, Together for Girls

A bold, honest, and courageous tale by an unusual human being. Dr. Paul Zeitz bares it all in this story of his life's struggles to find inner peace whilst fighting injustices of this world. From a dedicated AIDS activist who fought so hard to help so many in Africa, *Waging Justice* is captivating and full of surprises, making it difficult to put down.

—Ngozi Okonjo-Iweala, Chair, Global Alliance for Vaccines and Immunization (GAVI) and Former Finance Minister, Nigeria

Waging Justice provides an intimate slice of the history of the global fight against AIDS, and is a story of personal healing, frankly told. Dr. Paul Zeitz is a hero in the fight against the AIDS pandemic who transformed personal pain into a global commitment to boldly tackle the injustices that have allowed this pandemic to persist. Coming at a time when the United States government is wavering in its commitment to bring the AIDS pandemic to an end, this book is an important appeal on behalf of millions of people whose lives are at stake.

—Reverend Charles King, President & CEO, Housing Works

Waging Justice is a savagely honest account of faith, love, and conviction. Dr. Paul Zeitz's quest to sustain passion and compassion through physical, mental, and professional barriers reads like a roadmap for anyone seeking to know thyself in order to serve others. Through the decades of navigating turmoil both global and internal, Dr. Zeitz exemplifies qualities of youth with the boundless energy and magnetic optimism that continue to permeate his work.

—Katherine Kennedy Townsend, Executive Director, Open Data Collaboratives

Waging Justice is a significant book that inspires and charms, but most importantly, it is a book that helps us know the personal as political. The courage it takes to transform the world is the very same courage that is needed to heal ourselves. With beauty and humor, Dr. Zeitz shows us that it is only through our own personal healing that we find the hope, resilience, and valor to change the world.

—Rabbi Shefa Gold, Author of *Are We There Yet? Inspirations for Travel*

A very personal and mission-critical story, *Waging Justice* traces the genesis of one man's fierce social justice activism to its roots in his own lived experience of injustice and pain. Dr. Paul Zeitz takes us through the maze of trenches on the front line in the war against HIV/AIDS and reveals a rich tapestry—from the very personal to the brutally political struggle of the world's 36 million who live everyday with HIV. *Waging Justice* is a story of commitment, determination, vision, and belief—it inspires hope in all of us that one little step in the right direction can transform the self and the world for better and for good.

—Jon O' Brien, President, Catholics for Choice

Waging Justice is an amazing book that you'll want to read twice. Once holding your breath as a poignant story of abuse, incest, and reconciliation unfolds. A second time to savor the vision, integrity, honesty, and energy of a man of justice who inspires us all to fight a little harder for the world's children.

—Jennifer Margulis, Ph.D., Award-Winning Author, *Your Baby, Your Way*, and co-author, *The Addiction Spectrum*

Dr. Paul Zeitz has been at the center of transforming health rights denial and climate chaos, two of the planet's greatest challenges. His story that is deeply personal and political at the same time. *Waging Justice* is relevant in a world where we have the knowledge and financial resources to keep the entire world safe, healthy and dignified, yet millions die needlessly.

—Irũngũ Houghton, Executive Director, Amnesty International Kenya

Reading *Waging Justice* is an opportunity to walk in the shoes of a doctor turned humanitarian and turned fighter for social justice during the height of the AIDS crisis and beyond. It's an intimate journey through the Dr. Zeitz's fascinating life and how he came to make the choices that so few often do. It's inspiring to witness his transformation and provides the reader with hope for our future. Waging Justice is highly recommended for all to read.

—Susan McPherson, Founder and CEO, McPherson Strategies

I honor Dr. Paul Zeitz, a bold and courageous physician and activist, for the way he has chosen to share his truth and passion in such a vulnerable, riveting memoir. The tremendously inspiring *Waging Justice* motivates all of us to join together to combat the many ills and injustices of our society. From a psychological perspective, this memoir beautifully chronicles how facing our inner demons empowers us to be able to thrive even more in our personal and professional lives, and intimately demonstrates the power of love in overcoming significant life barriers. Today more than ever, Dr. Zeitz's story stands as a testimony for how one man can make a tremendous difference, offering hope in a time when it can be difficult to hold on. And although one person can achieve greatness, when he or she joins forces with other passionate, loving, justice-seeking pioneers, the impact on millions is felt globally.

—Dr. Howard Fradkin, Author, *Joining Forces: Empowering Male Survivors to Thrive*

Waging Justice

A DOCTOR'S JOURNEY
TO SPEAK TRUTH AND BE BOLD

DR. PAUL ZEITZ

BALBOA
PRESS
A DIVISION OF HAY HOUSE

Balboa Press books may be ordered through booksellers or by contacting:

Balboa Press
A Division of Hay House
1663 Liberty Drive
Bloomington, IN 47403
www.balboapress.com
1 (877) 407-4847

Printed in the United States of America.

ISBN: 978-1-9822-0542-3 (sc)
ISBN: 978-1-9822-0544-7 (hc)
ISBN: 978-1-9822-0543-0 (e)

Library of Congress Control Number: 2018906485

Balboa Press rev. date: 07/31/2018

Contents

PART 3   DEMONSTRATION

For Mindi Eve Cohen

I am my beloved and my beloved is mine.

—Song of Songs, 6.3

PART ONE
Formation

*The future belongs to those who believe
in the beauty of their dreams.*

—Eleanor Roosevelt

CHAPTER 1

Things Are Not Always as They Appear

MOM wanted another child after my sister, Marci, was born. Dad was ready to stop trying, but Mom was determined. Her persistence paid off and three years later, on May 17, 1962, I was born in Northeast Philadelphia, the second child and only son of Sandy and Mark Zeitz. Eager to be part of this world, I arrived about a month before my due date.

We lived in a small, recently constructed twin row house in a burgeoning multi-ethnic neighborhood. My earliest memory is of a day when I was about two years old. I was outside and saw Mom was in the passenger seat of a car pulling out of our driveway. I was panicked and confused, because I didn't know where she was going. I started running down the block after her as fast as my toddler legs could carry me, past a dozen rowhomes, until I finally tripped on a crack in the sidewalk and fell flat on my face. My two front teeth lay on the concrete, their tiny baby roots still attached. Bloodied and terrified, I watched the car carrying Mom turn the corner and vanish.

A stranger rushed to my side, and then my mom's mother, Grandma Rose, who was watching me, came running down the block.

Mom never saw me fall.

A rushed trip to the dentist turned out to be futile, as we were told that my two front teeth couldn't be reattached. I lived with an embarrassing gap until I was eight years old and my adult teeth mercifully arrived. Seven years later, I ended up with a minor speech impediment and a mouthful of expensive braces.

My parents were in the Philly cheesesteak and hoagie business. By the time I was born, they owned two shops in Northeast Philadelphia, both called Mark's Luncheonette, named after Dad, though everyone called him Mickey. My parents worked long, hard hours, coming home at night wearing the overwhelmingly pungent smell of fried onions.

Grandma Freda, my father's mother, lived directly above one shop, so Marci and I would spend weekends at her place while my parents worked downstairs. Her husband, Pop-Pop Ben, was in a nursing home, suffering from end-stage diabetes. His legs had been amputated and he was in a vegetative state. I never recall meeting him. Dad rarely visited him, and when we did, Mom, Marci, and I waited in the car while Dad went inside for a little while.

Dad inherited his first hoagie shop from his parents and bought the second one in partnership with his older brother. But the second Mark's Luncheonette failed when I was very young. Something bad must have happened, because my father and his brother didn't talk to each other for more than twenty years.

There were other mysteries. When Mom was only four years old, her mother and father separated, then later divorced. I met Pop-Pop Marty for the first time when he unexpectedly showed up on our doorstep. Mom hovered nervously as I watched this unfamiliar man wander through the house, talking to the pictures on our living room wall. Marci ran to her room in fear, but I was more curious. I stayed close to Mom, trying to figure out what was going on. Mom served him lunch, and we tried to make sense of his mumblings.

Later, Mom told me that Pop-Pop Marty had been hospitalized several times for severe schizophrenia. He probably had other mental illnesses, too, but had somehow escaped permanent institutionalization. Pop-Pop Marty spent his days selling Philly soft pretzels at the stadium, and his nights sleeping in a halfway house on Erie Avenue.

Marci was always my greatest friend. Three-and-a-half years older than me, she cared for me, made my bed for me, and played with me. I was her living doll whom she spoiled endlessly. On Saturday mornings, we would throw a blanket on the carpet in front of the small black-and-white TV. When we got bored with cartoons, we played "Boat" or "House."

When Marci played with her friends, I was the tag-along little brother. But I was a shy little boy and usually preferred to stay at home, reading or watching one of the handful of TV stations we received via the VHF antenna on the roof—often reruns of *Gilligan's Island* and *The Lone Ranger*. Cartoons like *Scooby-Doo* and *Dennis the Menace* were my favorites. Mom wanted me to be more social, so she became a Cub Scout den mother. For a while, groups of blue-uniformed boys would tromp into our home once a week, but that didn't last long. I never enjoyed the group activities. I felt more comfortable being a quiet observer, hanging out with Marci.

My father, an avid fisherman, owned a series of mid-size fishing boats, named Mammy I, Mammy II, Mammy III, and so on. The family often went on fishing trips to the Delaware River, the Jersey Shore, and the Chesapeake Bay, but I never liked fishing as a kid. I was terrified of the deep water and thought the fish guts and scales were gross. I even hated the taste of fish.

But my dad always seemed happier and freer on the water. On land, he was a more volatile and angry man.

We were Conservative Jews, moderately religious but very committed to the cultural and family bonds of Jewish holidays and rituals. We kept kosher in the house, but my parents were flexible with the rules, letting us occasionally eat Chinese food with pork and shrimp at the card table in the downstairs den—as long as it was on paper plates with plastic forks. If the pork wasn't in the kitchen and didn't touch the kosher plates, it was okay with my parents (and, presumably, with God). We celebrated all the Jewish holidays with our extended family and immersed ourselves in the cultural, food-oriented side of Jewish life.

I went to a Jewish nursery school at a place called the Neighborhood Center but entered the Philadelphia public school system in kindergarten. My first-grade teacher was a middle-aged, African-American woman named Mrs. Ridgely. I liked her, because she was always kind to me. One day she gave me a special present—a book called *The Wishing Well*.

My favorite first-grade subject was science, but I also enjoyed our art lessons. One day, we were doing a project that involved drawing large, multicolored flowers with crayons. We then covered the flowers with black India ink and scratched the ink off with blunt scissors. The flowers reappeared with a very different look and patina. I was happily coloring my flowers in bold red, green, and yellow tones when the kid next to me asked me why I was using the same colors that Mrs. Ridgely had used in her example. I became indignant and thought, *I didn't do that!*

With the last name Zeitz, I was seated in the back of the room. I marched all the way up to the front, past forty pairs of inquisitive eyes, to gather more evidence. I looked closely at the teacher's flowers and reaffirmed that yes, hers were different colors from mine. Seeking to confirm what I already knew was true, I confidently asked Mrs. Ridgely if my colors were the same as hers.

She looked at me quizzically. "Yes, Paul, they are," she said gently.

I was stunned and twisted with confusion, even as my teacher patted my shoulder and reassured me that it was quite all right to use the same colors.

I walked back to my seat with my head down and slumped in my chair, my untrustworthy eyes squeezed shut.

I had no possible explanation for why my classmates' eyes and brains were seeing things differently than I was. The young scientist in me was deeply shaken. This was the moment I became aware that not everything was as it appeared. And no two people ever see the world in an identical way.

The following week, hanging around the hoagie shop, I was talking to one of Dad's part-time employees, Dan, who was studying optometry. Even as a six-year-old, I had respect for men of science. Mom had the idea to ask Dan if he thought there might be something wrong with my eyes. He brought out a special color-vision testing book and pointed to pictures of several circles containing dozens of different-sized, multicolored dots, which looked like bubbles to me. He asked me if I could see the number formed by the dots. On many of the pages, I couldn't see anything.

I learned that day that I was severely red-green color-blind. I don't see the world in only black and white, but I have a hard time distinguishing many shades of color. I frequently see something as blue when others see it as purple, and I'm always unsure of what color I'm seeing with shades of brown, red, and green. I can easily see red traffic lights. I can see the red-feathered breast of a robin if it is flying nearby. But I have a hard time distinguishing the red breast of a robin if it is sitting in a tree, surrounded by green leaves. I don't see all the shades of a rainbow. Sunrises look very different to me than they do to most people: I can't distinguish the subtle pink, reddish, and orange shades that I'm told can be seen. When I'm getting dressed for work, I must ask someone if the colors in my tie, jacket, and shirt are matching—as I tend to go terribly awry without assistance.

Although Dan had crouched on one knee while he gently explained that there was nothing wrong with me—that my eyes simply worked differently from other people's—the truth is that this information made me feel different, alone, and afraid.

I knew this wasn't "normal." All I ever wanted to be was "normal."

I learned a profound lesson that day as a six-year-old: I could never "blindly" trust what I saw with my own eyes; I had to investigate beneath the surface.

After that, whenever anyone heard that I was color-blind, they would point at their clothes or at an object and ask me over and over, "What color is this?" "What color is that?" I usually couldn't tell. While this was a great game for my friends, who would guffaw with laughter, their eyes wide with disbelief, it was very annoying for me.

Meanwhile, things weren't as they appeared at home either.

While both my parents were very smart, they never went to college. They worked hard, and the hoagie shop supported our little family. Like most young children, I thought my family was solidly in the normal range. I imagined that my parents were happy and successful. But, also like many families, there was a lot going on behind closed doors.

CHAPTER 2

Defiance Burger

OUR parents deeply loved us—that I never doubted. But my father's rage seemed to simmer perpetually below the surface. He threw plates of food in outbursts during dinner. Fist-sized holes appeared in the walls. Months later, the holes would be patched with uneven plaster, but I could always see where they had been.

Dad never actually beat me, but he regularly threatened to, screaming at me whenever he was in a foul mood. He kept a black belt and a police baton in his bedroom that he promised would be used on me. "You *stupid* kid!" he would scream, picking up the belt and snapping it in my direction. I don't remember what it was that I did all those times to enrage him so, but I do remember that he terrorized me regularly. He didn't need to unleash these weapons on me. His anger was enough.

I remember one time when his mother questioned or challenged him in the hoagie shop, he exploded. He frequently yelled at her, in front of customers, when they battled over issues about the business.

By the time I was eight years old, I began preparing the lunchmeats at the shop, and with each year came more responsibility—making hoagies, cleaning tables, and even taking orders.

But food wasn't my friend then. A picky eater and naturally scrawny, I liked simple food—homemade chicken noodle soup *without* chicken and no carrots please, or plain spaghetti with butter. My Grandma Freda, who had immigrated from Romania as a young girl, constantly pestered Mom by asking if she was feeding me. "That boy is too skinny," she would say, shaking her head.

Mom tried, making a home-cooked dinner most nights and insisting I eat what she put on the table. One night, when Mom had made hamburgers for dinner, I refused to eat. I hated hamburgers. They were gross, especially the chunks of fat and gristle. But eating the prepared meal was the rule, and no one was to be excused until the act was completed. On this night for some reason, Mom decided to test the full measure of my will. Long after Mom, Dad, and Marci had finished their food, I sat, unresponsive, unmoved. Mom cleaned the entire kitchen and turned off the light, leaving me in the dark at the kitchen table with my plate and the single bun-less burger.

As I stared at that cold, gray disk of meat, a deep surge of defiance began swelling up from deep inside me, and a single truth crystallized in my mind: *I would never, ever eat that burger.*

After leaving me sitting for more than an hour in the dark—which felt like forever to me—Mom relented. She turned on the lights, cleared the lone burger from the table, and angrily told me to go to my room. I left the table, hungry but victorious.

Defiance of stupid rules set by the status quo would become a theme of my life. That trait would mostly serve me well in waging justice—but not always.

I was an extremely jealous and sensitive child, and I always thought people were doing things to hurt my feelings—except for Marci, who was always kind to me and made me feel safe. It was only when she started dating boys that I felt excluded. I was no longer her spoiled little doll; I became the annoying little brother who spied resentfully on her antics in the den.

For much of my childhood and adolescence, I struggled with painful, malevolent emotions I didn't understand. I knew that I hated my father. But I also hated myself, feeling implicated in everything happening around me at home—the yelling, the pointless rules, the forced fishing trips, the pretense that we were a happy family like everyone else. I even hated how much I hated Dad. I would lie in bed, fists clenched, telling myself, *I will never be like him! I will never be a father like that!*

As I progressed through grade school, I became profoundly introverted, choosing hobbies that kept me isolated in my room. While I didn't like going fishing, I convinced Dad to get me a fish tank. I loved taking care of the fish, and they were the subjects of my first scientific studies. I created a daily chart that tracked the number of living fish, sick fish, pregnant fish, and eggs hatched. I had a stack of mimeographed blank charts to fill in with daily status reports. I was a young epidemiologist (although I didn't know that word at the time), falling in love with the science of studying disease and risk factors in my fish. My neon tetras always got sick and died from something I called "ick." The black and white striped angelfish proved to be the hardiest.

I eventually got a chemistry set that came with small bottles of dozens of different chemicals. In my room I conducted secret experiments and concocted toxic potions. I also liked pretending I was a schoolteacher—I had about 30 imaginary students, and I developed lesson plans for them, regularly giving them exams and quizzes. The most fun for me was scoring these exams and diligently recording the daily details of each student's attendance and performance in a grade book someone had given me. Mom was so worried about my involvement with my imaginary students that she had a conference with my teachers. They reassured her that I was a just being a normal, albeit highly creative, kid.

CHAPTER 3

Young Patriot

My other great interest was American history. Growing up in Philadelphia, we went on annual school field trips to Independence Hall when the Liberty Bell was still there. I remember running my hands over the bell, wondering how it would sound, desperate to know how it got cracked.

I was awed by the idea that George Washington, Thomas Jefferson, John Adams, and James Madison had walked in the same streets that I walked. I loved visiting the house of my hero Benjamin Franklin and looking over all his cunning inventions. But my favorite place was Betsy Ross's house, near Elfreth's Alley, a street in Philadelphia that dates to 1702. I would crawl up the circular stairwell of the snug Colonial home, imagining her sitting by the woodstove sewing the first American flag.

We visited the quiet, upright Christ Church, which the guide told us was built in 1695, with its white marble gravestones, hand-carved balusters, and dark oak pews. I touched the gleaming wood where George and Martha

Washington had once sat. They were actual, real people, just like me! I wondered if they hated going to church as much as I hated going to synagogue.

I especially loved the parchment replicas of the Declaration of Independence, the Constitution, and the Bill of Rights, along with the Revolution-era money. But unlike my other classmates, I was never interested in the muskets or any other tools of violence.

Dad was a prolific and ostentatious gift-giver to everyone, and he often bought me presents, including weapons. For a while, I had a small replica iron cannon that sat on my bedroom floor, untouched. One day he brought home a replica of a seven-foot whale harpoon and hung it on my bedroom wall. I hated it. Just the thought of killing whales made me sick. But once, Dad came home with a replica of Gilbert Stuart Williamstown's portrait of George Washington, which I cherished.

Israel was a constant source of tension in my household. Dad had been obsessed since he attended a Zionist camp in New Jersey when he was nine years old. One day, he asked the counselor why there was no flag for Israel among the national banners on display. "In your lifetime, we will have a flag," the counselor promised, "And you will live to see it." That was 1945. Three years later, the State of Israel was born. For 12-year-old Mickey Zeitz, this prophecy-come-true ignited a lifelong passion for Israel, anchoring him to the idea of a Jewish homeland.

Mom was not so impressed. Dad wanted to take her to Israel for their honeymoon in 1957 when he was 21 and she was 19, but Grandma Rose nixed the idea. She would not allow her daughter to travel to such an unsafe and distant country. They had to settle for Miami Beach. But Dad managed to get Mom to Israel on their tenth wedding anniversary in 1967, a few months after the Six-Day War. On that trip, Dad connected with his Israeli family, including his father's half-brother. He came home talking about our family emigrating to Israel.

Then a Jerusalem-born Palestinian immigrant assassinated Robert F. Kennedy. My parents had cast their first votes for John F. Kennedy in 1961. Two years later, they went to the U.S. Capitol in Washington, D.C., to pay tribute to his body lying in state. Mom saved a suitcase full of newspaper and magazine clippings from the months after JFK was assassinated.

So in June, 1968, we watched black-and-white images of RFK's funeral on our small TV, unable to hear over the sound of Mom sobbing uncontrollably. Finally, unable to contain her grief, Mom sent me to the neighbor's, where everyone sat in quiet shock, which was just as bad.

The loss of another Kennedy, in a senseless act of political violence, left Mom in despair for the future of the United States. For the rest of 1968, I remember hearing on the radio a version of "What the World Needs Now Is Love," intermixed with speeches by JFK, RFK, and Martin Luther King, Jr. Mom always turned up the volume.

Mom's passion for these lost heroes rippled into my DNA. I was too little to understand the sort of justice and freedom the Kennedys and MLK stood for, but I knew that they were the kind of men Mom loved and respected—men of integrity.

Soon after the RFK tragedy, Dad started planning another visit to Israel. Mom refused. Stubbornly, Dad bought a single ticket and packed several suitcases. Standing at the door the night of his departure, he bent down and looked me in the eyes, his expression grave. His words were ominous: "I'm leaving. You're the man of the house now. You have to take care of the family."

What did I know about taking care of a family? I was seven. I felt scared and inadequate. Mom sobbed as Dad departed; my sister and I clung to each side of her. I felt abandoned, but also a little relieved. Unlike the Kennedys, Dad was not the kind of man Mom respected.

He had left the impression he was never coming back. Still, my shoulders relaxed as the taxi drove him away. I would be the only boy in the house. Mom and Marci could focus on spoiling me.

But Dad returned a few weeks later. I drew deeper into myself than ever before, doing everything I could to avoid him around the house and trying to pretend he had never returned. His rage was worse than ever. Many of my memories of the next year buried themselves and remained hidden for the next four decades.

CHAPTER 4

Israel

Two years later, in 1971, Dad got his way, and all four of us went to the Holy Land for a ten-day summer trip. I think he still yearned to move our family to Israel, but I didn't care. At nine years old, I was just excited to travel so far away from home. We flew first to New York City. At JFK airport, we had to sit on the terminal floor for 12 hours because of flight delays. Groups of likewise stranded hippies with long hair sang folk music all night long. It was fun to me and I joined in when I knew the words.

We started our journey through Israel in a tiny rental car, with Dad negotiating a narrow, two-lane road to Jerusalem, stopping a few times to enjoy the vistas and investigate the bombed-out trucks and tanks from Israel's wars along the road. As we headed north, Dad insisted on picking up hitchhiking Israeli soldiers with machine guns. At first, it was terrifying to be crammed together with young, intense-looking Israeli men and women—strangers with huge guns—but I got used to it after a few days.

We visited not only the Western Wall—where Mom and Marci had to stay behind in the segregated women's area—but we also got to see the Dome of the Rock, an Islamic holy site that is much more difficult to visit nowadays.

The greatest part of the trip was meeting our newly discovered relatives, Israel Zeitz—half-brother of my grandfather Ben Zeitz—his wife Massy, their only daughter, Shiffra, her much older husband, Yonaton, and their beautiful teenage daughter, Arnona. At their small apartment in the heart of Tel Aviv, we shared a feast, including my favorite, chicken noodle soup, without the chicken. I was fascinated that I was related to these people who spoke with funny accents and loved me at once. They gave me a gold Jewish star necklace and a bunch of gold-laced postcards of the holy sites. Arnona showed us her bedroom and she sang us some folk songs as she played her guitar.

Soon after our return to the U.S, our family moved to a new neighborhood. From our small, urban house, we upgraded to a single-family home in the suburbs of Huntingdon Valley, Pennsylvania. We were like the Jefferson's from the TV sitcom, "movin' on up" to a richer neighborhood. Our new house overlooked a large back yard with a creek and a forested hill. My new surroundings pulled me out of my room, and I fell in love with nature as I hiked through the wooded areas around the tract of homes.

One afternoon, soon after we moved in, a gang of three kids around my age knocked on our door. I had watched them approach our house from my bedroom window, and by the time they got to our doorstep, I was hiding under my parents' bed. I was so shy, I had never had close friends beyond my sister and her crowd. But I was intrigued by these brave kids who boldly approached my house simply because they had spotted the "new kid" in the neighborhood. When the trio said they wanted to meet me, Mom came to find me, finally dragging me from under the bed and sending me downstairs. They convinced me to venture outside and into the neighborhood with them, and that day I met all their families and pets, and our lifelong bonds of camaraderie and fun began.

Barry, Kenny, Ellen, and I were inseparable over the next few years. We practically lived at each other houses. We liked the same foods and sang the same songs. I was fascinated by Barry's talent for comic impersonations of people we knew and his way of making up new words and imaginary characters. When I came home from hours of play, Mom would yell, "Stop talking like Barry!" when I said nonsense like "Doouba day!" as I pretended I was on an exotic vacation with the imaginary character of "Vivian Bardell Otzmiooti Bibble!"

For as long as I can remember, I liked to create and name new organizations, so I started calling us The Committee. With these soul friends, I yearned to seal the bonds of trust and commitment by creating the four of us as an entity.

Two years after The Committee first convened, my family and I went back to Israel, this time for a five-week trip over the summer of 1973. We rented an apartment in Herzliya, a suburb on the Mediterranean Sea just north of Tel Aviv. Dad was still trying to make his dream of a life in Israel come true. By this time, I was defiantly opposed to such a move, not wanting to leave The Committee or our school. Still, I was entranced by the beauty of the Mediterranean, the soft sandy beaches, and the gentle cooling winds that blew through the warm night.

On this trip, we visited Yad Vashem, the Holocaust museum in Jerusalem. It confused me. At age 11, I could not grasp why so many people had been killed. *Just because they were Jews?* It made no sense.

I got very sick with a virus that summer and spent a full three weeks of our five-week vacation in bed in the small apartment. The trip was not going according to plan, and tensions between my parents were simmering. Mom used my illness as a reason to prove to Dad it wasn't safe to move to Israel.

When I didn't get better, my parents took me to an Israeli doctor to check for mononucleosis. It was the first time I can remember having blood drawn. Mom told me not to watch, but I couldn't help it. I was horrified—and riveted. As we left the doctor's office, images of dark fluid squirting out of me and filling a collection tube lingered unwanted in my head, and I felt myself getting dizzy. The world faded around me before I passed out on the street.

Within seconds, a gaggle of Israeli women surrounded me, screaming for help and smacking my face and wrists. Someone brought me a cold soda, and after a few minutes I had recovered. My queasiness with blood would remain a challenge for the rest of my life.

By the end of the trip, it was clear our family would not be moving as a unit to Israel. But I was more fascinated than ever by the place, and by my Jewish heritage. Unfortunately, along with that heritage came the obligation of spending three afternoons a week at a conservative Hebrew school, on top of public school.

At Hebrew school we learned about the Holocaust from an elderly woman named Judith, with graying blond hair and numbers tattooed on her forearm. She was an Auschwitz survivor. Her accent was so heavy, I had to listen carefully to understand her stories, but I wanted every detail. I wanted to understand.

For several classes, she showed black-and-white films of the Nazi death camps and piles of bodies being moved by tractors for burning. She told us how she was evicted from her house, separated from her family, and forced to endure long marches from one camp to another. A miraculous series of coincidences and twists of fate aligned to secure her survival and that of others she helped.

During a long winter march through a forest she fell into a ditch. She was exhausted and cold but she decided to stay hidden, even though she was separated from the people she knew. Hours later, she walked alone toward a river, and, extraordinarily, found someone with a boat to take her across. During the crossing, the boat was commandeered by the Nazis. The young girl slipped overboard and somehow swam to shore and escaped capture.

Judith wept as she told us her stories. I was horrified by the level of suffering that she endured but awed by the lucky happenstances that allowed her to survive against all odds. This woman had witnessed the death of her family and the destruction of her entire community.

At age 12, her experiences hit deep into my soul.

What would I do, faced with her journey?

How would I behave?

Would I lose my faith when surrounded by so much hopelessness and evil?

Would I leave people behind to save myself?

Would I just give up?

Honestly, I couldn't fully imagine the situation that Judith, nor the other Jews, gypsies, Poles, homosexuals, and others endured—nearly 10 million people in total—hunted down and murdered by the Nazis. And there were millions more who were imprisoned, tortured, and abused, carrying the scars of that trauma to their graves.

"Never again," I remember Judith saying. "This can never happen to our people again!"

But my young mind jumped over that profound mantra and settled on something that seemed more important:

How did they let it happen?

What forces were at work that allowed millions of people to know there was a genocide going on right in front of them, but do nothing about it?

Who were these heartless neighbors?

Didn't other powerful countries know what was happening?

How could they turn away?

Judith left an indelible mark on me because of her willingness to openly share those traumatic moments from her life—she constantly wept and dried her eyes, going through a box of tissues during each class, week after week. It occurred to me that she must have told her story hundreds of times, yet it still shattered her. Still, she showed me how a "normal" person can find the spirit and drive to wage justice, even when all the odds were against her, and the barriers seemingly insurmountable.

As we grew older, Barry, Kenny, and Ellie would tease me about being obsessed with death. Whenever we drove by a cemetery, I would ask them what they imagined about the people buried there and wonder aloud about what our lives would have amounted to by the time we were six feet under. I was The Committee's existential philosopher, trying to figure out the meaning of life and death.

CHAPTER 5

Becoming a Campaigner

In 1980, the fall after high school graduation, I landed at Muhlenberg College in Allentown. I moved into the dorms on a sunny morning in late August, unloading books and boxes into my tiny third-floor dorm room at the far end of Prosser Hall. After unpacking and meeting my roommate, I allowed my fastidious mother to make my bed for the last time.

My parents barely held themselves together for the send-off. As we hugged goodbye, Mom cried and Dad looked blank—he was ready to go. I turned around and walked away from it all.

I felt eager and hopeful. A new chapter of my life was beginning. I was going to set my own path, away from the emotional tumult that engulfed me during childhood. Although Allentown was just an hour north of Philadelphia, I felt free. I planned to study biology and I was going to be a doctor and a campaigner for people who needed my help.

As a pre-med, I was required to take a full year of calculus as a freshman. Our professor was new to Muhlenberg and a poor teacher. He couldn't even explain the basics or solve the problems he was supposed to be teaching us.

I was paying for part of my college education, working on campus, and my parents were struggling financially. It outraged me that I was investing money in this lousy professor who couldn't teach. Knowing my goal of becoming a doctor would be compromised by bad calculus grades, I decided to mount a campaign to oust my professor. I wanted to protect not just myself, but future students from suffering. The situation was unjust. We all just wanted to learn.

I mobilized a group of classmates to meet with the dean of students, who subsequently launched an investigation. Classroom observations proved our point, and the professor was gone by the end of the spring semester. I ended up with two semesters of Cs in calculus, significantly pulling down my GPA, but it didn't matter. I felt happy. I realized I had the power to get an incompetent professor fired. Though I had wasted two semesters when I could have been learning math, I had set in motion institutional change that helped others: Future students wouldn't have to be subjected to incompetent instruction.

Being away from my family and in college opened something up in me. This former introvert made lots of friends, joined a fraternity, and started to get involved in causes. I even ran for student government in my freshman year under the banner of *Vote Zeitz, He'll Fight for Your Rights!* It sort of rhymed, right? I enjoyed walking the halls of the dorms and catching friends at the cafeteria and encouraging them to vote for me. I didn't win, but an upper classman I respected came up and congratulated me on a great run as a freshman and a newcomer to student politics. I still really like the slogan…*Vote Zeitz, He'll Fight for Your Rights!* Catchy, right?

Spring semester freshman year, Marci was rescued from the family home by a man, her knight in shining armor. Not long after her wedding, my parents announced they were getting a divorce. Their marriage had been dead for a long time, and now they'd done their duty of raising us children to adulthood. Marci and I were not surprised: We'd both seen this coming for a long time.

Because money was so tight, Mom and Dad co-habited for nearly a year until they could sell our childhood home. They fought over family heirlooms and a framed painting of a rabbi. Their relationship was so explosive that when I came home from college for breaks, I stayed at Marci's house.

This was definitely not normal. I felt sad and embarrassed. I also felt angry at Dad for hurting Mom. My sister and I ferociously defended Mom. I felt my mother had been unfairly treated.

Gradually, though, I began to see Dad's experience differently. After a lifetime of effort to support our family he had suddenly lost his wife, his house, and his children. He was lonely, broke, and was now living uncomfortably with the older brother he'd cut off decades before. It was a sad state of affairs, and a wave of empathy for him welled up within my heart. Wanting to be fair, I consciously set a goal of breaking down the walls built up between us. While I was at college, we started to have dinner together a couple of times a year. At first, it was awkward. We engaged in the most banal conversations imaginable. Part of me still hated him. But I knew he needed my support, and I was willing to give it.

One of Dad's most irksome traits was buying things he couldn't afford. This was why we grew up in a tiny house where we never had dining room furniture, but always had boats and at least one sports car. It's also why, my sophomore year of college, he bought me a brand-new Z/28 Camaro, flashy and green, without mentioning a word about it to me beforehand.

I hated that car. I was struggling to pay for college and I felt like a fool driving around the streets of economically depressed Allentown behind the wheel of a pricey muscle car that expressed the exact opposite of who I felt like inside. To top it off, the car was a lemon. I made more than half a dozen trips to the dealership to fix factory problems. The car's bad mileage, the waste of my time, and the stress of it breaking down all the time galled me. Finally, Dad replaced it—with another Camaro, this one glittering and bright red. It was a relief when I finally traded that car in for a common blue Volkswagen Fox a few years later. Dependable, sensible, and understated, Volkswagens were more my speed.

I tried to maintain close ties with Mom and Marci throughout my peacemaking attempts with Dad. I felt caught between two warring camps. Things got nasty at times, and I was dismayed that people who used to eat dinner together every night and lived together as family for nearly 20 years could hate each other so much. Holding grudges was a habit in my family. One that I wanted to change.

I deliberately positioned myself differently. I committed myself to be a bridge connecting both sides of my nuclear family. At that time, I was naïve and hopeful. There was a lot I didn't know about what had really gone on inside my childhood home.

CHAPTER 6

Becoming a Healer

MY academic snags continued sophomore year of college, when my pre-med advisor contacted my parents to tell them my grades were not sufficient to pursue medicine, and I should select another academic track.

I was outraged. How could anyone decide that I couldn't be a doctor, just because I had a lousy and incompetent calculus teacher? I believed my pre-med advisor was himself incompetent for making such a rash judgment about my future. *He barely knew me!*

My defiance gene, first sparked years ago by that unjust and bun-less hamburger, was now fully activated. I told myself *I* would be the one to decide what academic path to pursue. No one else. I told my parents to ignore my pre-med advisor, and I buckled down, worked hard to improve my grades, and got back on track.

I was on my way to becoming a scientist, alongside my two best college buddies, Marty Duvall and David Weber. Both from rural Westminster, Maryland, Marty and David were childhood best friends and neighbors. We all pledged the fraternity Zeta Beta Tau, where they were among the very few non-Jewish brothers. We bonded during an intense hazing: We were tarred with corn syrup and feathered, made to swim in a freezing lake, and collectively forced to drink a huge vat of cold, chunky split pea soup.

David was my lab partner in organic chemistry. When I got frustrated with the complex experiments, he taught me to practice patience and precision. Marty was my study buddy. When I was overwhelmed by the masses of information we had to memorize for organic chemistry, Marty spent hours with me in a conference room on the top floor of the science building organizing the volumes of formulas onto a one-pager. Their science minds rubbed off on me as I learned to discipline myself, synthesize the materials, and study with a determination to succeed. I delved into molecular and cellular biochemistry, my intellectual passion at the time, without looking back.

While academics and socializing were the main focus of my college years, I also wanted to serve others. Being so intrigued by the Kennedys, I was attracted to the Special Olympics, founded by Eunice Kennedy Shriver, sister of JFK and RFK, and her husband Sargent Shriver.

During my junior and senior years of college, I raised money for the Special Olympics by organizing 24-hour dance marathons at ZBT. Everyone who wanted to come got a sponsor sheet and signed up as many people as they could to give them a donation for every hour they danced. Then we danced with the energy known only to 19-year-old testosterone-fueled college guys from morning until the next morning, when we could barely stand up, legs buckling in a hangover of muscular exhaustion. We raised hundreds of dollars.

I volunteered at Special Olympics sports events too. At first, I was drained by feelings of empathy and sadness for the children suffering from physical and mental handicaps. But I soon was awed by their zestful optimism and the way their parents were in full-throttle support.

This experience proved to me that I could be successful and have fun mobilizing and organizing others into actions to support the most vulnerable people in our society. I had no idea that in a few short years I would realize it was my life's work to help those on the margins.

After graduation from Muhlenberg, David and I celebrated by taking an eight-week backpacking trip through the U.K., France, Spain, Italy, Greece, Germany, and the Netherlands. It was my first truly nomadic journey. We managed to survive on just $10 a day, sleeping rough in trains, boats, cheap hostels, and sometimes even in the street when we couldn't find an affordable place to stay.

One night we took a ferry across the purple Ionian Sea from the southern tip of Italy to the island of Corfu. I met an American woman my age from Chicago. She had curly black hair and beautiful blue eyes. I fell into a deep lust that night, and poor David had to deal with my ongoing obsessive search for her in Athens and again on the beaches of Santorini.

A week later, in the pre-dawn hours of a Sunday morning, we arrived in Venice after two sleepless days and nights on the slow, rattling train from Brindisi. Exhausted, David and I decided to take a nap on the cold, narrow steps of a closed bank in a quiet piazza. I was startled awake by the strike of a policeman's club on my foot. We had to keep moving.

David and I survived those months on fresh bread, local cheeses, and cheap wine. Every few days, we would treat ourselves to a real meal with fresh fish or steaks—our malnourished appetites ensuring that we would later declare those feasts in Europe to be the best of our lives.

I loved living on the edge, all senses alerted, connecting with fellow travelers, learning about the history and cultures of other countries, and seeing that people everywhere were more the same than they were different. I was becoming a globalist. It struck me that people abroad were seeking love and happiness, just like me. The idea delighted and warmed me.

So it was like waking suddenly from a pleasurable dream when David and I found ourselves traveling on a very crowded bus heading toward Southern Germany and Dachau. Emotions suddenly attacked me, passing through the barrier of my intellect and into my soul. The unexpected fear was like an alarm bell ringing in my mind. The harsh voices of the German tourists made my heart race. As we pulled up to the camp, I started sweating. Here were the ovens that were used to burn my Jewish ancestors. Right here. My mind returned to the question of my childhood when Judith had told us the horrors she had lived through, *How could they let this happen?*

I walked the camp, tirelessly questioning the tour guide about how so many people, including the Germans living nearby, the Pope, the U.S. corporations who sold equipment to the German army, and even President Roosevelt, knew what was happening—but all did nothing. The complicity of others in allowing and enabling the Nazi death machine to march forward irritated, puzzled, and frightened me. I started to feel afraid of the German tourists around me.

That was a dark moment in a trip filled with light. My excursion through Europe that summer broadened my horizons. I returned to Pennsylvania feeling brave, competent, and experienced. I overcame my fears and discovered my curiosity about other cultures. It seemed that in foreign lands, where I was stranger, I felt most free to be me. A travel virus had entered my bloodstream.

College was over, and my new life was about to start. And this time, no one was going to tell me how to live or what to do. From now on, my choices would be mine alone.

And I had chosen to be a physician. Muhlenberg's pre-med advisor thought my grades weren't good enough. But I didn't care. I was going to make a difference in people's lives.

Not only that, I was going to be an osteopathic physician—a DO, not an MD.

The DO medical training is mostly identical to what allopathic medical doctors receive, but osteopathic medicine adds a more holistic approach, which involves using the hands to diagnose and treat patients. DOs are trained to view the human body as an interconnected system. They are taught how illness or injury in one part of the body can influence and affect other parts. While most conventional MDs rarely touch patients, DOs learn to palpate and perform physical manipulation to align the bones and joints to relieve muscle spasms and pain.

That really appealed to me. Mom's cousin was a prominent cardiologist in the osteopathic medical world. He once told me that being a DO was a great opportunity, as osteopathic medicine is a much smaller pool than allopathic medicine. "You can be a big fish in a little sea, or you can be a little fish in a big sea," he said. I knew even then I would rather be the big fish. It was also a bit easier to be accepted into osteopathic medical schools, and with my bad calculus grades, I felt this was the fastest way to fulfill my dream of being a doctor.

In the 1980s, osteopathic physicians were viewed a little doubtfully by much of the public, and were outright disrespected by the mainstream medical establishment. I didn't care. I followed my gut and was accepted to several osteopathic schools. I chose the Philadelphia College of Osteopathic Medicine—PCOM. I was attracted to osteopathic approach of whole-body medicine and to the idea of charting my own course. It was even better that it did not conform with the path that most people thought best.

And I loved medical school. I didn't even mind the incredibly hard work of my first year and the endless fire hose of complex information that gushed over us day after day. If I was going to take care of peoples' health, I was eager to learn everything I possibly could.

Anatomy was by far my favorite class. At first, the intense formaldehyde smell made me nauseous, but that was quickly overcome by the thrill of delving into the organs, arteries, and muscles of Bert, the cadaver of a 72-year-old man who had died of pneumonia. We dissected every part of Bert three days a week, learning how the heart pumps, how ligaments connected to the bones, and how the brain was connected to the spinal cord. Fortunately, with no blood flowing, I didn't have any pangs of queasiness to overcome.

Still, I struggled to stay focused on academics. Yes, I liked anatomy, physiology, and biochemistry, but my interests also trended toward social activism—and women.

My second year, I was elected by my fellow students to represent our school at a national convention in Chicago organized by the Student Osteopathic Medical Association (SOMA). My main motivation was the opportunity to travel to a new place—and try to meet up with the blue-eyed woman I'd traded phone numbers with in Greece during my summer of backpacking. Ten months later, I still could not stop dreaming about her crystalline eyes.

On the sidelines of the convention, I went to her row house in a crowded Chicago suburb for dinner. It was an awkward meeting. The magic of the Ionian Sea was gone. She was very tied into her Chicago family life, and we didn't seem to have any common interests. We really didn't even know each other. One love interest ended that week, but my relationship with political organizing was just beginning.

At the SOMA events, I met students from Oklahoma, Iowa, Michigan, and California—places I had never been. We shared both a common cause to become healers and a love for the profession. We deliberated on what we could do to improve our medical education and how to influence establishment doctors to develop better programs and policies.

Over the next year, I attended more national meetings in all parts of the United States, and ultimately was elected to serve as SOMA's national president for two consecutive terms during my third and fourth years of medical school.

This was my first experience of feeling powerful and effective in a busy, hyper-creative space. I was on clinical rotations all day and writing student opinion pieces for our SOMA student magazine at night. As we raised more money, we expanded our national organizational team from three to ten people. I found that I could attract the smartest students by giving them a platform to help their fellow medical students across the country.

Together we transformed the osteopathic medical student movement from a stagnant professional association into a vibrant national voice for student activism in the 1980s. We reinvigorated SOMA's 15 chapters around the country, published a monthly journal, convened two national conferences per year, and launched an international health program that paired medical students with physicians in Rwanda, Burundi, Turkey, and Nepal.

I also returned to my interest in the Special Olympics, launching a national partnership with medical students who organized events, raised money, and helped children with disabilities. The scope of this effort landed me an invitation to Special Olympics headquarters in Washington, D.C., where I shook hands with Sargent Shriver.

I also walked past the open door of the office of Eunice Kennedy Shriver, who was busy reading some papers. I couldn't believe that little Paul Zeitz, son of a hoagie maker, was a few steps away from Mrs. Shriver, the sister of JFK. I was utterly starstruck, awed by the fact that my work as a student activist brought me so close to such influential people. I thought about my mom sobbing when Kennedy was shot. This was how I could be the kind of man that Mom would respect.

I also fell in love with Washington, D.C. during this visit. Here was a place where people who wanted to help others could have a big impact. I couldn't believe I could have so much fun learning to be a doctor while at the same time developing my justice skills. I was leading a relatively small and dynamic team, bringing larger-than-life social justice action to people all around the country. For the first time in my life, I felt like I was finding my full power. Working with a small dedicated team to wage justice would become my blueprint.

CHAPTER 7

Behind the Iron Curtain

As the national president of SOMA, I created for myself an opportunity to travel to Moscow in May of 1987 for a conference that would bring together more than 2,000 physicians from 70 countries.

It was the Seventh World Congress hosted by International Physicians for the Prevention of Nuclear War (IPPNW), which was at that time the fastest-growing medical organization in the world. This global federation of medical groups from 64 countries, representing tens of thousands of doctors, medical students, health workers, and concerned citizens, shared the common goal of creating a more peaceful and secure world freed from the threat of nuclear annihilation.

President Ronald Reagan was in the White House. He was aggressively challenging the status quo of the decades-old Cold War. This was the year he famously stood at the Brandenburg Gate in West Berlin and ordered the Soviet president to "Open this gate! Tear down this wall!" It was the eve of *perestroika,* the cultural and political movement spearheaded by President

Mikhail Gorbachev that ultimately broke up the Soviet Union. But when I arrived, the Soviet Union was still a country on lockdown.

There was little food on the shelves apart from black bread, potatoes, and onions. People lined up for hours, sometimes days, to get ration coupons for basic staples like sugar and salt. This was my first international conference, and I could barely grasp that I was in Moscow—a place few Americans got to venture—behind the Iron Curtain of the USSR.

It was surreal at times. To wait 45 minutes in the street for ice cream, only to be handed a plain vanilla cone, was shocking. I expected to be able to pick from at least a few different flavors. I waited so long only to have no *choice*.

That was a freedom I had never considered before. I was an American conditioned to expect the freedom to choose, from the 31 flavors at Baskin-Robbins to the sort of career I wanted to pursue. I walked down Gorky Street licking the ice cream. It tasted stale. I felt a strange sort of homesickness that was new to me.

Senator Al Gore gave the keynote address at the World Congress, speaking passionately and firmly for a world free of nuclear weapons. As a student delegate, I was sitting in the nosebleed section at the top of the crowded stadium full of healers from around the world. Senator Gore made me proud to be an American in this global village. And I realized that this was a guy who was going places. A few weeks later he announced his first presidential candidacy.

The next day, I attended the World Conference of Health Workers on Social Well-Being, Health, and Peace, organized by Dr. Milton Terris, then editor of the *Journal of Public Health Policy*. I spent a lot of time with the gray-haired and wise Dr. Terris, an elder statesman of global public health. During one of the breaks, he handed me a copy of his journal. The cover story he wrote reported on the global crisis in preventable childhood deaths. Later, we had dinner together, eating Russian sweet and sour cabbage, boiled potato, and hard-to-chew meat.

Dr. Terris explained his research: 37,000 children under age 5 were dying every single day across the globe from diseases that were vaccine-preventable and even mundane, like diarrhea and pneumonia. I was mesmerized by his worldly knowledge and fascinated by this crisis of children.

How could we let it happen?

Over 13 million babies and young children were dying unnecessarily each year. Wasn't that like a modern Holocaust? I was dismayed to be so ignorant. I knew nothing about these global problems, the families that were losing their babies. My heart raced with the possibility of saving children's lives.

What kind of medical education was I really getting?

What could be done?

What could I do?

Stopping the unnecessary deaths of millions of children was just the challenge I could spend my life working on.

I had another mission while I was in Moscow that week, but I needed to get away from my stalker to accomplish it. She was a young woman about my age with short, straggly brown hair. She shadowed me, under the guise of being a tour guide. We both knew she was really a government-sponsored "minder" who was watching my every move. Her quiet scrutiny spooked me.

In breaks during the conference, I had successfully eluded my stalker a few times to explore the city and its beautiful art- and sculpture-filled subways by myself. But now I had a more important mission. Outside a subway station during one of my illicit excursions, palms sweating, I placed a call on a public rotary phone with a clunky black receiver. I dialed the secret number a Jewish agency in America had given me. In halting English with the person who answered the phone, I arranged a clandestine meeting with some Jewish *refuseniks*—people who wanted to emigrate out of the Soviet Union but were being refused because of their Jewish heritage.

The next day, I again slipped away from the hotel and the minder and traveled by subway to the outskirts of Moscow. I was met by a woman in her 30s with deep brown eyes, dark brown wiry hair cut to her shoulders, and the strained look of someone living in daily struggle.

She took me on a tour of her life, moving through an otherworldly, forlorn urban landscape of rows and rows of indistinguishable white apartment buildings under a perpetually gray sky. The shops serving the Jewish community were nearly empty. She showed me a bread shop that had no bread. A cheese shop with one small hunk of cheese for sale. A butcher shop with no meat. She explained that the refuseniks spent all their time waiting in line at these shops when small shipments of food arrived. They were not allowed to work, which was fortunate in a sick way: Their time was fully occupied with a daily hunt for food and survival.

It was heart-wrenching to witness this modern-day oppression of Jews. I was flummoxed that this was happening to them, while I was living across the world with an abundance and variety of foods to choose from. As an American from Philadelphia, it was in the Soviet Union that I truly understood at gut level why the human spirit yearns for liberty and thrives on freedom. Listening to her story felt like a gift. As I said goodbye, I was felt sad and sorry, wishing I could do something to help the refuseniks, but with no idea how.

As drab as things still were for many, Gorbachev's policies of *glasnost* (openness) and *perestroika* (reformation) meant I got to see a wild rock concert in a Moscow back alley music venue that just a year before would have been banned. I also attended an exquisite performance of the Bolshoi Ballet, where the dancers twirled and leaped with an artistic beauty I had never seen before, or since. My hands were left sore from applauding so vigorously for so long.

Such extremes: oppression and authoritarianism alongside Russia's devotion to beauty and the promise of glasnost. The future of world politics teetered on a precipice of hope in that small slice of time, just before the fall of the Iron Curtain. Peace was possible.

On my return to medical school, I became a zealot for the elimination of nuclear weapons. While my classmates focused on learning surgical skills and how to manage diabetes and high blood pressure, I tried to get a resolution passed by the American Osteopathic Association (AOA) that called for physicians to take a stand against nuclear war as an existential threat to human life.

The activist in me was on fire. But the prestigious doctors running the AOA smirked at me and refused to sit down for a real discussion. I was contemptuous of them. These conservative doctors weren't true healers, in my estimation. They were uninterested in the danger we all faced as human beings. I wondered:

Did I pick the wrong profession?

These people are so narrow-minded!

Faced with people telling me to slow down or stop focusing on the urgency of problems as I saw them made my defiance gene kick in every time. The bun-less hamburger flashed through my mind. I would never let institutional rejection stop my forward motion.

So I mobilized a tribe of young, engaged medical students on campus—too inexperienced to be jaded, too passionate about saving the world to be cautious—and we launched a national advocacy effort to advance the anti-nuclear cause through student activism. At the next national meeting of the AOA, I stormed onto the delegate floor and passed out copies of a resolution we students had presented to the Governing Council. I was sure that my sheer willpower would convince the medical elites to break out of their limited viewpoints.

The resolution failed to get physician support. I vividly remember the feeling of being stared down by the "experienced" doctors. Their complacency and opposition were fuel splashed on the fire of my rebelliousness. That day, I realized that I was nothing like them. If you push me aside, I will come back stronger.

CHAPTER 8

Walls and Cages

THE first two years of medical school, as any student will tell you, is a grueling marathon of 12-plus-hour days in lecture halls, labs, and libraries, reading and memorizing facts about anatomy, pharmacology, and the full range of clinical medical topics. The volume of information to be learned and exams to cram for was overwhelming and relentless. I spent most nights and weekends completely engrossed in brainwork, struggling alone.

Until I met a woman.

The heartbreaking fracture of my nuclear family and my childhood home, witnessing my father lose everything and everyone, and the constant brokering among my closest kin had left me extremely wary of having a girlfriend. I'd had a few romantic "friends" in high school and college, but had never been in love. I wasn't even sure I was capable of it.

Like being color-blind, I thought I could never really experience what my friends seemed to feel when they easily opened their hearts—often to people they barely knew.

Attraction, passion, love, heartbreak—the cycle was familiar to me, but only as an observer. The inner anger and self-loathing I wrapped around myself felt comfortable, like a security blanket, but it was closed off to love. My heart was well protected.

Laura Robin had a mop of wild, wavy brown hair, deep blue eyes, a merciless wit, and a keen intelligence. She was the perfect study buddy. We spent weekends together in drab hospital conference rooms reviewing the names of each bone, explaining the immune system to each other, and making up memorization games, such as a mnemonic song to remember all names of the 26 bones in the foot. This was the proven medical student method of embedding the maximum amount of information into our tired, caffeinated, sleepless minds.

Lonely and overwhelmed, I leaned on Laura, and a deep friendship developed. We laughed endlessly and let off steam together as we both struggled in the hothouse environment of med school. Over time, our relationship evolved from friends to lovers. As that was happening, I realized how much I wanted to be in love with her. My heart could not make that frightening, dizzy decision to open. I loved Laura, but the part of me I needed to share with her was locked behind a wall.

Instead, I was caustic, demanding, angry, and mean to her at times. I didn't like myself and I didn't understand why I acted this way. The suppressed rage and self-loathing I had carried through childhood had not dissipated one bit in adulthood.

After months of enduring my temperamental treatment of her, Laura wisely closed off emotionally and withdrew to protect herself. When our class completed the second year of med school and went out on clinical rotations to learn our trade firsthand, Laura and I also parted ways.

The experience left me depressed and ashamed. I blamed myself and my hyper-defensive protective walls for driving this amazing woman away. It was all on me.

I realized I needed outside help if I was ever going to open myself up to love. As a physician-to-be, I knew that I had to fix myself before it was too late. My sister Marci was having children during these years, and I loved being an uncle. I realized if I couldn't open myself to love, then I would never become the kind of father that I dreamed of being.

But I didn't know how to find help. My parents had tried marriage counseling to help their relationship and came away from the experience disappointed and cynical. I wasn't sure about trying something that had failed them so profoundly.

I knew I had to do it my way. I wanted to chart my own course. I wanted more than to change. I wanted to grow as a person, emotionally and spiritually. I was determined to keep my mind open.

A female friend from high school had been seeing a therapist, around the age of our mothers, and this therapist was really helping her find confidence. My curiosity turned to amazement when I learned that not only did my friend's therapist share my mother's name, Sandi, but she had once been the director of the nursery school I attended. And there were more *Twilight Zone*–type coincidences to come.

Sandi had two offices where she saw patients—one in downtown Philly and one at her residence near Wissahickon Valley Park in a tall apartment building called the Kenilworth. That is where I found myself on the day of my first appointment. As I sat down to wait in an elegant reception area, I felt shy and unsettled. My heart was racing, and my palms and armpits were slick with sweat. I closed my eyes and reminded myself that I really wanted to do this kind of work. I needed it. And as I sat, I felt a warm, welcoming energy. My eyes opened wide, and I sat up straighter, suddenly calm. This was going to work. It had to.

Still, the first sessions felt awkward. I was always nervous before every visit. I didn't know what to share, and I reflexively held back on telling the truth about my inner demons. I was ashamed and embarrassed about parts of myself.

But one day after a session, I was writing my usual payment check when it dawned on me that I was paying for this support. So, I might as well open up and share the full monty of what was really going on.

My self-exploration centered on a deep-seated barrier I had erected against vulnerability and a lack of self-love that would not allow me to accept myself as a worthy individual. My inner critic constantly badgered me:

Why was I so stupid?

Why was I so mean to women?

Was I destined to fail?

I hated myself. But I was also deeply committed to changing—to waging justice for the little boy inside me and the man I was trying to become. So, with Sandi's help, I forced myself to be assertive and ambitious as I dug deeply at the roots of my mental barriers.

I trusted Sandi. Week after week, she made me feel safe. Under her kind coaching, I began to open the locked doors of my childhood feelings and experiences. I did some deep work on bringing down my inner walls and sharing my deepest anxieties, inner conflicts, and terrors. After sharing the pain of my failed relationship with Laura, a metaphor for understanding my wounded psyche crystallized.

My heart was protected by a solid steel wall that wouldn't allow vulnerability, weakness, or feelings of dependence to enter. Sandi worked with me to reconstruct my steel wall to have some openings. Ultimately, I created the image of a steel mesh—a flexible cage that would be protective, yet still let love flow in and allow me to share my love—at least cautiously.

Despite hours in therapy, my life was still a paradox. I was doing well in school—I was one of the best in my class—and I was the national president of a prominent student organization, traveling around the U.S. and the world trying to improve policy. But I was living two lives simultaneously. On the outside I was "normal"—productive and preparing for success. In the inside was negativity, anger, shame, and self-loathing. The dissonance between my external and internal worlds made me feel off-kilter. I could perform well and seem strong, but I was seething with rage and mistrust, which often brought me into conflict with people around me. With Sandi's support, I was now imagining steel mesh around my heart. But I needed to do more.

I began to understand that I had full control over my heart. I found I could open it completely, like unfolding and spreading powerful eagles' wings. With time, I learned to control these wings, opening them to allow love to flow through the splayed feathers, but able to close them fully so they cradled my heart in protection when I did not trust someone. This approach allowed me to feel safe from the hurts of my wounded childhood, my difficult family relationships, and my risky search for someone who could be a partner for life.

I'd spent 18 months in therapy, seeing Sandi for an hour every week, sometimes twice a week. Now it was time to wrap it up.

At one of our last sessions, Sandi mentioned for the first time that her youngest daughter was a fellow student at the same medical school. She said she hoped one day our paths would cross. And they sure did.

CHAPTER 9

An Ounce of Prevention

By my first surgical rotation, through sheer mental will, I had mastered my queasiness around blood and foul odors. Now in my fourth year, I was on my way to becoming a clinician.

One afternoon, I was observing my first upper abdominal surgery near the liver, pancreas, and gall bladder—a major junction in the body where the superhighways of vessels that carry blood, bile, and digestive enzymes cross and cross again. The surgeon dutifully pointed out the red arteries, the greenish-brown bile duct, the blueish veins, and the different shades of the organs.

It was a gray mush. I couldn't distinguish any of the colors.

My arms straining from the hours of holding the retractors, I was hit with a thought of startling clarity: *I am never going to be a surgeon.*

Then in my dermatology rotation, I found it impossible to distinguish the colors of rashes, especially on darker shades of skin.

But later that year, I found my calling. I had a month-long, hospital-based rotation under a brilliant nephrologist originally from Ukraine. Dr. Zenia Chernyk was extremely wise, graceful, and compassionate. I was impressed with how she would sit beside a patient and thoroughly and patiently answer every question.

I was responsible for tracking a middle-aged man with alcoholism who was hospitalized for end-stage cirrhotic liver disease. For weeks, Dr. Chernyk and I tried to get his out-of-whack electrolyte and metabolic systems normalized through salt and sugar balancing and adding and removing different medicines.

On a Friday afternoon, at the end of a long month, we were finally making progress. On that day's rounds—the medical training ritual where a group of eager students follow the attending physician responsible for the patients—we discussed my patient's case in the hallway outside his room. Dr. Chernyk suggested we could discharge the now-stable man.

I was irked. I blurted out, but as calmly as I could, "What's going to happen to him when he goes home? Won't he just start drinking again?" I wondered what measures we would take to treat the underlying cause of the metabolic diseases we had been managing.

She looked directly at me, her dark eyes leveled at mine. "Well of course," she said with certainty, "He'll be back here on Monday."

I looked at Dr. Chernyk in disbelief. We had spent so much time—and money!— stabilizing a chronic disease situation while doing nothing to prevent or address the patient's alcohol consumption—the primary driver of his disease.

My young medical student mind rebelled against this system that seemed designed only to respond to end-stage disease, rather than pursue disease prevention and healthy living with equal vigor.

Born and bred in Philadelphia, I had been saturated with lessons on the life and aphorisms of Benjamin Franklin since elementary school. I had always admired the way he lived his life, translating bold visions into simple ideas while traveling and enjoying the pleasures of the world. In that bedside moment, Dr. Franklin's perfectly sensible pearl popped into my mind: *An ounce of prevention is worth a pound of cure.* I was with him. Prevention was going to be my path.

I re-immersed myself in the writings of Franklin and learned he had advocated for creating a citywide organization of volunteer firefighters in Philadelphia, arguing in a pseudonymous newspaper editorial that it is far better to head off a catastrophic inferno than to rebuild a city burned to the ground. He personally brought together 30 local men to create Philadelphia's first volunteer fire department.

Franklin was a man who felt empowered to implement bold, creative, transformative ideas that would change the world. I wondered, *What if we were all liberated with that kind of freedom?* That was the kind of doctor—the kind of person—I wanted to be.

CHAPTER 10

Love at First Sight

I KNEW of Sandi's daughter from seeing her around campus, and I had briefly dated her best friend. But at first Mindi Cohen had no idea who I was.

Like me, she was from a conservative Jewish family in Philadelphia. She had started her undergrad degree at the University of Tel Aviv, then transferred to, of all places, Muhlenberg College. She'd spent two years there at the same time I was an undergrad—although we never crossed paths—before graduating from Philadelphia College of Textiles and Sciences.

In April 1988, I was in my final month of medical school and had traveled to Toronto for my last conference as national president of SOMA. At the Friday night opening reception at the top of the needle at the CN Tower, I spotted Mindi and noticed her gorgeous blue eyes, her sweet smile, wavy brown hair, and petite frame. I knew who she was, and assumed she was aware that her mother had been my therapist. After all, I had dated one of her best friends.

Armed with knowledge of our connections and feeling good about my upcoming graduation and my high profile as SOMA president, I confidently approached Mindi amid her gaggle of friends. I sat right next to her to introduce myself. As we made eye contact, I think I instantly fell in love.

As we talked, I learned that she was finishing up her second year at PCOM, and we connected as she shared her experiences living in Israel during college.

Mindi loved Israel, but she had found Israelis to be abrupt and abrasive. I shared impressions from my latest trip to Israel with Dad, so we had a lot to talk about. We talked about our respective adventures in Cairo, navigating the pyramids and the captivating perfume sellers. I told her about my overnight camel ride with the Bedouin people in the Sinai desert, where I saw shooting stars and learned to eat with my right hand only, as the left hand is only used to wipe after a bowel movement. Ours was an easy, uninhibited conversation, the kind that old friends share.

After the main reception, we joined other students back in my hotel suite. The others were milling around, drinking and eating, coming and going, and having side meetings, but amid all this hubbub, Mindi and I were happily marooned alone on the desert island of my couch, lost in conversation. We were hyper-focused, oblivious to all else, listening to each other in a way that I had never experienced.

Something magical happened to me that night. I was dating another medical student at the time, but with Mindi, something in my soul opened, and my whole self was set ablaze. It was complete and immediate. Her wavy brown curls, her spiffy fashion sense, her natural beauty—all combined with a keen and curious intellect, love for global travel, and our shared

Jewish heritage—pretty much made her a bull's-eye target of my lust.

This kind of passion wave was a rare event in my life. I had never experienced, before or since, this kind of instant, intense attraction that hit the physical, emotional, intellectual, and spiritual part of me all at once.

But I could tell she was holding back, because every time I moved nearer to her that night, she pulled away. She was not interested.

A few weeks after returning from Toronto, Mindi told me why. She was in a long-term relationship with a South American man she had met as an undergrad who was in the U.S. on a temporary student visa. They planned to marry soon, fulfilling on their love and hoping to resolve his shaky immigration status at the altar.

I was stunned and crushed. I felt stupid, angry, and extremely confused. I was falling in love for the first time, but I had chosen someone who was unobtainable. I searched for a reason for this wretched turn of events.

Although I had completed my therapy several months earlier, I wondered seriously if my attraction to Mindi was psychological transference. I scheduled a check-in session with Sandi, and we openly discussed the strangeness of what I was experiencing regarding her daughter. She told me I should trust that my feelings for Mindi were real, because her daughter was indeed a unique and endearing person. She ended our session by giving her blessings to our new friendship.

As I walked out of her office, it dawned on me that Sandi—a woman who knew more about the light and darkness within me than any other person on the planet—accepted me as a person who was worthy of friendship with her daughter. This hit deep inside my soul.

I didn't know if things would work out with Mindi, but I wasn't giving up yet. We kept talking, diving deeper into each other's minds with every drawn-out phone call.

Just weeks later, it was graduation day. Mom threw me a party, and we invited Mindi. I didn't know if she would come, because she knew I was on the hunt for her. Still, I wanted my people to meet her.

She showed up in a sleek, sexy dress, black and white, which appeared to me as the yin and yang symbol of balance and peace. It wrapped tightly around her tiny figure, leaving her shoulders open to the air. Her Diva perfume smelled wonderful. I was intoxicated.

My friends and family checked her out and gave her a big thumbs-up—in contrast to my previous girlfriends who did not always pass muster. But she *wasn't* my girlfriend. We were in friendship limbo, growing closer with every searching conversation. But she belonged to another man, and I had to make plans for my future.

A month later, I began my new identity as Dr. Zeitz, medical intern. Now I was to spend the next year in a training program of long night shifts and more than 80 hours a week as the first line of care for patients at two Philadelphia hospitals. I thought, *What better time to escalate my relationship with Mindi?*

I decided to ask her out for a mid-week dinner date between my shifts, since my weekends were filled with hospital duty. She said yes, and we agreed to meet at Chun Hing, my favorite Chinese restaurant near one of the hospitals. We drove into the parking area at the same time, and as our cars passed, we rolled down the windows. Mindi called out, "Hi! I wanted to let you know that I invited my boyfriend to join us for dinner!"

What the fuck? I thought. *No.*

Dr. Paul Zeitz

I was not going to sit through dinner with the object of my intense desire... and her *boyfriend*. I choked down the angry outburst that was mounting and explained this to her clearly and calmly. Then with as much dignity and good manners as I could muster, I drove away.

I wanted her (and her boyfriend) to know without a doubt that for me, this was not just a friendship. I wanted Mindi romantically, but obviously she didn't want me. Frustrated and sad, I knew it was time to take a step back.

We stopped communicating. I assumed my dream of marrying Mindi, if not my desire, was dead and buried.

I continued my busy internship year, pulling day and night duty at the hospitals. It wasn't long before Mindi, now in her third year of medical school, showed up at one of them for a rotation. I could only laugh at my strange luck when she was assigned to be my medical student. My only words to her that first day were smug and dismissive: "Welcome, Mindi, to the obstetrics and gynecology ward. It's time to get to work!" I had the upper hand. I'd show her I was all business and no play.

But of course, I couldn't keep up the facade. Over the next few days, we started flirting and having fun together. I got to teach this brilliant, confident woman how to draw arterial blood, and how to assist in delivering babies and managing post-delivery care of the moms.

One afternoon, the doctor we were both reporting to asked us to assist on a vaginal exam of an extremely obese patient. While I held up the patient's huge apron of belly fat, Mindi held aside the fat from one of her thighs. A second student held the other thigh. The doctor began conducting his exam, his hands pushing back flesh and his head straining to get a view. Suddenly, the patient let out a huge fart! The doctor rose up from the pungent mist with an awkward smirk. When the patient started laughing, we all simultaneously lost it, and Mindi and I had to run out of the room in complete hysteria. We may have been in our 20s, but we were still kids in a lot of ways. We laughed our way through the rest of the day, and we relished our silly shared moment.

Our connection reestablished, Mindi and I resumed our regular phone conversations. Over time, our talks became even longer, deeper, and more intimate. One night, we talked for six straight hours into the early morning. I lay in the dark on the loft bed in my apartment, staring up at the glow-in-the dark fluorescent stars on the ceiling and the map of the world hanging next to me. Together, we took long, imaginary journeys through places across that map, drawing verbal pictures of a large family laughing around us. As we were both drunk on fantasies, we went further, on to imaginary celestial star travel—imagining the union of our energies.

This was all surprising and very intense for me. We had never kissed, and we weren't even dating, but our conversations were as revealing and intimate as any lovers'.

It was the end of 1988. Mindi was spending a lot of time with her Grandma Anna, who lay dying in a nursing home. During this time of her vulnerability I sensed she was opening up to me. Once she invited me to join her on a visit to her grandmother. As I walked into the quiet room, I saw Sandi and her sisters at their bedside vigil, holding Anna's hand and comforting her.

This was a big moment for me. I felt that Mindi was allowing me to enter her private family life. I was happy to be there for her while her partner was out of the country.

Anna died peacefully a few days later. I attended the funeral, with a few of Mindi's other friends. The very next evening, for the first time, she accepted my invitation to come to my tiny loft apartment in downtown Philly on the scrappy, gentrifying edge of 15th and Broad St., where bombed-out cars and back alley drug deals were still common. As Mindi entered my apartment, I felt the winds of hope pushing against my back. *Was my persistence finally paying off?*

We had never been alone in a room together, and I wasn't sure what to do next. Awkwardly, Mindi accepted my offer to massage her feet. We talked about hospital rotations, her family, and our respective plans for the following year until—too soon—it was time for her to leave.

I was afraid to push at this delicate time, and after the door closed behind her, I was overwhelmed with frustration once again. We still had not kissed. I pounded my fist into the doorframe.

But a minute later, I realized Mindi had left her handbag with her driver's license. I imagined she had done it on purpose, so we would have to see each other again, preferably at my place. And because sometimes my dreams *do* come true, Mindi returned the next morning to my pad, in the light of day.

We realized something had changed. We both wanted to explore a romance—finally! But first, Mindi had to talk to her boyfriend about seeing other people. Other people being me.

When he returned in early January, Mindi told him she wanted to "see other people." Other people being me. He was stunned and upset. He had come back with a renewed commitment and hope that they would build a true married life together. Indeed, Mindi had made a promise to marry him and help him become a legal U.S. resident, and Mindi always kept her promises.

Honestly, I was perplexed by the idea that Mindi could seriously open her heart to me while at the same time keeping her commitment to marry another man. But as vexing as this time was for me, Mindi showed me that me that she is a compassionate woman who keeps her word. Ironically, it was one of the reasons I had fallen in love with her.

And now in the ultimate irony, I could only be with the woman I loved by accepting that she had made an unbreakable promise to another man. Mindi's character—her integrity and tenacity—just opened my eagle-winged heart to her even wider. Exposed and tender, it hurt like hell.

We started dating, hanging out together in and out of the hospital in every free moment. I sensed that Mindi was falling for me, warts and all. My parents' unhappy marriage and contentious divorce still haunted me. I knew I only wanted a life partnership if it was bulletproof and eternal. The litany from my childhood repeated itself in my head: *"I will never be like him!"* I believed in forever.

CHAPTER 11

Hiroshima

MY year of working in the hospital reaffirmed for me that I didn't want to pursue a career as a traditional clinician. Although I loved connecting with people from all walks of life, I was frustrated by the state of the American medical system.

Many of my classmates, and lots of practicing physicians I knew, had dispensed with the idea that practicing medicine was practicing the art of healing. Instead they were fixated on making as much money as quickly as possible while protecting themselves from malpractice lawsuits. I saw firsthand how this led to human suffering: Patients were being subjected to procedures and tests that I felt were unjustified, expensive, and unfair.

I was outraged by a group of gastrointestinal doctors who would frequently order both an upper endoscopy (scoping of the esophagus and stomach) and a lower endoscopy (a scoping of the large intestines and colon) as a first diagnostic when patients really only needed some antacids. *These jokers are just scoping for dollars*, I angrily huffed under my breath. Unnecessary testing like this was just one of the signs of a broken medical system that heavily rewarded uncalled for invasions of the body to identify and cure diseases, rather than focus on prevention. I had invested years of time and borrowed tens of thousands of dollars for my medical education, and now I was at a professional crossroads. After intensive soul-searching and consultation with my loved ones and mentors, I chose not to go forward with seeing patients as a medical doctor, which had been my expected path. Instead, I broke ranks with all my peers, went with my gut, and chose a career in preventive medicine and public health—a field that studies the health of whole populations.

Remembering how I felt inspired during my trip to Moscow to pursue public health, I applied and was accepted to the Master's in Public Health program at the Johns Hopkins University School of Hygiene and Public Health in Baltimore, a couple hours south of Philadelphia. I was back in the classroom way sooner than I had anticipated.

After a week of school, each Friday evening I would fight traffic on I-95 North from Baltimore to Philadelphia, where I worked 36-hour weekend shifts as a moonlighting doctor at two different South Philly hospitals. I needed money for my apartment, my car, food, and my long list of student loans. During seemingly endless weekend shifts, I would get just a few hours of constantly interrupted sleep, waking to admit patients and handle emergencies. Ambulance sirens barreling down Broad Street and the beeper in my pocket were the enemies, attacking throughout the night.

But my relationship with Mindi was flourishing. Occasionally, she would come downtown to visit me in the hospital in the middle of the night. We would hunker down, eat Chinese food, and grab some quality time in the tiny, cramped sleep room. Early on Sunday mornings, buzzed with exhaustion and caffeine, I drove to the apartment at the Kenilworth where Mindi lived with her parents. I would take a long, hot shower and sneak into her bed, trying not to wake her—but happy when I did.

Despite the demands of going to school full-time and working most weekends, I was eager to travel again. One of my first classes was on the sociology of public health, and we had to pick a topic for an in-depth study.

At the messy end of the Cold War in the late 1980s, many of us were worried about what would become of the rapidly dissolving Soviet Union and its scattered, poorly managed nuclear arsenal. Through my ongoing involvement with Physicians for Social Responsibility, I learned that the next global meeting of International Physicians for the Prevention of Nuclear War was in Hiroshima, Japan—ground zero in President Truman's choice to use the first atomic weapon in human history. I felt called by some force to attend.

Something strong was drawing me to that place, where almost 150,000 innocent people died from a single explosive dropped from five miles above. I wanted to know what it felt like to be standing on that earth, under that sky, where devastation fell.

With very little money and very big dreams, I started researching any option I could think of to participate in the Hiroshima conference. I dreamed that somehow, Mindi could join me. I wondered if we could really fulfill our dream to travel the world, at least once.

The next time I saw her, I talked as fast as an auctioneer, stumbling over my words in eagerness to explain the importance of the conference and how it would help me complete my research for my sociology class. I told her forcefully, "We have to find a way to make this happen!"

A few days later, Mindi called with some astonishing news. Sandi, in addition to her therapy work, was also the co-director of a small international adoption agency, Adoptions International, and they needed at least two people to serve as orphan escorts and travel from Korea to the U.S. with four very young children whose adoptions had been approved. In those days, families did not travel themselves to the country where they were adopting a child—all transactions were managed by agencies. We were offered the opportunity to serve as orphan escorts.

Sandi proposed booking our air travel through Japan so that we could attend the Hiroshima conference. Another dream was coming true!

In early October, Mindi and I took our first international trip together. Yes, Sandi, my former therapist, was completely supportive of my now-thriving relationship with her daughter, and she made this adventure happen for us.

Before picking up the orphans, we flew to Japan. The conference overlapped with Yom Kippur, the holiest day of the Jewish year, which focuses on personal atonement and purification of the soul. On the morning of October 9, the anniversary of the bombing, the Jewish doctors and students attending the conference gathered for an outdoor interfaith service at the cenotaph in the Hiroshima Peace Memorial Park, the very spot where the atomic bomb fell. An elderly man with tufts of gray hair, dressed in black, began conducting the ancient service. Rabbi Leonard Beerman compelled us to remember the wrongs we have done to one another and resolve to change.

At 8:15 a.m., a single peal of a bell rang out across the park, marking the exact moment of the explosion.

Behold I set before you life and death…

Rabbi Beerman chanted in Hebrew and English.

Choose life, that you and your descendants may live…
then you shall endure in the land.

I prayed hard. I could not stop seeing, over and over again, the image of a blinding flash of light. I imagined that all of the doctors with me, from all across the world, felt the full weight of responsibility and the implications of what happens when we fail to take ownership over the way our militaries exert their power in the world.

As an American, I felt a sense of shame and remorse that my country had forced the world into a nuclear arms race. My mind's eye winced at the blinding flash that changed our world in a nanosecond, and I saw how the decisions of our leaders from decades earlier affected us in that moment. Mindi and I stood side by side, gripping each other's hands.

During that week, we heard testimonials from elderly survivors of the Hiroshima and Nagasaki atomic bombs. Almost uniformly, they spoke of hearing a loud explosion, and as the sky turned gray, a knife of superheated air stabbed into their school yards and neighborhoods, and everything caught fire. After a hushed silence, all they could hear were screams and sirens.

Many of the survivors who spoke had been small children at the time. Their words became soft and garbled as they returned to that day, their bodies small and defenseless again. Some were disfigured by burns and radiation. But even just surviving was a trauma, when so many others were instantly vaporized or died soon after, vomiting blood and in excruciating pain, from radiation poisoning.

Hearing the survivors' words and seeing their wounds hurt my heart and inflamed my rage. The power of these weapons of mass destruction to wipe out humanity was utterly terrifying to me. I was scared. I was angry. Now 27 years old, I fiercely resolved to dedicate my life to creating a more peaceful world.

CHAPTER 12

Orphan Escorts

AFTER the emotional visit to Hiroshima, it was a short flight from Tokyo to Seoul, and suddenly our humanitarian mission was underway. Mindi and I visited the orphanage on the outskirts of town, atop a forest-covered hill. It reminded me of a small hospital—everything was white and sterile, and not too inviting for children, I thought.

Our job was to escort three healthy infants and one mentally disabled four-year-old boy halfway across the globe, almost 7,000 miles. The young boy's skull was visibly malformed, with a large flattened area on one side, possibly caused by forceps during a difficult labor.

The next day, six tickets in hand, we were met at the gate by several middle-aged Korean women—representatives of the orphanage. They presented the two of us with four children, and I understood immediately that the math was not on our side. We were outnumbered and totally responsible for these kids. It was truly intimidating.

I held the boy's hand, and the women and Mindi carried the babies as they helped us board our flight. We were given a full row of bulkhead seats, plus two adjacent seats. The women disembarked, and we were on our own.

As I helped the boy with his seatbelt, I was overwhelmed with admiration for the American family I had never met who had chosen this challenged little boy—a child who would likely need their support forever.

Our itinerary would take us from Seoul through Los Angeles, then to Philadelphia—an 18-hour trip through three airports. But Mindi and I made an amazing team. The three infants needed constant care: feeding, diaper changing, and holding, and Mindi was a natural with them, while I was drawn to the young boy. He seemed lost. He was agitated and could not fall asleep except if I held him on my chest. He didn't know how to use the bathroom, so he ended up peeing on me while he lay across my lap.

I felt such a deep empathy for this helpless boy, knowing he must have been terrified to be cared for by a large, hairy, white man who didn't look like anyone he had ever seen and who spoke gibberish to him. Feeling desperate and inept, I called upon the South Korean flight attendants for help. They happily jumped in, taking the boy for walks down the aisles and even into the first-class front of the plane, offering hugs, giggles, and, to my gratitude, a familiar language.

A few hours into the first flight, things settled into a steady rhythm. The infants were all sleeping peacefully, and the young boy was settled into his seat, finally dozing. Mindi and I looked into each other's eyes and smiled. We were tired and harried, but we were having fun. It was at that moment I think we both realized that we could get married. We could raise a family together. I finally believed then that I could be a father utterly unlike my own.

Sandi had explained to us that when we arrived in Philadelphia representatives of Adoptions International would come onto the plane to take the children and deliver them to their parents, who would be waiting at the gate. She had also warned us that escorts often experience intense attachment to the children, and at times have a hard time giving them up when handing them over to their adopting families. I thought that sounded absurd.

We arrived in Philadelphia, and as the other passengers departed the plane, Mindi and I stayed back to wait for Sandi and the agency representatives. The four middle-aged women who boarded the place seemed friendly and competent—the storks who would make the final delivery of the kids to their parents. I rushed to tell them about each of the children, what they liked, and how they liked to be held.

And when the moment came to pass the children on, I was shocked by a surge of fierce, manly protectiveness within me. A biological flood of paternal hormones was pouring through my arteries. My mind raced with worry. Handing the young boy and the babies over to strangers brought on anxiety. I was their rightful adult caretaker, and I needed to know that these children would be cared for properly and be safe. An unexpectedly deep, internal, biological bonding had transpired.

Our arms empty, we walked off the plane. Then we saw the families gathered together, holding their children in a haze of joy. As we greeted each of them, I sighed with relief. My jolt of separation anxiety was waning, and I was thrilled to see the new families bonding. We had succeeded in ushering these children into new lives and loving families where they could flourish.

Mindi and I didn't know if we would ever see those Korean orphans again, yet we knew we had done a drop of service in their lives. Our loved deepened, and I let myself imagine, as we walked through the airport together, that we could become great parents together. I smiled and squeezed her hand, imagining that we could even help create a world that would be safe for all children.

Months later, we broke up.

CHAPTER 13

A Proposal

MINDI left for Zuni, New Mexico, to complete a student rotation, with the Indian Health Service. It was February of 1990 and I was in Baltimore studying and plotting the next phase of my career. Unexpectedly, Mindi stopped returning my calls. She gave me lame excuses for why she couldn't walk to the nearby payphone to call me. I became angry at her non-communication and vented my frustration at her. I asked her if she was intentionally pulling back.

I had not felt this vulnerable about losing her since we began dating a year earlier. Something was not right with her, and it took several confrontational discussions over the phone before we decided to stop talking for a while. In my mind, it was clear that breaking up was a better solution than not being treated respectfully. With a broken heart and a fierce determination to put Mindi out of my mind, I traveled to Antigua, Guatemala, on my first overseas excursion to work on children's health.

Several of my professors at Johns Hopkins were global health leaders who confronted the biggest disease challenges, despite what seemed like insurmountable odds. I'd been lucky to have several classes with Dr. D.A. Henderson, dean of the School of Hygiene and Public Health, who had been a leader in the global effort to eradicate smallpox—the first contagious disease in human history to be completely stamped out. I was deeply inspired by his mission to bring smallpox vaccines to every child in the world. Now I had the opportunity to work on the world's next major disease control program—polio eradication. This effort would begin in Latin America and the Caribbean, building on the successful program in the U.S. and Canada.

The brilliant public health expert who was leading the effort, Dr. Ciro de Quadros, was the chief of the childhood immunizations for the Pan-American Health Organization, and he had mobilized the support of Rotary International to eradicate polio in the Americas by 2000. They had a big, bold agenda, and it was working. I loved their concrete and time-bound focus. I felt honored and humbled to finally get approval to work with him.

My first step was to improve my Spanish. I arranged for a month-long immersion with a private tutor in Antigua, who patiently walked me through hours of daily lessons. I even—sort of—fell for her. Middle-aged Maria had long, brown, silky hair and deep soulful eyes. Her accent was dreamy.

I tore myself away when lessons were over to begin conducting a research study on how to improve polio vaccine coverage in every province of Guatemala. I was learning on the front lines that it was possible to close the senseless gap between the availability of technologies and solutions—such as poliovirus vaccines—and the actual delivery of those things to the right people, at the right time, in the right way.

Mindi and I did not talk during my entire time in Guatemala, and I endured a daily struggle of convincing myself to accept that our relationship was over. I had to move on with my life and bury my fantasies of living and traveling the world with her. I was living the dream I had imagined for myself: learning and growing as a public health expert. But I was also heartbroken.

Toward the end of my assignment, I was surprised to get a call from Dad. Mindi had reached out to him, wanting to find out what I was doing. He told her I would be flying home to Philadelphia at the end of June via Miami, where she recently moved to start post-graduate training in family medicine.

On that warm, sunny day, Mindi was there at the airport to meet me. She looked extremely beautiful—but so did I. Since the nearly 6 months we'd been apart, I was fitter and tanner than she had ever seen me. I had become fluent in Spanish, trained dozens of medical students about polio eradication, traveled to every province in Guatemala to study the program, and completed a report with recommendations on how to achieve greater results. I was feeling great.

After a nice lunch at an outside bistro, she eagerly showed me her new apartment—complete with an enticing waterbed and new sheets with a Southwest Native American pattern of a pale blues, greens, and reds.

I am naturally stubborn (and crazy), so I remained fixed on my determination that we were *over*—even though all my physical signals were telling me otherwise. My defiance won the battle with my libido that day.

We did, however, reconnect emotionally, and we re-established regular, long conversations over the phone. But these had a more serious tone. A choice was coming.

Over Labor Day weekend, we met in Philadelphia. We took a walk in Wissahickon Park near where we both grew up. It lasted for five hours. We reflected on all of our moments of passion, adventure, and future-dreaming. As we fed the ducks near Valley Green, we imagined one day bringing our children to the same spot. After hours of careful and deep discussion, we agreed to resume our relationship. But this time we agreed that it was for real.

Before we could be formally engaged, Mindi had to finalize her divorce from her boyfriend. He was safely a legal immigrant and she had finally resolved her emotional tangles with him.

We agreed to meet in Miami and drive to Key West for New Year's Eve. In the meantime, I paid a secret visit to Sandi and Jerry Cohen's apartment. I asked for their blessing. Although my relationship with Sandi started as therapist/patient, this was not even a blip on the radar for her. They were both ecstatic.

The drive from the Miami airport through the Keys was awkward. I had pinned the engagement ring and box in a plastic bag to the inside of my shorts. I was afraid Mindi would see it—and frankly the sharp edges of the box were painful. I pretended that I hadn't been able to confirm a hotel, but that we had a couple of options. I drove her as I'd planned to a cute bed-and-breakfast called Whispers. While she waited in the car, I ran in "to see if they had a vacancy." When I returned, I told her that there was only a tiny room the size of closet with no windows. Mindi was annoyed. Which was exactly my plan. I was the bad planner and we were short on other options. I managed to convince her that we should check it out.

She climbed the stairs to the third floor and I eagerly followed. As she opened the door to the beautiful suite I'd secretly booked, her jaw dropped. She spotted the vase of a dozen white roses and was even more confused. As she stood there trying to figure out what was going on, I could not contain my energy and passion. I dropped my pants and fumbled to remove the ring box from the plastic bag safety-pinned to my underwear. I went down on my right knee and asked her to be my partner for life.

She had suspected a proposal was coming soon, but I am proud to say that I totally surprised her in that moment, and she quickly accepted.

As we lay together that afternoon, I told her I had another big secret. In my most serious and hushed voice, I said, "All these years, when I was talking about my interest in global health...well...I've really been working for the C.I.A., and I finally have permission to inform you."

Somehow, she didn't believe me.

Later that day, we celebrated on a dreamy champagne sunset cruise, welcoming a new decade and a new life together in the New Year as the soft winds and blue seas swirled around us.

My plan was happening!

I worked hard to reach this moment.

I can open my heart.

I can compete and win the heart of my beloved.

I can turn my dreams into reality!

For the first time in my life, perhaps, I felt like all was well in the world.

CHAPTER 14

I'm in Heaven

Now I was enrolled in a preventive medicine residency program at Hopkins and it was time to get experience in the world. My first residency assignment was in Florence, Italy, at the United Nations Children's Fund (UNICEF) Innocenti Centre—a think tank where I was going to work on a national capacity-building project focused on child survival and development with the famous Ethiopian expert, Dr. Aklilu Lemma.

The offices were on the historic site of the nearly 600-year-old Ospedale degli Innocenti, established in 1419 as one of the first secular orphanages for the illegitimate children of noble or wealthy citizens, along with the children of families too poor to care for them adequately.

The plan was for me to spend six months at the Innocenti Centre with Dr. Lemma, while Mindi completed her family medicine internship year. Then we would move together, as newlyweds, to the African country of Uganda, where I had my next assignment.

I had worked in Latin America, but I wanted to go to the places on earth where the problems were the worst; where children were dying unnecessarily in the largest numbers. I felt called to sub-Saharan Africa, so this was my dream job. My life felt like a movie, and I was the director and lead actor. All my plans were falling into place, just as I had imagined.

A couple of months into the Italy job, I made my first visit to Uganda to prep for our move. As we touched down at Entebbe airport, I was seized by a gut-level fear. I recalled the horrors of the barbaric Idi Amin regime and the heroic rescue of hostages by the Israeli Defense forces in 1976. My pangs of anxiety quickly evaporated though, after I disembarked and began to meet and connect with African people from all walks of life.

I was struck by the beauty and the pride of the Ugandan people, even though they were living in abject poverty, laden with poor health and infectious diseases—including a horrifying AIDS epidemic—which snatched away the lives of their young children.

Ultimately, my job would be working under Dr. Jessica Jitta, a young African pediatrician who pioneered the creation of the Child Health and Development Centre at Makerere University in the capital city of Kampala. My mission, funded by the Government of Finland through UNICEF, was to support Dr. Jitta's vision to establish a new national program for child survival and development. When we first met, I was struck by her brilliance and clarity about what was needed to the stop the unnecessary deaths of children throughout Uganda.

For the first time, I was connecting person-to-person, directly with the people behind all those statistics of hardship. I was living my purpose; I was going to be part of a program to save as many Ugandan children as possible.

To prepare for our move there, I went house-hunting on my first free day with an energetic young man named Moses, a proud member of the Baganda people. Moses told me about the history of the city and his people and about the different neighborhoods where Mindi and I might live. We sped along in his banged-up white Toyota through the curvy hilltops surrounding Kampala on a magical, mist-filled morning. Together, Moses and I searched for the perfect house on a hillside with a view of the city below where I would bring my bride and begin our lifetime of adventure.

We arrived at a two-story, all-white house on a nice size plot of land, with a high wall surrounding the property. The steel bars on all the windows, including the second-story bedrooms, made me wonder if I had considered all the security risks.

I didn't let those transient fears take hold as I walked around the yard. I was imagining that Mindi and I would have a couple of kids running around it before long. I filmed the house with a new video camera, so I could show Mindi the exciting prospects of our new life.

We were married near Philadelphia on September 1, 1991, with a large gathering of our family and friends joining to celebrate our wedding and send-off to Africa. By this time, my parents had been divorced for many years, and even though they barely talked, I was able to cajole them into walking me down the aisle together.

All of us were hyperaware of the long journey my family had taken—through a fracturing divorce and years of divisive hatred—to reach this moment of joy. I was 29 years old, Mindi was 28, and for the three years we had known each other, we'd gone through our own tribulations. But we were confident in our commitment to each other and filled with anticipation about our next big challenge—starting married life together and doing important global health work in Central Africa.

It was one of the greatest days of my life. The band played the Hora, the music for the traditional Jewish circle dance, and then moved to African beats as everyone wished us a *bon voyage* to Uganda. Mindi and I shared an intimate newlywed dance in front of all 217 people who witnessed our sacred marriage ceremony. We slow-danced heart to heart, eye to eye, soul to soul to Joan Armatrading's "Heaven."

I was making decent money by then, so we decided that right after honeymooning in Jamaica, we would head to Uganda with a stopover in the Seychelles Islands—an oasis of heaven in the Indian Ocean. Mindi had completed her internship year in medicine but decided to hold off on completing her full postgraduate training in obstetrics and gynecology to work as a family physician while we were in Africa.

So, there we were, poised to sail off to exotic worlds, the heroes of our new marriage. Sandi bought us eight giant blue steamer trunks to carry our belongings across the oceans as if we were Victorian explorers.

But before we could pack the trunks, just days before we were due to travel, we got devastating news.

With the breakup of the Soviet Union on the horizon, the Finnish government decided to shift its funding from the Africa-focused child survival effort to support its neighboring Baltic States like Estonia and Latvia. The funding for the child health program in Uganda—and my work—had been withdrawn. Our big dream vanished in an instant.

It was gratifying that the oppressed Soviet people—especially the refuseniks I had met just a few years before—seemed on the cusp of liberation and freedom from authoritarian rule, but I was completely crushed for myself and my wife.

Suddenly, we were scrambling newlyweds. We had no jobs and no place to live. We cancelled the Seychelles part of the honeymoon.

I tried to rationalize that everything was going to be okay, but I was trapped in despair. I felt like a failure. While I knew that international development programs can come and go on the whims of unknown forces, I irrationally felt like it was somehow my fault. I was so drawn to working in Africa; I needed a way to get us there somehow.

I ruminated on different plans for weeks that turned into months. Questions dogged me endlessly.

Were we going to be stuck in Philadelphia forever?

Should I give up my dream of living in Africa?

Do I need to get a job in the U.S. to support my new wife and our kids-to-be? Why was this happening to me?

It was the first time in my life that a plan I had meticulously created for myself utterly collapsed. I felt like a crime victim, robbed of the opportunity to follow my dream of saving lives.

Until that time, I lived with an intense planning mind. My defiance and determination had always produced successful plans that were realized. Now that my scheme to move to Uganda didn't manifest, I struggled to figure out my next steps.

PART TWO
Unification

*It was during those long and lonely years that my hunger
for the freedom of my own people became a hunger
for the freedom of all people, black and white.
I knew as well as I knew anything that the oppressor
must be liberated just as surely as the oppressed.*

—Nelson Mandela

CHAPTER 15

Nigeria

Marooned in Philadelphia, just a few miles from where we spent our entire childhoods, rather than in exotic Central Africa as we had planned, Mindi and I did our best to adjust to newlywed life. Mindi got a job at Covenant House, an urban community health center where she provided family planning services to mainly African-American and Hispanic clients, and I enrolled in a global health fellowship program through Johns Hopkins. At home, we explored new domestic hobbies, like buying old pieces of furniture, stripping and staining them, and fixing the hardware.

It was fun working on projects with Mindi, but the truth was, I was completely frustrated and angry about my situation. I pestered my supervisors at Johns Hopkins, and at last, I landed a field assignment in Nigeria. But I was going by myself; it was just a four-month assignment. In early January 1992, I left Mindi, who had just learned she was pregnant, alone in Philadelphia. Mindi encouraged me to go but I also felt guilty, wondering if my dream of working in Africa had become a selfish priority.

As I walked through the Murtala Muhammed International Airport in Lagos—hot, chaotic, and still crowded after midnight, I was both delighted and overwhelmed. I had been warned about pickpockets and thieves, so after leaving baggage claim, I was on hyper alert, wheeling my huge assortment of luggage out of the airport into a throng of taxi drivers and hucksters grabbing at my bags with the intention to help me. With relief, I saw a young man with my handwritten name on a sign. He escorted me safely to a van.

My supervisor at Johns Hopkins, Dr. Stella Goings, had arranged for me to stay for a few days in the house of a Nigerian Ministry of Health official in the posh zone of Victoria Island, about a one-hour drive from the airport. The roads were still densely crowded, even this late at night. *Did Nigerians ever sleep?* As we drove south toward the congested urban island on the Gulf of Guinea, we passed miles of squatter huts and slums that seemed too ramshackle to be used as human dwellings. The data I had studied about entrenched poverty came to life right before my eyes, but I wasn't prepared for the immensity of the human deprivation I was seeing. I felt my first wave of culture shock.

A few days later, I traveled from Lagos to Maiduguri, the capital of Borno State in the northeast corner of the country where I was to take up my temporary post.

My day started at the new wing of the Lagos airport, which had recently opened to support a rash of new private airlines— the result of government privatization of the domestic airline industry, which had once been controlled solely by Nigerian Airways. It's safe to say that they were still working out the kinks, because the check-in zone was complete mayhem.

People were clustering at the counters, yelling and fighting among themselves in the crush to get their tickets. There was no signage, and piles of tagless bags were heaped in front of the check-in stations.

After surviving the chaos, I entered the departure lounge to wait for an announcement for my flight. But after a few minutes I realized that there *were* no announcements, or even an information board indicating when or from which gate flights were departing. *How in the hell am I going to find my plane?*

Others were equally unmoored. I began to follow groups of passengers, hoping to hear about the flight to Maiduguri. Packs of lost people poured out onto the tarmac and moved from plane to plane trying to get information. After about an hour of wandering, I finally found a group of fellow passengers heading to Maiduguri. We decided to stick together. For the next several hours in the blazing sun, our group of 25 men and women of all ages (but just one white person, me) ran after each plane that arrived, darting under the wings of moving jets and sliding on the tarmac oil slicks.

When our plane to Maiduguri was finally identified, the crowd grew to about 75 people. They were so eager to board, a massive fistfight broke out, forcing the flight attendants to raise the steps and close the door against the pandemonium. I was shocked by the raw anarchy and found myself wondering what my fastidious mom would think of this place. I also wondered if I would survive to tell her about it.

A middle-aged Nigerian women saw that I was a fish out of water, and she kept me close to her side. Eventually we boarded the plane and we all had a seat.

My first lesson about this country was that Nigeria was nothing like the calm and laid-back Uganda. But there was a vibrancy and intensity that enthralled me.

Maiduguri turned out to be a dusty university town in the Sahel. It is a predominantly Muslim area, and very hot. People keep cool in beautiful, long, flowing traditional clothes and tall caps to block the sun. As a young American in Western garb, I wondered if they saw me as equally exotic and interesting. Or something else.

The U.S. had recently helped the Nigerian government set up new democratic institutions, including the establishment of national political parties, unimaginatively named Democratic and Republican. Nigerian friends I would meet later liked to joke that democracy was a good concept, but not particularly useful in a world where hierarchical tribal chiefdoms had dominated all decision-making for millennia. Their point was proved one day when we drove past the abandoned headquarters of the newly formed political parties.

Living on campus at the University of Maiduguri, I had a small, comfortable apartment with a nearby bathroom and shower that worked. A tiny white kitten adopted me and became my best friend. I had to shop for my own food, and a nice young woman would help me prepare it, if I asked. But after a couple of weeks of eating what I could get at the market—typically beans, cabbage, and occasionally some scraggly chicken and rice, I set out on a mission to find some cheese, my favorite staple food back home.

One Saturday morning I jumped into the backseat of a rickety taxi. When I looked down, I saw a huge hole in the floorboard. The driver smiled at my horrified reaction and assured me that I would be safe.

We drove to the two supermarkets in town—no cheese. We prowled the outdoor market—no cheese. Finally, after asking around, we drove 45 minutes out of town and into the countryside to a German-owned farm. There, we were shown a shelf containing a single type of cheese, cut into jagged lumps.

Cheese! I felt like the happiest mouse in town. From then on, I dropped my Western yearning for hundreds of varieties of cheese in seductive supermarket displays. I was happy with what I could get.

My work took me about an hour southwest of Maiduguri into the Bama local government area of Borno State, which is known for its remote prison. I was working with the health managers who wanted to learn how to improve the quality of their services. They were smart and interested in their patients, and every day they taught me something new about delivering public health care with scarce resources.

One night, I decided to maximize my time and reduce my commute by staying over in a local hotel. The tiny room had no running water and no working toilet—just puddles of water to piss in. The windowless screens let in mosquitos and other flying insects, cockroaches, and lizards who basically ruled the room. *This must be the worst hotel experience of my life,* I thought. I was right.

It was in Northern Nigeria that I first began to learn about Islamic culture. In early April, I noticed my colleagues weren't taking a lunch break, and they were all sluggish by early afternoon. The holy month of Ramadan had begun. I had never heard of Ramadan, and I was embarrassed by my ignorance about the customs of their religion. I learned it is a time of fasting, introspection, and prayer. My friends were not eating or drinking from sunrise to sunset—which seemed impossible to me in the intense heat and humidity. They explained that they break their daily fasts by sharing meals with family and friends. I was disappointed that I never earned an invite to one of these feasts.

A few days into Ramadan, I received a fax message from a colleague in Lagos that I needed to call Mindi as soon as possible at her parents' apartment. I was instantly alarmed. Mindi and I talked once a week. We hoarded our news for these short, exorbitantly expensive long-distance calls, talking at night when the rates were lowest.

But it was mid-afternoon on a Tuesday. I ran to the local offices of the Nigerian Telephone Company and made a collect call to Mindi's parents in Philadelphia. It was morning there, and she answered. She told me she had begun cramping and bleeding and was heading to the hospital. I could hear the anxiety in her voice. Our worst fear was coming true—a miscarriage. I promised to come home immediately and would call her back the instant I had flight arrangements to come home.

I was distraught, panicked, and confused. I didn't know what to do or where to start. Even if I managed to get the only flight out of Maiduguri that afternoon, Philadelphia was still two travel days away. And if I didn't get out, I would be stuck until the next flight, several days later. I *needed* to get out of Africa and back to the U.S. to be with Mindi during this crisis.

In that moment, I was filled with regret and shame for my decision to leave my pregnant wife alone, thousands of miles away. I contacted the local airline and found a seat on a flight leaving in a couple of hours. Before rushing to the airport, I called Dr. Goings, my supervisor at Johns Hopkins, to tell her what was going on.

Sensing my panic, she tried to calm me down, assuring me that Mindi would be fine, as miscarriages were fairly common. (*Not to me! Not to my wife!*) As I tried to digest this impossible fact, Dr. Goings swiftly followed up in a businesslike tone: "If you leave Nigeria now," she said, "You won't be able to return to complete the project, because there is no funding available for the return travel expenses." *What?*

I was outraged. Once again, I was being told what to do and being held back from where my heart wanted to be.

My next call was to Mindi, who was considerably calmer than I was. She agreed with Dr. Goings that I should stay and complete what I had started. She was at the hospital where they were going to do a D&C, a minor surgical procedure to clean the inside lining of the uterus. She had things handled.

I didn't sleep well for days and talked to Mindi as much as possible. I did my best to support her while we grieved the loss of our child over the phone across the miles. I still had two months to go to complete my research and training. It was heart-wrenching to be forced to choose my work over my wife, but Mindi's quietude and assurances helped me return to pragmatism and accept the circumstances.

Two long months later, the assignment complete, I headed home. Mindi met me halfway in London. We met up in a quaint little hotel near Paddington station, and when the door of our room closed behind us, we hugged and cried together. We made love and vowed to move on with our plans to build a family.

Before my Nigeria trip, I had been accepted into the Epidemic Intelligence Service (EIS), a highly regarded job training program with the Centers for Disease Control and Prevention (CDC) in Atlanta. I would be working as a field epidemiologist—an expert in studying risk factors and patterns of disease in whole populations. The world would be my fish tank!

CHAPTER 16

Unconditional Love

WHEN I joined CDC, I expected to be assigned at headquarters in Atlanta to continue my work in international public health, but the CDC had other plans. In the summer of 1992, Mindi and I found ourselves in Phoenix, assigned to the Arizona Department of Health Services in the infectious disease epidemiology section. I felt like my ability to plan my own life had evaporated, yet I acknowledged these random job assignments were creating opportunities for me to grow.

In Arizona, Mindi began a residency program in family medicine. We'd only been settled for a few months when she started calling me from pet stores around town, telling me about the cute puppies she wanted to take home. This was strange behavior for her. Mindi was afraid of dogs! We soon found out she was pregnant again. Under the influence of hormones, she was determined to create a family nest.

We searched for the right puppy, and finally found a four-month-old bichon frise, a white fluffball we named Yote, short for coyote, in honor of his Arizonan cousins. We were finally a family of two plus one, and another one on the way.

Mindi's second pregnancy was uneventful, and even fun. We made a project of responding to her cravings for milkshakes, searching for the best in Phoenix on the weekends. We soon found ourselves in a competition for who was gaining the most weight. Then, in early May, she went into labor five weeks early. After a toe-curling 36 hours of back labor for Mindi, Lian Bem Zeitz was born, perfect and whole.

I was surprised that his eyes were wide open as he emerged, and when we first looked at each other, my heart melted. *Who is this mystery soul that just opened my heart wider than ever before?* I wondered in amazement. It seemed to me that we looked into each other's eyes and knew each other deeply, primally. In that moment, I felt that our souls were connected forever.

I was a father!

My heart was wide open; my eagle's wings were splayed, unhinged toward infinity.

Any anxiety I felt about how to be a good father was suppressed for now. And although he was a bit yellow—from a common condition called neonatal jaundice—and very tiny, coming in at less than six pounds, we were approved to take him home the next day.

Since he arrived so much earlier than expected, we hadn't bought all the gear to support a new baby. We stopped at a children's store on the way home from the hospital, searching his tiny face for signs of endorsement as we shopped for a crib and other apparatus. Then someone at the store gently pointed out that we probably shouldn't expose our day-old newborn to the germs rampant in a store full of kids. Here we were, two licensed physicians, clueless about how to keep our premature son safe during his early fragile days.

At home, Mindi and I basked in our good fortune. In those first days, I was intoxicated. Swinging in our hammock, under the desert moon, holding my baby boy close to my heart, I imagined that baby Lian smiled and even laughed.

Our wonderment spilled over into our entire extended family. All four grandparents and all of our siblings traveled to Phoenix from Philadelphia over the next couple of days to celebrate Lian.

On the eighth day following his birth, we held a *Brit Milah,* or bris—ritual circumcision. A local rabbi and a *mohel* (a Jewish lay person trained in circumcision) came to our home and removed the foreskin from Lian's penis in a minor surgical procedure. I had spent months researching the history and basic practice, and Mindi and I had long debates over whether we would uphold the custom. We debated benefits and risks: Might Lian be traumatized by the experience? Were there any medical benefits? Ultimately, we chose to follow tradition so that Lian would be connected to me as his father, his Jewish peers as he grew up, and to the generations past and future of our tribe through this ritual. We buried his foreskin under a sapling pomegranate tree in our yard, as our ancestors have done for thousands of years, or so I imagined.

As his grandparents gave him blessings, the rabbi chanted and blew a *shofar*—a rams' horn—to call in the angels. I felt mystically blessed and filled with joy. With Lian, there was no prior history, no baggage, no drama—just a pure soul, wide-eyed with curiosity, awed to be exploring the universe for the first time. I had never felt such a liberated and deep soul connection as I felt in those first weeks of my son's life. I experienced unconditional love for the first time.

But soon after the parties ended, and the relatives left, I was hit with a tidal wave of anxiety. I realized I didn't know how to be a good father. I had no adequate role model.

As I lay with Lian in my arms, I was overcome with fear, thinking of the millions of ways I could fail him. But the scientist in me knew it was time to investigate. I began a search for books on fatherhood. That's my approach to new things: I need to study and learn. But as it turned out, there were very few books on the subject published at that time, and no Internet to surf.

After some effort, I found a book that was perfect for me, *Earth Father/Sky Father.* In its pages, I discovered how to be present in the home and to father my child day-to-day as an Earth Father. This meant I could find joy when Lian was screaming and needed his diaper changed. It meant finding purpose in shopping around town for organic baby food and mashing homemade veggies into his meals. With tiny Lian asleep, heart-to-heart on my chest, his head tucked under my chin, I chanted sacred Hebrew prayers, and prayed for a peaceful world.

I discovered that I could also be a Sky Father—the father in the world—out there doing things and fixing things for our planet and humanity. And I learned about the need to find equilibrium between the two fathers.

I realized my dad was a Sky Father almost exclusively—out of the house running his hoagie shops, and fishing. I worried that I would do this too—put all my energy out into the world and not reserve enough to support and wage justice for my family in the home. My mind flashed with the memory of me, pounding my fists and declaring, "I will never be like him!" In those early days of Lian's life, I made a commitment to try to find the right balance between Earth and Sky.

Those days, new fathers didn't get any time off, so I was back to work the following Monday. And less than two weeks after Lian came into our lives, I came face to face with my first public health emergency.

Chapter 17

Unexplained Illness

An unexplained illness had struck a group of Navajo Indians near Crownpoint, New Mexico. Over the course of just a few weeks, several dozen people had become very sick with bleeding into their lungs. Many of them died. Alarm bells were going off in the public health community.

As an infectious disease epidemiologist with CDC, I was called to join an emergency response team in Gallup, New Mexico, a major city on the Navajo reservation. We quickly identified a hantavirus—a hemorrhagic fever virus like Ebola and Lassa fever, though one that presented with symptoms that were less severe. We had the culprit, but we had no clue how or why people were becoming infected. As part of the investigative team, I would have to stay on the reservation as long as needed as we worked to get the outbreak under control. We suspected an explosion of field mice that spring was part of the chain of transmission, and the investigation team was trapping and studying mice around each of the affected households.

I bounced between the joy of welcoming my new son and the empathetic pain of consoling grief-stricken families facing the sudden, unexplained deaths of their loved ones. It was a hard time. But during it I experienced a heightened awareness of the preciousness of life. My heart yearned to be with Lian and I regretted abandoning Mindi again for my Sky Father work. I was grateful when she brought Lian up to Gallup a couple of weeks into my assignment.

We stayed at a tourist resort near the Petrified Forest National Park, so I could escape from the ramshackle hotel in Gallup and the frenzy of the investigation team working 18 or more hours a day. My heart opened as I reconnected with my little family after what seemed like an eternity. My little boy with his dark blue eyes and bald head was more alert, gaining weight, and growing stronger. Mindi was beaming with joy as her dream of being a mother was unfolding.

On our first night together, I slept fitfully, troubled by a nightmare that I had already had time and again: Hantavirus-spreading mice were taking over the planet and putting mankind in peril. Suddenly I felt something on my chest. I woke to see a gray, beady-eyed creature on top of me. I hurled the mouse away from me and leapt out of bed, screaming like a horror film extra. Mindi, who was up nursing Lian, started laughing hysterically. Lian stared wide-eyed at me. The mouse was a "gift" from my wife. My fear quickly melted as I realized Mindi's prank helped relieve some of the tension I had been feeling.

The hantavirus struck some Caucasians and Hispanics, but disproportionately affected the Navajo. Breaking news updates tracked the day-to-day developments of the epidemic and our evolving investigation. The pressure was on us to figure out what was causing the illness and death, and to stop it. And even though the CDC's public reporting stressed that all ethnicities and races were affected, the public became frightened of this deadly "Native disease."

During this time, a group of Navajo school children traveling to Los Angeles to visit a Jewish day school as part of a cultural exchange arrived at LAX to a swarm of media. As cameras rolled, these innocent children were turned back—the whole group of students and teachers were held at the airport until they could board a return flight—by local health authorities in fear that they could be transmitting the "Navajo disease."

I was angry and shocked. The media had purposely ignored the facts to propagate a racist, ratings-grabbing view of what was happening. I now understood why so many Navajo families were reluctant to share health information with our team. They felt stigmatized and feared being publically shamed.

I was meeting regularly with affected families in their traditional *hogans* as I tried to gather and standardize the data from all the hantavirus cases. But these families were grieving and afraid, and in my effort to communicate the urgency of needing to know more from them, I failed to reassure them. Instead of having an inventory of each family, an exact date of the onset of symptoms, a health assessment of those who had died, I was walking away with half-filled out forms and incomplete health histories.

My CDC bosses grew frustrated and I felt distressed, both about the outbreak and about my failure to get the information needed to control the epidemic.

I was moved by the emotional anguish of the families whose loved ones had died so suddenly and so mysteriously.

Could this happen to me, or to Lian or Mindi?

I believed I could never survive losing either of them. Never. I had to work hard to keep my heart from closing in self-protection. I needed to stay open to love, for and from everyone, despite my fear of death. I was 31 years old with a beautiful young family, a medical degree, and a masters from the most prestigious public health school in the country. I had meaningful, interesting work and my whole life ahead of me. But despite the outward success, fear of death gripped me inside.

I had to drive long distances to interviews, alone through blank stretches of prairie and the broad, open-sky New Mexico vistas. To quiet my anxious mind, I started chanting over and over "The Priestess Blessing" by Hanna Tiferet—the song the rabbi sang at Lian's circumcision.

> *Guiding the cycles of darkness and light, a sacred dance reveals that we are all one.*

On those long rides, a realization was forming. I needed to work on myself and cultivate within me a deeper level of appreciation of life and death. I wanted to appreciate each moment of life given to me. Any one of them could be my last.

On one of those drives, I made a personal, lifelong declaration:

> *Living and acting today, I shall overcome my fears and push the boundaries as far as I can, because tomorrow may never come.*

Finally, after months of research, our investigation revealed that an El Niño event had led to a very wet spring, which led to an abundance of piñon nuts, the main diet of field mice. The abundance of food, sparked the mouse population to grow 10 times larger than normal, so they moved into human households to survive. When humans cleaned out mice-infested cabinets or closets, they inhaled aerosolized mice urine, which transmitted the hantavirus. Once we confirmed the cause, we found a solution. We issued emergency guidelines to the public to reduce the risk of hantavirus by keeping mice out of the house and avoiding mouse feces. In a very short time, no new cases were reported and I could move back home.

CHAPTER 18

Family Expansion Project

AFTER two years with the CDC in Arizona, working on a slew of infectious diseases including bubonic plague, meningitis, and mumps, our little family moved back to the East Coast, to Takoma Park, Maryland, on the outskirts of Washington, D.C. I had been hired by the U.S. Agency for International Development (USAID)—one of the largest funders of child health programs around the world—to serve as an expert in protecting the lives of children under five years old.

Finally, seven years after meeting Dr. Terris in Moscow and learning about efforts to prevent millions of unnecessary child deaths, I would be doing this amazing work every day. My choice to risk everything by giving up the normal clinical practice of medicine was paying off at last.

I settled into my new job with its 50-minute daily commute on the Metro to my office in Rosslyn, Virginia, just across the Potomac River from Washington. One morning, in July 1994, as my train chugged across the city, I was reading the *Washington Post*. Several pages in—certainly not on the front page—I read an article that made my heart race. A genocide was underway in the small Central African country of Rwanda. I'd been hearing snippets about the attacks for weeks, but they seemed too unbelievable to absorb—neighbors were brutally slaughtering each other with machetes. Up to a million were dead.

On this day, somewhere in my soul, an alarm bell started ringing. A memory surfaced. In that moment, I was back in my childhood Hebrew school class. Judith was saying, "Never again. This can never happen to our people again!" And I recalled my own questioning. *But how did they let it happen?*

I suddenly felt a chill deep inside my body. I realized that *I* had become "they." I was fully aware of the murders in Rwanda and the passivity of leaders who let it continue, but I had remained uninvolved, even complacent. I was doing nothing to stop this crime against humanity. I was complicit and therefore partly responsible.

I'd finally gotten the answer to my boyhood question: I understood, *This is how it happened.* Here I was, doing nothing more than lament about the problems of the world, carrying on with my busy family and work life as innocent people died.

I was deeply troubled by this new awareness. *What could I do? Why didn't I do something?* Haunted by these thoughts, I continued, unabated, with my daily routine.

Mindi had completed her family medicine residency in Arizona, and she was yearning to work in adolescent health. She landed a position at the student health center at the University of Maryland's main campus in College Park. Lian was now 15 months old. A stout toddler already known for his daredevil antics, his favorite activity was jumping from tall walls and laughing when he fell and scraped his knees. He had endless amounts of energy, loved to play with other children, and was fearless. We thought Lian needed a sibling.

We got pregnant again that fall. Everything progressed perfectly smoothly, and in the spring, we decided to celebrate our waning months as a manageable three-person family with a road trip to Charlottesville, Virginia, to visit my first cousin Robbie and to see Thomas Jefferson's estate at Monticello. Mindi was in her seventh month, and we had a bouncing, high-energy, nearly two-year-old Lian to chase around.

That day at Monticello, after climbing the hill and exploring the house, Mindi suddenly started feeling queasy and light-headed, almost passing out. A sharp pain in her abdomen—contractions—sent us rushing back to Maryland by car and to Holy Cross Hospital in Silver Spring. Mindi was admitted with pre-term labor. This was serious and scary. If born now, our baby would only survive with intensive neonatal care, if at all. I thought of the dying babies around the world, and I felt lucky that Mindi and our unborn child had access to world-class medical services.

The goal was to stop the contractions and keep the baby inside as long as possible. Mindi was put on intravenous magnesium sulfate, a potent drug to stop contractions. I knew from my obstetrics rotation that mag sulfate had to be carefully titrated: An excessive dose could harm the mother and the fetus.

During the next five weeks, I became the primary caretaker of Mindi and Lian and lead patient advocate for Mindi and our unborn baby. I kept working full-time to help the other children of the world, although Dr. Al Bartlett, my USAID supervisor, allowed me to have a flexible schedule. I chanted "Or Hadash," a Jewish spiritual call for peace and compassion by Hanna Tiferet, over and over again, while driving Lian to and from our daily visits to Mindi, who had to stay in the hospital. The chanting helped calm my nerves. I could feel my heartbeat slow down and the anxiety slip away. These prayers, which connected me to so many generations of men who came before me, helped build my strength and resilience.

Days passed. The medical staff were having trouble finding the right dose of mag sulfate to completely stop Mindi's contractions without harming her. One afternoon when I arrived for a visit, she was barely responsive.

For the first time, I was terrified that my wife could die. Equally unthinkable, we might lose our baby. I urgently called the nurse and told her, as calmly and firmly as I could in my panicked state: "My wife is nonresponsive. You have 30 seconds to turn off the mag sulfate."

"I won't be able to do that," she said just as firmly. "I have to check with the doctor, and that will take some time."

Wrong answer. My defiance gene kicked in. Barely able to contain my anger, I growled:

"I am a doctor.

"I have been sitting with my wife over these past several days, and I have never seen her nonresponsive.

"It is clearly due to the mag sulfate levels being too high.

"You have 30 seconds to turn this off or I will do it myself!"

Stone-faced, the nurse complied. Mindi quickly returned to full coherent consciousness. I collapsed, shaking, into the chair by her side.

After five weeks in the hospital on complete bed rest, Mindi gave birth to Yonah Arael Zeitz. Yonah was born on the exact same day as Lian, two years later. When I held him for the first time, I rubbed his mop of long black hair, touched his small sweet face and wept with joy. I had been so afraid that we would lose him. I'd had to dig deep within myself and mobilize all my capacities to make sure that Mindi and our baby would be healthy. My global passion for children's health was now hitting me in my own heart, in my own home.

Lian was overjoyed with his new toy. He finally understood why his life had been so tumultuous, and why his mommy had been in the hospital for so long. He loved to poke, prod, and kiss Yonah. We had to make sure he didn't bop Yonah too hard.

Weeks before, I had planned a birthday party for all Lian's nursery school friends. Instead, we brought Lian's birthday cake to the hospital where we celebrated his day—and Yonah's—with the nurses and other hospital staff.

On Yonah's eighth day of life, our close family and friends arrived at our home in Takoma Park to celebrate his arrival and to witness his bris which we held in the backyard. It was a sunny spring day, with the birds chirping and daffodils blooming. Dad and Jerry, Mindi's father, each held Yonah as he was passed to the *mohel* for the surgical deed. Lian climbed on the table to watch.

We buried Yonah's foreskin in our yard under a cherry tree sapling. All my prayers had been answered. My family was healthy and safe, and we had survived a very difficult phase. But things were stormy inside my heart. I was toiling with my relationship with God, or what I call the "love force." I had chanted and prayed for Mindi and Yonah, and my prayers were answered. I knew I should be grateful. I knew I should accept God. But something held me back.

I asked myself, *Can I overcome my skepticism of living with faith to some unknowable higher power?* The answer was unclear.

CHAPTER 19

I Fight for Child Survival

ONE of my first assignments in my job at USAID was to travel to New Delhi, India, to help USAID with the design and launch of a national polio eradication campaign, modeled after the program I had worked on in Guatemala and other successful campaigns in Latin America.

Delhi was totally overwhelming at first, with its massive human congestion, honking horns, and surging sea of rickshaws. People wore face masks to protect their lungs from millions of exhaust pipes pumping out pollution. We spent endless hours in standstill traffic crawling to and from meetings with the World Health Organization and the Ministry of Health. America was a latecomer to the efforts, but our support was welcomed by Indian and international government officials.

The chaos of New Delhi reminded me of Lagos. While the work went well, I felt exhausted by the poverty, noise, and heat. I was in a constant state of vigilance. It was hard not to long for home, or dream about working in a quieter country where I could have as big an impact, like I had imagined Mindi and me in Uganda.

I began traveling to Africa regularly for various USAID assignments. On my first trip to West Africa, I visited Senegal, Niger, and Mali, three former French colonies. In Dakar, the capital of Senegal, I joined Dr. Ron Waldman, a prominent global public health leader I greatly admired. Ronnie was directing a multi-million-dollar, USAID-funded global child survival initiative. Ronnie was a mentor, somewhat older and a family man like me. Over the years he had become a good friend. He had a daughter Lian's age, and back home on the weekends we would meet up with the kids to feed and pet the horses at the stables in Rock Creek Park. He was a man of impressive professional and physical stature, wise and sharp-minded. His balding scalp and bristling eyebrows, along with his sardonic wit, could be intimidating, and I had seen him win many battles in forceful (and sometimes loud) arguments with my USAID colleagues back in Washington.

In the mid 1990s, most Senegalese were living in utter poverty. Families had between five and seven children, expecting that half of them would die before their fifth birthday. This cycle of so many births and deaths perpetuated economic stress and structural poverty. My job focused on helping stop thousands of Senegalese children from dying each year.

Our goal was to strengthen U.S. government support to Senegal to expand vaccination coverage and to prevent and treat diarrheal disease. But we had been warned that the mission director of USAID in Senegal was not interested in these issues. She had other priorities—and she held the purse strings.

She began our first meeting with an incantation of opposition to child survival programs—one that she had successfully executed in her prior position in Chad. Ronnie raised his eyebrows and gazed at her in momentary silence.

I held my breath. "I fight for child survival," Ronnie said softly. "I'm here to save as many lives as possible."

Child survival programs, Ronnie insisted, help increase the number of people using family planning services, allow the family to earn enough money to thrive, and reduce the number of women who die during childbirth. I nodded as he spoke, looking at him with awe and pride. Ronnie was standing up for values in opposition to a person of authority—and one who controlled all the funds. I could see she was listening. But all the evidence and argument in the world could not sway the USAID official and her entrenched viewpoint. She shook her head and made it clear that the meeting was over. Still, I was glad to be on Ronnie's side of the table.

When I told him later how dismayed I was that the U.S. government was represented by a person with such a narrow vision, he addressed me as the naive and innocent neophyte that I was, glibly responding, "Welcome to my world."

I shouldn't have been so shocked. There are endless competing priorities for the limited funding available. My urgency came from my duty to prevent unnecessary childhood deaths. But the mission director felt that economic development programs were a better, more direct way to help families overcome poverty and ultimately limit the number of children they have.

But I labeled her a naysayer, blocking what I knew needed to be done in the world. I dismissed her skepticism about the programs we were proposing. *She was a complete jerk,* I thought. Defiance roiled up in me. *Ronnie and I were right, and she was wrong!*

Ronnie returned to Washington, while I stayed one last night in Dakar. I took a small fishing boat for a short ride to nearby Île de Gorée, a small, 45-acre, car-free island dotted with ancient buildings that echoed with eras past. Gorée was the center of the European slave trade—an estimated 20 million Africans passed through the island between the mid-1500s and the mid-1800s.

Touring the site by moonlight, I realized I was at yet another landscape of human devastation. The anguish of so many who had been locked up, thrown into the bottom of ships, and hauled from their homelands was palpable in the energy crackling around me. *Why are humans so cruel to each other?* I wondered, yet again.

I also learned for the first time that Africans had sold each other into slavery. A small-scale tribe-against-tribe slavery had long existed in Africa, a tour guide explained. As competing tribes fought for power and against each other in the quest for European goods and weapons, they did not hesitate to sell their enemies into the hands of the colonial slave traders.

Paradoxically, it struck me that African-Americans whose ancestors had made those bitter voyages appeared economically better off and had many more opportunities than the families I saw entrenched in poverty in and around Dakar. But theirs was a different sort of pain—that of racism and exclusion in a world of plenty.

From Senegal, I traveled alone to Niamey, the capital of the even poorer landlocked country of Niger. Niamey was a sleepy town with traders passing through on camelback, and few cars. This was a complete contrast to the vibrancy and dynamism of Lagos and Dakar.

Here in Niger, USAID was on the brink of closing desperately needed child survival programs for no apparent reason. We had so many battles on our hands.

Immunization coverage was low, malnourishment was high, most Nigeriens did not have access to clean drinking water, and many lived in unsanitary conditions. The country had been struggling with ongoing outbreaks of measles, meningitis, and cholera. Thousands of children were being needlessly infected, and many died.

I was baffled that my government would want to close our program in the face of these crises. I decided to visit the local headquarters of UNICEF, whose purported mission is to protect children's rights and meet their most basic needs, since USAID was a large funder of these programs.

The UNICEF building was a single story, sand-colored structure, with dusty, open-air hallways and rows of large windows. Inside, I imagined as the driver parked the car, was a crowded operation center where furious action was being mounted to respond to the rampaging epidemics. But as I approached, I could see it was empty. I was coming unannounced. I stepped into the hallway, peering into empty offices with cluttered desks and a few older computers. A weekday, mid-afternoon, and all the staff had vanished. As the dry winds blew around me, I wondered:

Had they run out of funding?

Was it a vacation day?

Where were the epidemiologists, doctors, and nurses organizing mass immunization campaigns?

Where was the sense of urgency?

I left Niger without answers to any of these questions. It seemed that the United Nations was completely failing. This was the first time I felt utterly disillusioned with UN operations, but it would not be the last.

The final stop on my West African trip was Bamako, the capital of Mali, another large, arid, landlocked country. I met up with Karen Blyth, an experienced West Africa expert who worked on the same project as Ronnie Waldman. We joined a local team to visit villages where USAID child survival programs were immunizing children and teaching mothers about preventing diarrhea and pneumonia. The team had several clinics along the road to Koulikoro, about an hour's drive from Bamako to the northeast. We passed miles of rural poverty. Village after village of mud huts with no electricity or running water.

In Koulikoro, Karen arranged for a meeting with a village chief and his governing council. We sat in a large circle in an open area under a few baobab trees. They served us a generous lunch as a sign of respect and welcome. It was very hot and dry, and the cool shade was rejuvenating. A few village women served us each a generous plate of rice, local vegetables, and plump pieces of chicken.

After taking a bite, I looked over my shoulder. Just two steps behind me, a group of 40 or so children had gathered. All were visibly malnourished, with discolored hair and popping bellies. I stopped chewing and put down my plate, unable to continue. I quietly whispered my distress to Karen, who encouraged me to keep eating. It was the custom to offer guests the best possible food, and eating it was my part of the bargain.

My heart sank. I closed my eyes and meditated for a few moments, willing myself to breathe. The burning sun starting creeping under the shade where we were sitting. *Screw cultural norms.*

I offered my food to the children who cautiously accepted, and I promised myself I would never eat in front of starving kids again, even if that meant not following protocol. Karen became agitated: We were guests of the local chief and could not afford to upset him. But she was no more successful than Mom at getting me to eat when injustice was on the menu.

When everyone else finished, we began our discussions about improving the health of the local children. I noticed then that no women were present—only men could serve on the governing council.

I insisted that we meet with the mothers, grandmothers, and sisters of the community to learn their views. After some scuttling about, we were taken to the other side of the village, to a gathering spot beside a large field where women were harvesting cassava. We had been granted permission to talk with the village's ranking woman. As the proud middle-aged woman approached us, a large group of women gathered silently nearby. The village chief's men lurked closely, listening to every word. Using multiple translators (Bambara to French, then French to English), the woman proceeded to give us what I believe was her honest perspective of the need to keep the children in school as the best way to protect them.

This woman had wisdom and high status, but still, she could not participate in the decisions being made about her community. I was furious. The oppression of these women, and the plight of their children under a locally determined patriarchal system, felt incredibly unjust to me. I was a 33-year-old doctor and a new father trying hard to model gender equality in my own family. I cooked, shopped, changed diapers, and played with my boys in the same way Mindi did. I knew that the centuries-old way of life in this predominantly Muslim area had been organized to ensure survival of the community in a harsh environment. But I also realized that these traditions had no modern purpose.

This encounter opened my eyes to the gender discrimination that women confronted throughout West Africa. I felt despair and hopelessness about the magnitude of work the world still needed to do to achieve equality. But I knew a shift towards including women in decision-making was essential if we were ever going to improve life for Mali's rural children.

CHAPTER 20

My Djembe Drum

In Mali, on the road back to Bamako, Karen and I came upon a group of adolescent boys who were dancing, singing, and shaking traditional wooden castanets, the Bamana musical instruments, in celebration of circumcision and coming of age at 13. They were dressed in traditional clothing, headbands, and loincloths, and they smiled broadly as they danced in a row.

We stopped for few minutes to watch. I felt a strong spiritual connection to them, fresh from my ecstatic memories of Yonah's circumcision a few months earlier. Here was a global connection. Despite living in different universes, my family and the families of these four young men were entwined by ancient, sacred circumcision rituals to sanctify the life of our young sons. From my suitcase I whipped out my photo album of Yonah's ceremony and tried to explain to Karen and our driver how awestruck I felt.

Back in Bamako, Karen and I went out to explore the nightlife and culture of the town. I was longing to buy a large West African *djembe* drum—an instrument I had always wanted to learn to play—but had been told that they were hard to find in the city. We hired a driver to take us to the marketplace, but it was closed. Our next stop was a hotel where artisans gathered outside. I was surprised to see a single, tall, dignified *djembe* sitting by a stall. It was statuesque, strong, and full of beautiful rhythms waiting to be released. The gold studs and carvings around the base gave it a regal look. I bargained with the artisan and purchased the drum. I also asked for a local Malian mud cloth strap—and it had to have plenty of flair.

Drum in hand, I was overwhelmed with joy. The spiritual connection that I felt with those boys along the road had opened up the universe.

We strolled along the beautiful, full Niger River and through the city night. I played my drum as we walked. Some passersby snickered and smiled, entertained by the inexpert sounds. Others were frowning and shaking their heads in dismay at my novice drumming skills. As I walked around working on the rhythms, I spotted a *pinasse*—a long, canoe-shaped boat with a woven roof—which I hired for a ride down the Niger. Karen decided to come.

As we embarked, I spotted a man on the veranda of a nearby hotel carrying a guitar. Without thinking, I waved him over and gestured for to him to join our boat ride. He approached and boarded. Sitting directly behind me, he began playing his guitar and singing as my hands beat softly on the drum as if controlled by some ancient spirit. I had never been very musical growing up. I felt as if the divine was flowing through my fingers. I found a perfect rhythm. We drifted down the Niger and around the islands in the river. Malians waved and smiled from the shore as our musical joyride floated by. I was having a peak experience, completely buzzed and feeling a very strong, direct connection with the Divine.

Karen later told me that she was also aware of the uniqueness of a spiritual presence and the coincidences that made that river ride so unique. But she was also concerned about my mental status. She had stayed with me to make sure I would be safe—I was starting to lose myself in my own ecstatic world.

Later that evening, my last night in Africa, I sat outside the hotel playing on the *djembe* with a traditional Malian calabash guitar player, and two women singers, who also danced. Small groups of locals, and a few tourists, would come by to watch and join the singing for a few minutes before moving on. The four of us performed for hours, until the winds brought some rain.

In my hotel room, I was flying high. I had never felt this connected, this powerful. I throbbed with a sense of untapped knowledge and insight. I grabbed paper and started writing furiously.

What came out was a kind of manifesto, flavored by my insights from the day and night in Bamako. I knew as I wrote that I would be able to shape it into a plan to improve child health in West Africa. But it was much more than that.

Throughout my journey, something had been taking shape in my head: the outline of a New World Order. My document was nothing less than a treatise on creating global peace. From my jotted-down notes, I used my laptop to draft pages and pages of text.

By the time the sun started peeking over the low hills, I had a first draft. I faxed it to Mindi and asked her to make sure it was seen by policymakers as fast as possible.

Mindi was confused and alarmed. She was keen to get me safely to my plane that day and back home to Washington.

Throughout the Air France flight, I was in an altered, dream-like state. Thoughts of a better world were swirling though my mind. I kept asking myself, *When can we create a better world? How fast?*

Then, I had an actual vision. Clear and real. A vivid image of myself being shot, JFK–style, in the back of my head. A message came: *Take bold action NOW!* Then a second head shot: *NOW-NOW!*

A perfect view of the future emerged. We needed to create a sustainable, peaceful, global community. *Now-Now!*

I felt the connection and unification between my soul and all other souls. I saw that a global transformation was possible, in our time. I saw that gender equality was possible, in our time.

On that turbulent ride over Europe, and then crossing the Atlantic, I saw the possibility of unleashing the creative power of the unification of all children, women, and men to achieve peace and justice, in our time. I saw that the course we were on would lead to death and devastation, and we had to do much more to realize human rights for everyone.

And I had a detailed strategic plan to back it up.

On arrival in Washington, Mindi was waiting, in a semi-frantic state. When I appeared through the Customs and Border exit barefoot, she ushered me out of the airport, into the car, and home. We stayed just long enough to drop my bags. Then Mindi took me to her parents' house in Philadelphia. Within a few hours, Sandi shuttled me to a psychiatrist. At the time, I thought I was fine, though I was troubled by everyone's concern. I honestly didn't realize how strangely I was acting. By the time we arrived at the doctor's office, I was starting to feel anxious. His deep, steady voice shook me, penetrating the last bubbles of my elation. I slowly started coming back to myself.

I had cracked! I had lost my social navigation skills. I had become delusional for a couple of days. Mindi, my parents, and my friends were rattled. It appeared I had lost my mind. I imagined Mom was having flashbacks of fear as she wondered if I was going down the psychiatric path Pop-Pop Marty had traveled.

The psychiatrist talked to me for two hours. He determined that my bizarre behavior was in part a side effect of the anti-malarial drug, mefloquine, I had been taking for several weeks.

I lost my bearings for a few days. Looking back from the vantage of time, I realize it is true. But it is also true that I had a profound and lasting mystical awakening. The outpouring of epiphanies was divine, transcendent, and life-altering. I was utterly transformed.

Chapter 21

Zambia

AFTER my mystical awakening in Mali, returning to the daily routine of government bureaucracy was challenging to say the least.

Over the next couple of months, I struggled with feelings of helplessness and frustration in my white-collar Washington life. I was too removed from the front lines and caught up in interminable federal red tape while genocides, health emergencies, and famines raged on in Africa. I sat in endless meetings, strategy sessions, planning meetings, needs assessments—on and on it went. I started joking with my colleagues about creating a new reward system where you could collect "frequent meeting miles" to exchange for days off.

I knew I needed to get out of Washington and make it to the frontier of global health—or find a different career. I always wanted to be where the devastation was happening. I yearned to live and work in a place where my odds of success were the longest—testing the limits of possibility. But my traveling back and forth to Africa had been difficult on Mindi, left at home to cope with two small kids, a job as a doctor at the student health center at the University of Maryland, and managing my ecstatic escapades.

Later that fall, our child survival team at USAID in Washington was called into an unexpected meeting. By the time I made it into the conference room, I'd already learned that USAID had decided to establish a large new population, health, and nutrition program. We were going to meet Paul Hartenberger, head of the new program. The windowless meeting space, with its huge square table surrounded by 20 padded executive chairs and a row of seats behind for junior staff, was already full.

Paul was a senior official—tall, fit, with thinning gray hair. He had decades of front-line development experience, working and raising his family in India, Bolivia, and currently Zambia. Unlike so many other bureaucrats, his penetrating eyes still shone with passion for action. He mesmerized the room with his ideas.

Leaving the meeting, Ronnie Waldman whispered to me, "You should keep your eye on this program and latch onto it if you can." Within a few months, I was scheduled to take a five-week trip to Zambia—in mid-January 1996. My job was to go to Lusaka to help design the Zambia Child Health Program, a new $20 million, five-year effort to increase immunization and treat diarrhea and pneumonia in children under five.

I was in hog heaven. I couldn't wait to get back into the field. But I was also worried: I knew Mindi was going to be very stretched, going solo with a baby and a rambunctious toddler for over a month while working part-time. I checked in with her before I committed. Without hesitation, she encouraged me to go forward with the trip. She knew that my happiness was inextricably linked to my sense of purpose, and right now it was children's health.

I didn't take her generosity lightly. Mindi and I were still adjusting to parenting two small boys, neither of whom slept through the night. We were both dealing with chronic sleep deprivation. The Mali experience had rattled the foundations of our marriage, and we had some healing to do. I yearned to recreate the ecstatic part of my mystical experience in Mali, while Mindi persistently feared I might lose my social navigational skills again. Her worry left me resentful. But I, too, wondered if I would be able to stay sane if it happened again.

We decided we needed some time alone together. To usher in the New Year of 1996, we dropped Lian and Yonah off with Mindi's parents in Philadelphia and headed to New York City for the weekend. We went to Broadway shows, walked the streets of Greenwich Village, ate amazing Italian food, and caught up on our sleep and lovemaking. We remembered how much we liked each other, basking in our real, solid, sacred union.

Two weeks later I was in Zambia, a small, landlocked country in Southern Africa. This former British colony, called Northern Rhodesia until 1964, was sparsely populated— about 10 million people at that time. The capital city, Lusaka, reminded me of Niamey and the smaller towns in Nigeria. It was a sleepy capital city, with none of the vibrancy of Lagos or New Delhi.

I was delighted and a little starstruck to meet the Minister of Health, Dr. Katele Kalumba, and his leading deputies, Dr. James Banda and Vincent Musowe. They were giants in the global health universe at that time. Kalumba, Banda, and Musowe had devised a visionary, paradigm-busting health reform process that had become a model for Africa. They were committed to a universal health care system for all Zambians.

Paul Hartenberger and I spent a lot of time together on this trip, strategizing how to leverage U.S. support to save as many children's lives as possible. By the end of the five weeks, he had invited me to join his team in Lusaka at an unspecified time in the future. We agreed to start the bureaucratic processes to make this happen.

A few weeks after my return from Zambia, Mindi came out of the bathroom and held a familiar item in front of my nose. I saw the pink lines of the pregnancy test. I fell back on the color-blind excuse: "That looks negative, right?"

You would think that two doctors could have figured out effective contraception, but it turned out, thanks to our New Year's reconnection weekend, we were pregnant again. Mindi and I were blessed with a powerful brand of relentless fertility.

Truthfully, I was overwhelmed by the news. We were on the cusp of having three children under four years old. I was worried about being outnumbered, feeling stretched emotionally and physically, and being shredded by sleep deprivation, balancing jobs with family life, and financial concerns. My mind raced with worries.

How would we pay for all of the diapers, food, and day care?

How are we going to fit everyone in one car?

Will we ever afford to travel overseas again as a family?

Was Zambia now out of the equation?

I thought farther into the future and realized that our three kids would all be in college at the same time. My heart sunk under the weight.

The next day, my father came for a visit. Sitting at our dining room table over a Sunday brunch of bagels and lox, I told Dad how overwhelmed I felt as I adjusted to the idea of a third baby.

Dad dunked his bagel into his coffee. I sat back, irritated by this grotesque habit of his. "You and Mindi will figure it all out," he said. "Things'll be fine."

"You have no idea what I've been through," I snapped at him, annoyed. "Please stop assuming that you know the future." A few days later, after reflecting on this conversation, I actually heard my Dad's experience and wisdom come through. I realized he was right. We would make it work.

During the eighth month of the pregnancy, Mindi's doctors put her on bed rest at home to avoid a recurrence of pre-term labor. Recognizing that I was going to be stretched beyond my limits—Mindi immobilized, me working full-time, a three-year-old and a 13-month-old to care for—Mindi's Aunt Vicki moved in, bringing her 10-year old daughter, Jacinda, to support the next family expansion project.

Emet Shalom Zeitz was born in September. I was now 34 years old, the father of three sons. Mindi and I had evolved from a couple into a family of five in a little over 40 months.

We were excited about Emet, a healthy baby with a full head of brown hair, and equally excited about our assignment to Zambia, which was now confirmed. Adapting to parenting three boys, we began packing up our lives. We filled the blue steamer trunks Sandi bought us all those years before, as well as dozens of boxes. We bought a year's supply of diapers and pull-ups, put many of our cherished items away in storage, and sold our car. At the end of November of 1996, Mindi and I pushed ourselves out of the bubble of life in America. Lian was three and a half, Yonah was 18 months, and Emet was just 11 weeks old.

I was to start work immediately as an advisor to the Government of Zambia on HIV/AIDS, population issues, health, and nutrition. Yes, all of it.

The long plane ride to Zambia was a blur of changing diapers and managing bottles. Mindi and I caught each other's eye at one point, and we smiled knowingly, both remembering our time escorting the four Korean orphans to the U.S. It felt like my sheer will power, with a little luck and a bit of providence, had aligned to bring our youthful dreams into reality. The road was convoluted and unpredictable, but we had finally done it.

CHAPTER 22

Lusaka

Arriving at the Lusaka International Airport, we disembarked into a crowded customs hell. Zambian officials insisted on inspecting every one of our carry-on bags and all of our luggage—over a dozen trunks, boxes, and suitcases filled the hall. Feeling hassled, I took charge of shoving our belongings, along with three exhausted children, from one counter to the next as we were moved, searched, moved, and searched again. But although the officials were irritating in their officialdom, they exuded a unique brand of calmness, kindness, and patience—virtues that I was still learning.

Finally, we stepped out of the airport into the African sun and headed to the pick-up zone where a U.S. Embassy van was waiting to drive us to our new home.

We passed through neighborhoods with clusters of small homes made of clay and cement blocks with tin roofs—standard housing for Lusakans. Women stood by the road, balancing heavy trays on their heads laden with fruit and snacks to sell to passing traffic. The roads were filled with overcrowded white minibuses stuffed with people piled upon each other.

Then we arrived at our home, a large ranch house with five bedrooms, a beautiful outside veranda, large living areas, and a decent kitchen. It was a luxurious walled and guarded compound—complete with a sparkling swimming pool and a large yard, all set up and arranged by the U.S. government. This home was more than twice as large as any we had ever lived in.

Our dog Yote arrived on a separate flight a couple of days later. Like Lian and Yonah, Yote was thrilled with the large outdoor spaces of our compound.

Word of our arrival spread through the community like a wildfire burning through the tall grass. By the second day, a line of Zambians was waiting at our gate to apply for household positions.

Back in the states, Mindi and I had only ever hired a part-time nanny. But here we were expected to have an army of nannies, cooks, guards, drivers, gardeners, housekeepers, and pool cleaners. The idea of so many people taking over our daily family responsibilities made us a bit uncomfortable. But we assured each other that we were doing the right thing by giving work to our new neighbors.

We hired Bernadette, a middle-aged mother of three, and a younger woman named Rebecca, as nannies, Justone to cook, Peter to be our gardener, and Philip and Joshua as guards, alternating 12-hour shifts. Having so many employees seemed ridiculously extravagant. We were in Zambia to serve others, not to spoil ourselves. But we realized that both expat and Zambians who could afford to hire help did so, that it was what was expected.

With the help of our staff, we found we could be extremely productive in our jobs and keep up with the busy Zambian expatriate life with our young family of five.

Our house was equipped top to bottom with panic buttons. In case of a burglary or other emergency, the Zambian security company guarding the house would be mobilized. We also had walkie-talkies to contact the U.S. Embassy. Steel bars covered all of the windows. A steel door closed off the hallway leading to the bedrooms to create a "safe zone" that was locked every night with a padlock and key. Midnight snack trips to the kitchen or to let Yote out were like staging a heist.

One day, four-year-old Lian was exploring and playfully pressed one of the emergency panic buttons on the outside wall. A red light started flashing and a loud siren blared from the top of the house. Eighteen minutes later, six men from the security company arrived in a rickety old truck carrying sticks and wearing helmets with face shields. They were disorganized. No one was in charge. They did not make me feel safe. The incident left me fretting that my family would be unprotected if an actual crime occurred.

The majority of Zambians live in the urban areas of Lusaka and other cities in the copper mining zone. Although there are over 70 ethnic groups, most people speak English and either Nyanja or Bemba, the two main local languages. Most Zambians at the time were living in extreme poverty, earning less than $1 per day. They were in survival mode: literally trying to stay alive from one day to the next.

I began visiting community health programs in urban Lusaka, spending time in the marketplaces and talking with people about their lives. One young man told me he spent most of his time trying to earn a few *kwacha*, the local currency, to buy food each day. If he had enough money, he would splurge on a tiny plastic bag with a few ounces of oil to cook the food. When money was tight, his family didn't eat at all.

The nurses at the health clinic explained to me that young girls may sell tomatoes, or they may be pushed by family members to sell themselves in order to survive. One young mother at the clinic who was carrying a baby on her back wrapped in a *chitenge* (a sling made from local fabric) and watching over two small toddlers, told me she was just seeking a spoonful of sugar and a small amount of maize meal. From it, she could make the carbohydrate-rich *nshima*, a local staple to feed herself and her children.

On a visit to a community recreational center, where HIV prevention efforts were underway, I sat under a tall shade tree talking in English with a group of teenage boys. I had decided to be open and candid, so we started joking about how fun it is to have sex. But I shifted to a serious tone to talk about HIV, explaining that unprotected sex was a threat to their future and their lives. One boy insisted in Nyanja, which was translated for me, that skin-to-skin sex was so much better. It was hard to disagree with that point. Nevertheless, I kept trying to convince them about the importance of using condoms every time. One outspoken 17-year-old laughingly blurted, "I don't even know if I'm going to be alive in a day or next week, so why should I wear that rubber thing that will keep me from dying in ten years?" In that moment, I understood why our rich-country concepts of health and HIV prevention were utterly failing in Zambia.

Living in Africa full-time was a completely different experience than my prior visits, where I mostly stayed at posh hotels. Our new neighborhood was considered wealthy and safe, even though it was directly adjoining more impoverished areas. There was a stark contrast between our expatriate lifestyle and the survival mode of our Zambian neighbors. We were warned that desperation crimes—carjacking, burglaries, and pick-pocketing—were regularly committed against expatriates. I decided not to mention these details to my parents whenever we communicated by phone or email. My chronic fear would have only intensified their own worries and fueled my own in turn—a never-ending cycle of paranoia.

Mindi and I focused on everyday adventures. Learning to drive on the left side of the road with the steering wheel on right side of the car was a fun challenge. "Stay-left-stay-left!" Mindi cried while I was driving, and I did the same for her. The leading cause of death for expats in Zambia was car accidents. We assiduously avoided driving at night on the poorly maintained roads outside of Lusaka. This was probably the greatest threat to our lives.

We purchased a used Hiace minivan imported from Japan and had U.S.–approved car seats for each of the kids—a novelty to our Zambian staff. Mindi had a wooden carrier built in the back seat to hold a small color TV with an integrated video player. We thought ourselves so modern and innovative for having Disney films ready to roll when we ventured out of Lusaka on our daylight-only travels to Harare, Zimbabwe, ten hours away, to stock up on cheaper diapers and other household goods.

There were other dangers. One weekend, when was I traveling for work, Mindi and our nanny Rebecca took the boys for several nights of camping along the Chongwe River, a crocodile- and hippo-infested tributary of the great Zambezi River in southeastern Zambia. They pitched their tent below a patch of tall acacia trees, which held the favorite fruit of elephants. That night, Mindi woke to hear elephants feeding directly above their heads. One step forward, and everyone would have been crushed. Rebecca woke up, and immediately went rigid with fear, then began praying. People in the neighboring tent were also awakened. They whispered to Mindi and Rebecca to not move while they shooed away the elephants. The tents were pitched well away from the acacias for the rest of the trip.

The people I met in Zambia, from the young father at the market to my colleagues at the Ministry of Health, showed a unique sprit. Although most were living in poverty, they were also enigmatically happy. They yearned to create a better life. They did not want to stay in poverty. But they weren't despondent or bitter. They were living naturally in the present moment, rather than planning a future or lamenting the past.

Seeing this community of people coping with uncertainty yet being authentically happy was shocking and inspiring to me. I was sure I would constantly be miserable in a life entrenched in poverty. I realized I still had so much to learn: I could strengthen my own resilience by taking on some of the Zambian ways of being. Being miserable with my own life at times, I came to realize that, ultimately, happiness is more dependent on your internal state of satisfaction than on material things.

CHAPTER 23

Inner Racist

AFTER being in Zambia for just a few weeks, something extremely strange started happening to me. Unbidden, racist feelings and judgments started creeping into my thoughts. I was disgusted with myself, but it seemed out of my conscious control.

Naturally, I thought of myself as an inclusive, "color-blind" person in terms of race. I had already spent quite a bit of time working on and off in Africa and Latin America among people of many different backgrounds and ethnicities who I thought of as my peers. But one day, I walked into the Ministry of Health and greeted a Zambian colleague as I passed. He was actually a friend of mine. But in that moment, I watched and heard my mind label him with a racist epithet.

Where did that come from?

In that moment, childhood memories bubbled up. At Dad's hoagie shop in Philadelphia in the 1970s, I worked alongside many African-Americans. Now I could clearly remember Dad's voice griping about how the *shvartzsas* were lazy and never got their work done. *Shvartzsa* is a derogatory Yiddish term—basically the N-word. The realization that I had this imprinted racism going on in my head deeply shocked and embarrassed me.

This was not just one isolated incident. Racism seemed to be alive inside me like a sleeping monster. I became vividly aware of a veil of negativity through which I viewed my Zambian colleagues and friends. This was the first time I had lived for an extended time in a place where I was a racial minority, and I had to confront my hypercritical inner demons.

That night, as Mindi and I lay in bed talking after the kids were asleep, I shared with her my shame about how my racist mind was operating.

I was living in Zambia, representing the U.S. government. I was a tall, white, male, Jewish doctor. As we discussed our white privilege and our elite neocolonial lifestyle, I felt ashamed and troubled about my own blind spots. This could not continue. I committed to Mindi and myself that I would find a way to change my negative pattern of racist thinking.

Awareness was a big first step in addressing this flaw in myself. I set about consciously filing down and smoothing the damaged grooves in my psyche where racism had taken residence decades before.

Over the coming weeks, I experimented with intentionally invoking my biological color blindness. I worked hard to look at all people, including my Zambian colleagues, as the people they were—as their highest selves. I worked to rewire my brain to force it to halt racist, bigoted, and stereotypical thoughts. Mindi and I talked for hours as I fought to expose the hidden depths of my own unearned privilege. I tried to live in the full awareness that too many people of color are systematically oppressed due to their race.

My mind called up the image of Martin Luther King, Jr., talking about his dream of a time when all people of the world will not be judged by the color of their skin, but by the content of their character. I was now committed to live by this creed.

CHAPTER 24

View from the Apocalypse

W ITHIN a few weeks of our arrival in Zambia, Mindi took a part-time position as a medical officer at the U.S. Embassy, where she cared for the families of American diplomats as well as anyone working for USAID or other American government agencies. On her off hours she would visit local orphanages to see how care was delivered to Zambian children.

We enrolled Lian and Yonah in pre-school at the American International School where they met teachers and children from around the world, although we were disappointed to learn that the school's charter did not allow Zambian children to enroll. In those early days, the boys regularly invited the Zambian children of our nannies and neighbors to play in our large yard. Baby Emet stayed at home, doted on by Bernadette and Rebecca. He scrunched his eyes with happiness wrapped tightly in a *chitenge* cloth swaying peacefully on Rebecca's back as she hummed Zambian songs.

My job in Zambia was to support the country's efforts to reform the health system and deliver an essential package of basic health services, including both prevention and cures. I was intent on bringing my passion for action as an advisor inside the government's Central Board of Health. I was assigned a desk in a small windowless office shared with Zambia's child survival and nutritional advisor, Justine Mpuka. He was a young guy—a sharp dresser with a huge, happy grin—and his friendly nature welcomed me. I was the first American ever to work inside the Zambian Ministry of Health, so I wasn't sure how I was being perceived. I felt a little unsure about my new role but I decided to just be myself and do all the good for all the people I could.

Justine was totally aligned with that goal. While he wasn't a key decision-maker, we strategized and plotted on ways to address vitamin A deficiency and malnutrition in children with diarrhea, pneumonia, or AIDS. Before long, we were putting forward proposals for new programs, and the higher-ups were listening. Justine and I also shared stories of our sleep-deprived family life. We were both new fathers of young non-sleeping children and we became fast friends.

One morning I toured the country's premier health facility, the University Teaching Hospital (UTH). Though this was the best hospital in the country, it was known locally as the "departure lounge." Those days, it was for people on a one way-trip—Zambians of all ages and backgrounds went there to die.

I saw more seriously ill people at UTH in a few hours than I had seen during my three years working in hospitals in Philadelphia. The wards were filled with patients, sometimes two or three people sharing a single bed. Other patients were left on gurneys in the hallways, some were even lying directly on the floor. Families crowded around their sick loved ones with food and water, trying to offer comfort in this desperate situation. Some patients were lying in their own feces and vomit. As I walked through the halls, we saw almost no medical or nursing staff. There were literally no rubber gloves, let alone medicines or IV fluids, for maintaining basic hygiene and care. I was stunned.

My shock deepened when I entered the hospital's malnutrition ward. I walked into a dark room with a maze of 30 cribs filled with very sick children, some wailing, others flaccid and silent. The healthiest babies had cribs closest to the door and their moms were able to feed them water and a loose porridge or custard by mouth. Many of these young children were infected with HIV from their mothers and their young and weak immune systems quickly collapsed.

As I walked through the first row towards the sicker kids, several women in the last row started wailing. A small girl wrapped in a torn brown and red cloth took her last breath. Her mother stood over her weeping.

My heart broke. Nothing was being done to stop these children from dying.

If this is what is happening in the top medical facility in the national capital, how many children never make it here?

How many children are dying at home?

How many children are dying in facilities all over the city?

How many children are dying in rural areas where the health services were weak or nonexistent?

So many children dying, day after day. The grief I felt for them poured like wet cement into the depths of my soul.

Then anger surged in me as I thought about all the IV fluids, medicines, and other hospital products routinely available in the U.S. The hospital in Philadelphia where I trained threw away more hospital products in a week than UTH used in a year. Mindi had access to all the supplies she needed for Americans receiving care at the embassy, while here, just two blocks away, Zambian caregivers couldn't even provide adequate nutrition for dying children. The injustice enraged me! I had chosen to be at this site of devastation, and now I was going to put my foot down. I had to find ways to fix this crisis as fast as possible.

Death was everywhere in Zambia then. It seemed no one was safe from its hand. One morning, I was driving my usual route to my office at Central Board of Health past the UTH. Just ahead of my car, at the intersection of Burma Road, I could see young people from the Christian Aid Youth Project selling something on the roadside. I had noticed them there before, but this time I took a closer look at their merchandise.

I pulled over to the side of the road. Unable to stop myself, I started to weep. I had driven through this intersection dozens of times, but I hadn't actually seen what was in front of me. They were selling coffins—adult-sized, and ones small enough for children and babies.

The injustice I saw in front of me burned like a raging fire through my soul. The Holocaust bells from my childhood rang in my head. This time was different, I was no longer going to remain complicit in the AIDS holocaust. In a swirl of memories, I recalled a book I read during medical school by German philosopher Johann Wolfgang von Goethe, who said:

> *Until one is committed, there is hesitancy, the chance to draw back—Concerning all acts of initiative (and creation), there is one elementary truth that ignorance*

of which kills countless ideas and splendid plans:
that the moment one definitely commits oneself, then
Providence moves too. All sorts of things occur to
help one that would never otherwise have occurred. A
whole stream of events issues from the decision, raising
in one's favor all manner of unforeseen incidents and
meetings and material assistance, which no man could
have dreamed would have come his way. Whatever
you can do, or dream you can do, begin it. Boldness
has genius, power, and magic in it. Begin it now.

Seeing those tiny coffins, ready for the lifeless bodies of children who did not need to die, was the moment I committed my life to waging justice.

CHAPTER 25

The Death of a Friend

Two weeks later, in November 1997, my colleague and friend Justine died. He was only 38—a few years older than I was—with a wife and five young children. It was so ironic: He worked for the Zambian Ministry of Health but he died from an entirely preventable disease that was, and still is, wiping out millions of Africans: malaria.

Malaria is an infectious disease transmitted through mosquito bites. It was common for my Zambian colleagues to be out sick on a regular basis because of manageable bouts of the illness. No one knew why Justine died from it, possibly because the infection went into his brain. Or perhaps he died from another cause completely and malaria was the public story. That was common too.

On the day of Justine's funeral, my colleagues from the ministry and I headed straight for the cemetery. We were joined by hundreds of others, people arriving in droves, by car or bus, to bear witness to this tragic loss of a young father.

The funeral was held at the Leopards Hill Memorial Park cemetery, a new large plot in the northeastern part of town along the road where we drove our kids to school every day. We joined the procession of cars driving through the cemetery gates.

It was a warm and sunny morning, with a pale blue sky. Masses of people swarmed the grounds. After finally securing a parking spot, I walked around trying to find Justine's burial site. I was told I first needed to go to the viewing hall—a small, outdoor shed-like structure with no walls. We could see there were several rooms with four other viewings going on. Hundreds of people crowding around and I didn't recognize anyone.

Finally, I located Justine in one of the hot rooms. How still and serious he looked, so unlike the Justine who just last week had been working hard and making everyone laugh with his joking. His open casket was surrounded by a crowd of wailing, screaming women, some collapsed on the floor. His wife and young children stood nearby in stunned silence. I made eye contact with Mrs. Mpuka. I saw devastation in her numbed gaze.

The cries of despair from the other women sliced into me. These were a people who had seen too much death in recent years. Rather than dimming their emotions, each passing of a loved one unleashed fresh outpourings of anguish. I was surprised. In day-to-day life, I had found Zambians to be generally reserved—the total opposite of my own Jewish culture, where we are loud and cantankerous in our everyday life, but solemn at funerals where emotions are contained.

From the viewing hall, I walked slowly by myself to the burial site nearby. There were four simultaneous burials happening within stepping distance of each other. Each of the deceased had over a hundred tearful mourners performing different rituals. The graves and funerals were in such proximity that I slipped in the mud and almost fell into an adjacent grave as I looked for a spot to stand among the crowd.

One nearby service was being conducted by a Salvation Army preacher accompanied by a large group of uniformed people singing and playing tambourines. A smaller gathering of nuns dressed in all white adjoined Justine's group, with its glut of Ministry of Health officials and guards. I felt bewildered by the kaleidoscope of death rituals around me.

Justine's service was led by an elderly preacher dressed in long robes who offered a curious blend of traditional Zambian songs and Christian hymns. Several government officials from the Ministry of Health spoke. As the final tribute to my friend, Justine's casket was covered with dirt by group of family members until the mound rose three feet high. Then each mourner laid long stemmed roses of different colors. Some had brought whole bouquets. For those, like me, who had come empty-handed, there was a large white plastic bucket of flowers. I took my place in line, picked a single white rose from the bucket, and placed it on the grave on top of the others. My eyes were swollen with unshed tears as the sad service ended.

Exiting the cemetery in my car, we were stopped at the exit by a grumpy policeman to allow another funeral procession to pass into the cemetery. It was a state funeral for a senior advisor to President Chiluba, dead from AIDS. One of the buses carrying staff from the Office of the President sideswiped us, crashing into our car. As I sat in this traffic jam trying to leave, I was struck by the irony that I drove past this cemetery each morning with my kids, and while I had noticed bustling activity here every single day, I felt an even deeper emotional connection to the hundreds of thousands of Zambians who were dying before their time, and their loved ones. It wasn't until later that night, in the privacy of my own bedroom, that I folded, weeping in grief over the loss of Justine and so many other Zambians, as Mindi held me in her arms.

The next weekend, Mindi, the boys, and I paid our respects at the Mpuka home. Frequently in Zambia, a deceased husband's family of origin will seize the house and other property, leaving the widow and children destitute. And sometimes the widow would be forced to become the second or third wife to her dead husband's eldest brother. Her children would become lowest on the pecking order, with girl children at the very bottom.

I was relieved to learn that Justine's generous and fair-minded father had given the house and its contents to Justine's children. Justine's widow Doris was proving amazingly resourceful herself. She and I stood in the darkened foyer as she softly talked about how she was coping. She had decided to stay in her home and pursue training to improve her prospects of getting a job, so she could make sure all of their children could go to school, like Justine had done. Mindi and I were eager to contribute to the children's school fees, a small gesture of support. But it felt almost tokenistic, like putting a small Band-Aid on a gaping wound of despair.

CHAPTER 26

Intractable Problems

T HE longer we stayed in Zambia, the more of our friends got sick and died from AIDS-related diseases. My Zambian colleagues working for USAID, for the Zambia government, and for all our partner organizations, were dying. Most of their jobs remained vacant as there were so few educated and qualified people to replace them. There was a huge human capacity gap. In this wake of so much death, many children were orphaned.

AIDS hit close to my home. People we knew had siblings who had died from AIDS. A friend of mine, a sweet-natured single mother of a four-year-old—the same age as Yonah— suffered several serious ailments, though she never told me the cause. She was a loving soul and she won my heart when she hung a poem I had written where she worked. I was extremely insecure in my poetry skills and her positive acknowledgement of my words meant a lot to me.

During one of her near-fatal hospitalizations, the doctors determined she urgently needed high-powered anti-fungal IV drugs to survive. Mindi and I went to a private Lusaka medical clinic, bought the drugs, and brought them to her bedside. She survived that bout. But died two weeks later.

In Zambia there was no consistent access to antiretroviral (ARV) medications—a triple-drug cocktail that was readily available in the rich countries of Europe and the U.S. and Japan. It cost $12,000 per year to treat one person with ARV. Mindi and I felt miserable that we could not afford to help. The cost was also way beyond the capacity of the Zambian health system, and even beyond the insurance policies of local USAID employees. Fewer than 1 percent of Africans living with HIV were getting the lifesaving ARVs that were readily available in the developed world.

I felt myself going numb. To manage my daily sense of despair and preserve my empathy, I decided not to attend any more funerals. I had heard enough of the howling cries of grief at cemetery viewing halls, on and on and on, as the tragedy raged publicly and privately in every home and office.

When we modeled future projection of the AIDS epidemic in Zambia, the results sickened me. The death rate was not expected to peak for several more years, when one out of five people aged 15 to 44 would be lost. Taking out this huge proportion of the Zambian population would be devastating to families, communities, and the future of the nation. I imagined what the world's response would be if 20 percent of Americans or Europeans were destined to die because they didn't have the resources to buy these readily available drugs. Did anyone care about this gross geographical injustice?

In studying the epidemic's pattern in Zambia, we saw that pervasive gender inequality was contributing significantly to the crisis. Regions where women were most powerless had the highest rates of HIV, a trend that continues today. Girls in

Zambia were commonly the last to be fed, clothed, and sent to school. Many left home before they were teenagers, forced into early marriage or prostitution.

Survival prostitution was a fact of life for many young girls in the region. Women in general were controlled by men in many visible and invisible ways. It was common for young school girls to hang out at truck stops at the beginning of the school year to have sex with older men in order to get money to pay school fees and buy books and uniforms.

I learned about a local women's group, Asuito ("Let Us Try"), that had been active for a decade by then, creating education programs for children and adults, income-generating projects, and community-based health care. The results they were seeing were astounding: significant drops in maternal deaths, improvement in childhood malnutrition, and increased vaccination rates. I wanted to see how we could replicate these programs around the country.

There were many other community-led, women-led, youth-led, and faith-based efforts in Zambia. Yet on their own, the efforts were too small to permanently alter the equation for these dignified, hard-working people. I kept digging and exploring, and asking, *How can we let this happen?* I soon came face to face with the reality that poor countries like Zambia were trapped in a global economic system that kept them poor. It was pure economic and racial injustice.

If we as humans, living in this time of history, truly want to align our inner compassion with our outer reality, then we must take a hard look in the mirror and recognize our complacency and even comfort with the status quo—and the fact that this status quo prolongs the oppression of others.

My mind was racing with tough questions:

What could I do as one person?

What could we do together to create effective social transformation movements?

What will it take to reach the tipping point for a constructive transformation?

Can we organize ourselves to prevent an apocalypse?

Or do we have to go over the cliff, and then pick up the pieces in a new way?

I was in a war with myself—bouncing from a deep well of despair and hopelessness amid the holocaust all around me to a crystal-clear vision of how I would mobilize a massive response to save lives and bring hope and recovery to all Zambians. The ping-pong of my thoughts left me feeling impotent and angry at my inability to act. I could feel the downhill gravity pulling me into despair.

CHAPTER 27

Shroud Practice

MY mind was scrambling to make sense of the current state of the world and to find a way to improve life for Zambia's poor. To people around me, I appeared extremely intense, stressed out, and not fun to be around. I didn't want that.

By our second year in Zambia, I had gained 10 to 15 stress pounds. Whenever I walked into work at the Zambian government, many of my Zambian co-workers, cleaners, and drivers started greeting me with bigger smiles, saying, "Hey, you are looking fat!" I hated being called fat. It triggered the worst kind of self-loathing and shame.

At first, whenever I heard these words, I would keep walking forward with my head down, grumble a reluctant "Hello," and struggle to shove down my anger at being called this name. Still, it kept happening. I shared my distress to a Zambian co-worker, who explained that calling someone fat in Zambian culture is a huge compliment. Being fat is a sign of wealth and success because you can buy enough food to get fat. I roared with laughter when realizing that I was being given compliments, yet I was inadvertently receiving the words as insults. From that day on, I smiled and thanked the people who were admiring my fatness—even if I internally hated that (true) label.

To counter my misery, I began sifting through religious and spiritual teachings of many kinds. I learned about Buddhist mantra practices, where you repeat sacred phrases to program your mind. I continued learning and practicing the sacred Hebrew chants that had helped me in Arizona, connecting me to a higher purpose and taking me out of the machinations of my own mind.

But my intense inner battles raged on, whittling away at my sense of self and compromising my ability to function as a fat husband, father, and global health worker.

To manage the intensity of my emotions, I dived deep into silence. I traveled to Upstate New York to attend a seven-day silent meditation program taught by Rabbi David and Shoshana Cooper—spiritual masters who wove Buddhist meditation and chanting into Jewish religious practices.

This retreat was highly scheduled, beginning at 6 a.m. and going until 10 p.m. Structured, hour-long sessions began with the ring of a chime. I would spend that hour sitting silently on a cushion, tracking my breath, watching the thoughts that emerged, and aiming to keep my back straight and my posture erect. When the chime rang again, our group was guided in a walking meditation. We walked back and forth inside a ten-foot elliptical space, awareness rising with every step.

It was tough to transition from the frenzy of my life in Zambia to the extreme silence of the retreat. But by the fourth day, my mind started to slow down, and I could examine the patterns of my own thinking. I realized that before I traveled, I would mentally start packing my bags five days in advance.

In my mind, I would keep a running list of everything that I needed to pack, and I would repeat this over and over again. *What a waste of mental effort to ruminate on packing,* I thought.

I identified other useless mind patterns, which helped me realize how much time and energy I was spending on mundane tasks. But I had the freedom to choose. I could halt those mental tapes, stop my thought, redirect my attention to calmer things.

More importantly, the more time I spent sitting in silence, I was forced to grapple with my rapidly firing, jumbled, monkey mind; my vast network of negative thought patterns; and the deep roots of my anger. I also saw how frequently my mind was focused on negatively judging others, creating fictitious stories about them, and forming opinions about people based on what they were wearing or how they looked.

This outer judgment was really a mirror into my own self-hate. I gained fuller awareness of the inner demons who were telling me how inadequate I was and how hopeless the problems of the world were. *Who do you think you are, that you can help solve these global crises?* they mocked. While this awareness was enlightening, it was also very frustrating. I felt I could do little to tame them.

I also imagined that everyone else in the world was struggling just like me. I believed my crazy monkey mind was normal.

I traveled to these stateside retreats from Zambia several times. Mindi joined me on a couple to experience the power of silence for herself. During one of our debriefs at the end of one weeklong silent retreat, I realized that my wife didn't have the same kind of deeply entrenched grooves of negativity and hyper-criticism I had. I was starting to realize that I was not normal.

Whenever I returned to my family and work life, I could predict the exact number of hours it would take for my mind to go from enlightened back to petty and self-destructive. This frustrated me beyond measure.

I had some deep work to do on myself.

An idea began to form. To break the demons and the negative patterns, I would practice my own death. This way, I could fully embody my own limited time to live. During our second year in Zambia, as part of my meditation on life, I created a spiritual practice in which I willed myself to experience the finality and silence of death.

When Jewish people die, the body is ritual cleansed by loved ones and then is dressed in a white linen shroud. The garment has multiple parts: pants for the legs, foot coverings, a body wrap with strap, and a head wrap. I yearned to wrap myself in a burial shroud.

I don't know what Mindi said to her parents exactly, but Sandi and Jerry convinced a Philadelphia funeral home to sell them a shroud. On the day it arrived, I closed the door of my office, my heart racing as I slowly opened the package.

Holy shit, this is my shroud!

This is the cloth I will be buried in.

Am I crazy for asking for this?

Then, on a quiet Saturday morning, I went into one of the unused bedrooms in our home in Lusaka and locked the door. I undressed and slowly wrapped myself in each of the parts of the shroud. I laid quietly for more than an hour, focusing on my breath, and gradually imagining my own death. From this experience of embodying my death, I looked backward at my relationships, my accomplishments, my failures, and the intense feeling of loss as I imagined slipping my physical bonds with Mindi and the boys.

After I took off the shroud, that feeling stayed with me for the rest of the day, infusing my interactions with my family. I suddenly felt I had real clarity about how I wanted to create my life. Once a month, on the Jewish Sabbath, I wrapped myself in the burial shroud and lay in silence. Within a few months, I refined and embedded an internal memo to myself in my mind:

You never know when your time is up, so make the best of every day.

Live today as if it may be your last day alive.

Be bold and take action now.

I continued the practice every month for about six months during our stay in Zambia. This meditation helped me become more connected to the preciousness of my own existence and the need to genuinely live fully, each and every day.

CHAPTER 28

Morning Coup

Early in the morning of Tuesday, October 28, 1997, we were awakened by an emergency warning signal blasting from the U.S. Embassy communication system. The message was garbled, but we heard this much: "Please stay in your home in the internal gated part of the house." A military coup to overthrow the democratically elected government was in progress.

I became semi-frantic. Mindi was alarmed, but she remained calm. We rushed around the house gathering food, flashlights, and first aid supplies, checked on our sleeping kids, and locked ourselves inside the security gate protecting the bedrooms. Sitting by the radio, we heard a man calling himself Captain Solo announce that he had taken over the country and was dismissing the chiefs of the army and the police. President Chiluba's residence had been surrounded by military, and he had been given until 9 a.m. to surrender or be killed. Machine-gun fire echoed outside in the distance, along with a few faint explosions, followed by long silences. Four-and-a half-year-old

Lian awoke first, padding into our room and asking, "Daddy, what's happening?" It felt like we were living in a bad action movie.

Then began the stream of phone calls from friends and family in the U.S. and from colleagues in Lusaka who reported hearing machine guns and mortars, the same we were hearing at our house. In my mind, I imagined the rebel soldiers would overrun our compound and murder my family.

Oh my god! What have I done?

I wanted this so badly.

My selfish dream to work in Africa was risking the lives of my wife and children!

We called our friends Ellie and Trevor—who had been expats in Central America and lived through two coups—for advice. Trevor told us to sit tight and not pack yet. These events have bizarre ways of playing out, he said, encouraging me to stay calm.

At 8:00 a.m. our doorbell rang. I opened the security gate and slipped out, locking Mindi and the boys back inside. With trepidation, I tiptoed to the front of the house and peered through the front window. I saw our next-door neighbor, Captain Chewa, an independent member of the Zambian Parliament and a former military leader. I quickly opened the door and pulled him inside.

The normally calm government official was in a panic. He asked if he could shelter his family at our compound if matters deteriorated, fearing he would be a target for the coup leaders. I consulted quickly with Mindi, and of course we agreed. It didn't occur to us the danger we might be putting us all in.

An hour later, an announcer on the radio reassured us that President Chiluba was still in control. At noon, he gave an eloquent radio address, thanking the army for support. It turned out that Captain Solo was pretty much solo, backed only by a small group of soldiers with a few tanks who called themselves the National Redemption Council. Six plotters were arrested, including Solo. The erstwhile revolutionary had been drinking heavily the night before and had seen a vision of an angel telling him to oust the Chiluba government for its "corruption and criminality." He called his three-hour coup Operation Born Again.

After the President's address, we went to Captain's Chewa house, where his wife Patricia told us that her sister's husband was an army commander, and his home had been surrounded and invaded by the coup soldiers. He had escaped, but his wife and children had been beaten and the house ransacked. Had he stayed, they all could have been murdered. Lian had been playing there just a week before.

When Lian asked why school had been cancelled that day, Mindi told him that American kids get snow days, and Zambian kids get coup days. By the next morning, daily life in Lusaka had resumed.

But I was jarred with inner angst. I put myself through another round of questioning:

Was living in Zambia worth the risks?

Was I was putting my wife, my children, and myself in harm's way?

As normalcy rapidly returned, this wave of worry dissipated, and we moved on with our lives.

CHAPTER 29

Let Us Act

B<small>Y</small> the mid-1990s, Zambian orphanages were rapidly expanding to accommodate the large number of children left behind by parents who died from AIDS. Mindi, the boys, and I began taking family outings to a nearby orphanage, the Kasisi Children's Home, near the Lusaka airport. Kasisi housed around 150 children—more than half of them under age two.

Run by the indefatigable Sister Mariola and a group of nuns from Poland, it also housed a large medical ward to support children who were sick and dying from AIDS. The orphanage had four long, single-story buildings encircling a packed-dirt central square where there were lunch tables, play areas, and a couple of large shade trees. When the five of us would arrive, Lian would immediately find a few boys his age and they would go off kicking a ball or climbing a tree. Within minutes, their pack would grow to a dozen boys and girls all trying to be in on the games. Once Emet started walking, he would do his best to keep up with Lian, Yonah, and their mob.

The children were very well cared for, but desperately in need of individual attention for their physical, emotional, and mental growth. I would squat down and wait, and a few children would approach and hold my hand and then jump into my arms. Mindi was always surrounded by a group of kids who wanted to see baby Emet, who she carried in her arms. The kids would hang onto Mindi and me, each craving our attention and trying to get even a small taste of some tender loving care.

Sister Mariola was devoted to each of them, especially the HIV-infected children who required ongoing medical care. Mindi jumped at her invitation to come for weekly volunteer visits, where she cared for little patients as young as one week old.

The sheer number of orphans in Zambia at that time was staggering, estimated to be up to a million children, or about 10 percent of the entire population of the country. We wanted to do more than just a few hours of play. I felt we could unleash a real transformation in their lives.

One night after a visit to Kasisi, Mindi and I stayed up talking for hours after the boys were asleep. As we laid in bed, we hatched an idea. We would create a voluntary organization to expand awareness of the orphan crisis and get the local community engaged. We would call it KIDZLOVE, and we vowed to mobilize Zambians and expatriates, mainly Americans, to join forces.

Our first partner was an indigenous organization called Angels in Development, led by Angela Miyanda, the wife of Zambia's sitting vice president, Brigadier General Godfrey Miyanda. We planned to help her launch a new facility, the Kabwata Orphanage and Transit Centre. It would occupy three single-story, run-down buildings (both the land and buildings donated by the Lusaka City Council) on Burma Road, just a short drive from the University Teaching Hospital.

We surprised the local residents by organizing a volunteer work day to clean and refurbish the buildings. This kind of community teamwork wasn't common, and Mrs. Miyanda was skeptical; she wondered if anyone would come. But on a clear sunny day, nearly 50 volunteers showed up, mainly from the American community and from Mrs. Miyanda's church network. Together we cleared the weeds and created garden beds to plant crops to feed the children. We cleaned out the buildings and painted them inside and out. Lian and Yonah joined a bunch of American and Zambian kids running around and playing in the compound. We all saw the potential of this space where children could thrive.

We got a lot done on the volunteer work day, and Mrs. Miyanda was inspired to double down on her fundraising and buy beds and school materials. She started hiring staff to run the orphanage. Almost immediately, children who had been left behind in the streets filled the rooms at Kabwata.

Soon after opening, Mrs. Miyanda got a call from the obstetrics ward at UTH to pick up a newborn infant boy named David. He had been left at the hospital by his mom, who was dying from AIDS. David also had AIDS, infected in the womb like so many babies. I held him on a few of our weekend visits to Kabwata, and I was struck by the innocent sparkle in his eyes, identical to my own newborns'.

One weekday morning, a few months later, Mindi got a call from Mrs. Miyanda. David had been taken back to UTH with breathing difficulties. The doctors could do little to save him, and he died. Mrs. Miyanda could not bear to leave his tiny body in the hospital morgue, and she had asked Mindi if she could pick him up and ready him for burial.

I was heartbroken when I heard this news, but I was tied up in work meetings, so Mindi was left with this grim task. She drove the Hiace to Kabwata, picked up Mrs. Miyanda, and together they went to the mortuary at UTH to pick up the tiny body. Then they drove him to the coffin-maker, and finally to his lonely, family-less burial. Our noisy, boy-filled minivan had, for a day, become a somber hearse for David.

The ghost of David filled our lives throughout our time in Zambia. We now were living in an AIDS holocaust. Every day, Mindi and I forced ourselves to get close enough to feel the hot breath of hell blowing across our community. As I witnessed the devastation around us, my own despair spiraled. It would be so easy, I thought, to let numbness wash over me and put my conscience to sleep. So easy to blame others or decide that it was someone else's responsibility to solve this crisis.

No. How could I let this happen?

Defiance reared in me. I had to act. I needed to take on the whole system!

My first fight put me up against the USAID mission director in Zambia, the head honcho from the U.S. government. USAID headquarters in Washington had just made available a new batch of money from the Displaced Children and Orphans Fund to countries heavily affected by AIDS. We were being offered $1 million for Zambia. But the mission director refused to accept it. He wanted us to stay focused on the other things our program was trying to do in Zambia—including child health, family planning, and HIV prevention through condom promotion.

I went into full angry-activist mode. I was not going to allow this $1 million to be lost for the Zambian children. My boss, Paul Hartenberger, supported my efforts, and we hatched a multi-pronged strategy. We scheduled a Saturday morning briefing with the mission director. I enlisted UNICEF representatives to join us.

It was a tension-filled the room. We argued that this level of community collapse could destabilize the country, with national and global security implications. I promised that my team could handle this program expansion, on top of all the other programs we were responsible for. The director argued that our program was too diffuse already and we didn't have the capacity to take on more challenges. But we prevailed: USAID in Washington called on the mission director to approve U.S. government support for Zambia's children, and in the end, he was convinced to allow the investment to proceed.

With our $1 million, we established the first U.S.–funded programs in Zambia for children orphaned and made vulnerable by HIV/AIDS. We were waging justice within the government, with outside experts, and inside the community, increasing services for children in need.

My passion for science that began in childhood had morphed into a desire to heal people, and then to improve the health of whole communities. But now something else was happening. I was leaping up to a new level of ambition. I was doing work that would improve society and the human experience. And I was just getting started.

CHAPTER 30

From Jaw-Jaw to Now-Now

MY favorite Zambian expression is *jaw-jaw*. It's similar to the American saying, "All talk, no action," and refers to the human habit of useless dialogue that wastes time and energy. I convinced my Zambian colleagues to use a counter-expression to call for urgent action: now-now! I was living the vision of my Mali manifesto.

We weren't alone. The mood was shifting. In 1998, Bono, the lead singer of the superstar rock band U2, began spearheading a global effort called the Jubilee 2000 campaign. As the world looked to a new century, he was urging rich countries to wipe out $90 billion in debt owed to them by the world's poorest nations, including Zambia. The genesis of the idea came from the biblical concept of the Year of Jubilee. In Leviticus, this is a year of emancipation and restoration, observed every 50 years, when those enslaved because of debts are freed, lands lost are returned, and communities torn apart by inequality come back together.

To me, resolved to put an end to the desperation amid the dying fields around me, this campaign seemed like a solution. To stop the dying from AIDS, we needed a game changer.

The government of Zambia had its head in the sand—the "ostrich syndrome," I called it. They were denying that AIDS was having any impact at all on the nation, and very, very little was being spent to combat the epidemic. Their denial was almost farcical. The Zambian health system was near collapse. Local health providers had only received 30 percent of their expected budget, and they were unable to offer even the most basic primary care services.

Meanwhile, the country was laying out more than $100 million annually into debt servicing, basically paying the World Bank, the International Monetary Fund, and international donors—including the U.S.—to borrow money. This was the way the system was set up. And it *was* a setup. It was the very definition of economic injustice.

The wrongness of it all was unfathomable to me. The Jubilee 2000 campaign came as a ray of hope.

But what could I do?

Could I somehow link the debt relief efforts with the urgent need to combat AIDS?

I was trapped inside U.S. government bureaucracy where official policy dictated that Zambia had to pay what it owed, on time, no matter what the circumstances. Because the U.S. drove the policies of all international financial institutions, Zambia was entrapped in a neoliberal economic agenda called the Washington Consensus.

The Washington Consensus rejected the need for lifesaving AIDS treatment because it was "too expensive" and "not cost-effective," using a dollars-vs-lives equation. This was their global policy and they were not backing down. I was embarrassed as an American, that the name of our first president was being used to describe such a wretched, non-egalitarian set of policies. American policy was unjustly shackling millions of Africans in a system of utter economic enslavement.

I felt powerless, but Bono wasn't. He caught the attention of members of Congress and President Bill Clinton, as well as global media. The Jubilee 2000 campaign was mobilizing churches, governments, and international advocates. It seemed like a big policy change was possible.

I was staying up late at night drafting an in-depth proposal linking debt relief to the mounting of large scale AIDS programs to save lives. I was formulating a plan outside the purview of my official position, a big idea that needed attention. The idea was to negotiate agreements in which donors would let Zambia keep its money in country to fight the AIDS pandemic, rather than fill the coffers of the wealthy nations of the Global North.

In March 1999, Sandy Thurman, the White House AIDS czar brought on by President Clinton in his second term, made an official visit to Zambia. My friend Deborah Bickel, who was leading newly launched orphans programs funded by USAID, helped arrange a meeting with Thurman's lead advisor, the tenacious Michael Iskowitz, a progressive political operative who had spent years on Capitol Hill working for Senator Ted Kennedy. Excitedly, I shared my proposal, and Iskowitz seemed intrigued. I walked out of the meeting doing a happy dance. I was 37 years old and, despite being successful at my career, I had still felt nervous going into this meeting. Honestly, I couldn't believe someone so high up in the U.S. government found one of my rogue and bold ideas worthy.

Thurman was on a scoping visit to help design a presidential initiative to combat HIV/AIDS in Africa—which later launched as President Clinton's Leadership and Investment in Fighting an Epidemic (LIFE) initiative. On her return to Washington, D.C., Thurman wrote to me on White House letterhead, expressing interest in connecting debt relief to an expanded AIDS response. As I held the piece of paper in front of me, I yelped with glee. I couldn't fathom it! In a matter of months, my late-night rambling brainstorms on paper had been endorsed by the White House! I was the son of a hoagie maker, and now my ideas were reaching the top of the U.S. government.

The next day, I made a hundred copies of the letter and distributed them to everyone who crossed my path. With this signal from Washington, my colleagues and friends in the Zambian government started to respond. *Finally! We were going from jaw-jaw to now-now!*

Within a few months, the Zambian Ministry of Finance presented an official government version of my Debt for AIDS proposal to the Paris Club, an influential meeting of officials from wealthy countries who controlled debt payments. Feeling the pressure of the Jubilee 2000 campaign, the wealthy governments were searching for coordinated and sustainable solutions to the debt crisis that they had created.

By late 1999, the Jubilee 2000 Campaign had won a major victory. President Clinton and Congress agreed to rapidly expanded debt relief for African countries to allow them to increase spending on health, education, AIDS control, and other essential social services.

This victory catapulted the Zambian government's Debt for AIDS proposal to capitals around the world and back to

Washington. But when my bosses at USAID in Zambia saw my freelance handprints all over it, I was called into a meeting with the mission director at USAID, who forcefully insisted that I would no longer be working on any such project. This program was deemed "outside the boundaries of my assignment." What they were really saying was that it was outside approved U.S. policy in Zambia.

I had been spending a lot of time on the initiative, working daily with the Zambian Ministry of Finance, but suddenly I was blackballed. The U.S. government did not want to do anything beyond what President Clinton had agreed. The truth is that the White House letter of support for Debt for AIDS was only lip service. By the end of 1999, I was forced to leave my position at USAID.

Mindi was angry and upset that our life in Zambia was being disrupted. She witnessed my fervent efforts to find another assignment as our future clouded over. Mindi and the children had been happy with our stable and comfortable lifestyle in Lusaka. She felt I had risked it all with my rogue ambitions. She was livid with me for stepping so far outside the box. I felt betrayed by her anger. The foundations of our marriage were rattled. We both wondered out loud if our different approaches to life, and the crises around us, could be reconciled in one family. There was so much tension and so many arguments, I wondered if we could avoid a divorce.

The Joint United Nations Programme for HIV/AIDS (UNAIDS) mission in Zambia came to the rescue. In early 2000, they quickly created a new position and established a regional Debt for AIDS initiative—and hired me to lead it. Now my family could to stay in our home in Lusaka. I would be working out of the UN offices, under the supervision of Peter McDermott, the head of UNICEF in Zambia. I would be supported to bring Debt for AIDS forward in Zambia, Uganda, Tanzania, Mozambique, and Kenya.

I was in heaven once again, saving the world. The tensions with Mindi eased somewhat. But she remained on guard for the next curveball. Instead of talking at night, she withdrew, turning her back towards me when we went to sleep.

Peter was a strong supporter of any efforts to mitigate the AIDS crisis in Zambia. He had worked for years in UNICEF's emergency relief programs and had worked in Rwanda immediately following the genocide. He knew an emergency when he saw it and he was ready for us to mobilize. First, he set up a trip for me to Uganda to meet Michel Sidibé, then the UNICEF country representative. Uganda was already a leading country in becoming qualified for a debt reduction package under the IMF's Heavily Indebted Poor Country initiative. Our meeting was a huge success. Through Michel's extremely crafty advocacy and my strategic policy ideas, we managed to integrate debt relief for AIDS into Uganda's program. The Uganda template was then replicated throughout sub-Saharan Africa.

Debt for AIDS had gone to scale in a very short time. The winds of transformation were blowing around me. I was lifted by a sense of hope and optimism that the system could be changed.

We had funding. We had opportunity. But that wasn't enough. Down at ground level, the AIDS holocaust continued without pause.

CHAPTER 31

Another Family Expansion Project

In Zambia, so many young adults, just starting their adult lives, building homes and families, were being cut down by AIDS, going from healthy to buried in months. Grandparents and other relatives struggled to care for the orphans left behind, their resources stretched to the limit.

In late 1999, Mindi and I had begun talking about adoption, reawakening our dreamy long-distance phone calls from years before. We had three sons, so we thought about adopting a daughter. We felt blessed with a comfortable life and plenty of support, and we wanted to give a home to a child out there who needed us. Even though the boys were a handful, we felt like we could handle an even larger family.

Lian, the ringleader at six years old, used force to manage the others. Yonah, at four, did whatever he could to follow his elder brother at literally every step. He was still so little but he refused to be left behind, springing out of bed in the morning and throwing on his clothes even though he couldn't work the buttons, to be dressed as quickly as Lian. Three-year-old Emet was strong-willed: punching and hitting to gain equal advantage. We imagined that a younger sister would balance our family and calm the testosterone-driven posse of three daredevil boys. Working on an adoption together healed the frayed edges of our marriage. Mindi and I were completely aligned in our desire to battle the orphan crisis around us.

But I struggled with an internal barrier. Although I had always wanted to adopt, I was afraid that I could not love an adopted child as much as my three biological sons. I had wrestled mightily with this question since experiencing the magic of falling in love with my first child.

A couple of years earlier, at a conference in Kenya, I had cornered my friend Melinda Wilson, a longtime USAID colleague. She and her husband John had a busy and successful family life with five biological and adopted children from around the world. During a lunch break, Melinda and I took a walk, finally settling down on a sunny expanse of green lawn with glasses of home-brewed iced tea.

We shared updates about our families, and I started in with my long-winded and convoluted qualms about adopting. "I love my sons so much," I whined. "Mindi and I worked so hard to bring them into the world and to raise them well. I'm not sure I can open my heart as widely for a child that isn't mine."

Melinda interrupted. "Paul," she said, looking me straight in the eyes, "it is *not* the same. Get over it!"

I was dumbfounded by her clarity and tried to protest. Shouldn't it be the same?

Melinda calmly explained that the love you feel for an adopted child is different, that it grows over time as you deepen your connection and share your lives together. I took her words into my heart. Now, after two years of processing them, I felt ready. Melinda's wisdom finally broke through a major barrier in my psyche.

Adoption experts advised us that families should only adopt children younger than the youngest child, to avoid interrupting the birth order. We began making even more frequent visits to Kasisi Children's Home, spending hours playing tag and hide-and-seek with groups of 25 to 30 toddler girls—all so sweet and beautiful. Children in orphanage settings crave attention from adults, so these angels flocked to Mindi and me, held our hands, and sat on our laps. We always left overwhelmed by the decision in front of us. Despite endless hours of discussion, we could not come up with an approach for selecting only one of the endearing little girls to join our family.

How could we choose?

It felt too powerful. We were uncomfortable wielding that level of sovereignty over another's life, knowing that so many other equally lovable and deserving children would be left behind. It was unfair and unjust.

By this time, we had been living in Zambia for more than three years. Kabwata orphanage was established as a safe, secure, and reliable institution where children could get food, clothing, shelter, and love. At the end of 1999, we urged our family to forgo sending holiday gifts to us and the boys, and instead donate to Operation KIDZLOVE and the Kabwata orphanage.

Mindi and I decided to use our family's generosity and our own resources to offer an education scholarship for one Kabwata orphan. This was something we could sustain while we were in Zambia—and after we left—until the beneficiary completed high school.

After several discussions with Mrs. Miyanda, we agreed that she would select the child to receive this educational opportunity based on who she thought would benefit the most. She selected Cletus Chipeta, a tall, 12-year-old boy with a big, all-embracing smile. He had arrived at Kabwata a few months earlier, after losing his mother, Brona, to AIDS. He came with his own set of pajamas, which Mrs. Miyanda took as a sign that he had come from a middle-class, caring family. Most children arrived impoverished with only the torn and dirty clothes on their backs.

As a single mother, Brona had raised Cletus into a confident, friendly pre-teen. When she became sick, she started to make plans. Knowing that her already-stretched family could not take on another child—they were already caring for several orphans from other deceased relatives—she arranged in advance for him to go to Kabwata. We imagined Brona had been a smart, resourceful woman.

Cletus had dropped out of school to care for his mother, and by the time he arrived at Kabwata, he had fallen two years behind in his education. Scholarship in hand, Mindi and Mrs. Miyanda worked nonstop to find a private school in Lusaka to accept Cletus in a grade corresponding with his education level instead of his age. Finally, he started fifth grade at the Lake Road Elementary School, two blocks from our home but far from Kabwata.

For the first weeks of school, we drove Cletus back and forth from the orphanage to school in our van, traveling across town in the hustle of the morning rush hour. That got old fast, so we invited Cletus to stay in our extra bedroom during the school week, returning to Kabwata on the weekends. In our home, we had so much to share with him—plentiful food, cable TV, videos, games, a swimming pool, private rooms, and three happy, active boys.

Cletus opened up to our family quickly—his intelligence, humor, and affection for the younger boys was energizing for all of us. We began to bond. I remembered those children on that long flight from Korea and wondered if my feelings were simply protective. But deep down, I knew we were all falling in love with each other.

A few months into this arrangement, Cletus became withdrawn and quiet. We soon found out why: He was being teased by jealous peers at Kabwata. The conditions of the orphanage compared to our home depressed him, according to Mrs. Miyanda.

Had we done the wrong thing?

We were at a crossroads.

Mindi and I talked for hours. We both instinctively knew what we wanted to do: Abandon our plans to adopt a baby girl, ignore the advice of experts about maintaining the birth order of our family, and adopt this boy who was considerably older than all of our sons.

Mindi and I loved Cletus, and he loved us. He and our boys had become as close as brothers. We started with some intense discussions with seven-year-old Lian, explaining that he would always be our first-born son, even though Cletus would be the oldest if he joined our family. Lian said, "Sure thing, that would be great! I love Cletus."

Mindi and I decided to follow our own inner compass. We saw the fragility of Cletus, who had lost his mom at an early age, and our hearts simply opened. Every day I faced the delicacy of life—within my mind, around our family, and with our friends and colleagues in Zambia. We were ready to receive a new gift.

Now it was up to Cletus. One day, Mindi and I called him into our bedroom. The three of us lay on our bed, Mindi's and my arms wrapped around his shoulders and head, and we invited him to join our family, legally and forever.

We told the truth. He had a choice. We were white. We were Jewish. We were American. And we knew we would leave Zambia at some point. Cletus, a Zambian Christian, would have many challenges to face if he joined our family.

Without hesitation, he said yes. As we lay on the bed holding each other, we looked into Cletus's eyes and we all shed some tears. Mindi and I looked at each other and shared soft smiles and a steady gaze of knowing we had done the right thing for Cletus and for our family.

I realized then that our inability to figure out a way to select a child from Kasisi Children's Home opened our hearts and minds to being present to what was right in front of us at Kabwata. I think of Cletus as a child who came floating into our circle, like Moses floated down the Nile River into the hands of his adoptive family. We received the basket that was before us. It started with a tiny drop—a logistical solution—and washed through our lives, transforming all of us, opening our hearts.

CHAPTER 32

Second Chance

In April of 2000, Mindi and I brought the three boys home from Zambia to Philadelphia for a family celebration. The adoption process for Cletus was still underway, and he didn't have a passport yet, so he stayed behind at the orphanage.

Adam, the oldest son of Mindi's sister Nina, was turning 13 years old. In Jewish tradition, he would read from the Torah and would officially become a man at his Bar Mitzvah ceremony. Our extended family all stayed in the same hotel in Cherry Hill, New Jersey, near our home town of Philadelphia. The boys ran around joyfully with their cousins.

On arrival to Cherry Hill, we immediately noticed that Jerry, Mindi's dad, didn't look well. His pallor was ashen, and he was moving slowly. The Sunday morning of the big party, I was called into Jerry's room, where he sat on the side of his bed, his face almost green and his breathing labored. Mindi was away from the hotel, frenzied with last minute shoe shopping for the boys. Two other doctors in the family and I were called in to confer. We agreed that Jerry had to get to the E.R. He had a history of heart attacks, and we were scared.

Mindi arrived from shopping just as the ambulance pulled into the hotel parking lot. Scurrying, we decided that Sandi, Mindi, and I would follow the ambulance, and Nina would take our kids to Adam's Bar Mitzvah.

Jerry was having a massive heart attack. It took the doctors hours to stabilize him. The chief cardiologist decided that his situation was so dire that he needed to be airlifted across the Delaware River to Pennsylvania Hospital. As Sandi, Mindi, and I stood in silent shock watching Jerry fly off in a medical evacuation helicopter, I was dumbstruck by the crazy turn of events on what was supposed to be a day of celebration.

He made it through the night. The next morning, Mindi and I drove to the hospital to visit him. During the drive, Mindi's sister Nina called. She said she had some news and we should pull over.

We feared the worst had happened to Jerry. But it wasn't about him. Sandi's older sister, Bobby, her closest friend, had driven home from visiting Jerry after the Bar Mitzvah, went to bed normally, but never woke up. Bobby's husband Sid found her dead in bed in the morning. She likely had a massive stroke or heart attack.

Sandi's husband lay in critical condition in the cardiac care unit, and now we had to tell her that her beloved older sister had died. We contacted Jerry's cardiologist, who agreed to join the Cohen children and their spouses to share the news with Sandi. The ten of us convened in a small conference room. When Sandi entered, she knew that some kind of bad news was coming, presumably about Jerry. As Nina broke the news, all four of her children gathered Sandi into their arms. She melted in grief, and her pain shook my heart. My mind juxtaposed my father's fractured relationship with his brother to the closeness Sandi felt with her sister. Despite the horror of this moment, I was touched by how important deep family connections are in times of crisis. I felt blessed to be part of such a loving family.

The next day, Jerry still lay in critical condition while Sandi, Mindi, and all her siblings rode together to New York to attend Bobby's funeral. I stayed behind with Sara, Mindi's brother's wife and a top-notch nurse. We formed the family doctor-nurse team that would watch over Jerry.

We didn't know if he was going to make it through the day. Every hour seemed eternal as Jerry's blood pressure and heart rate see-sawed. Sara and I consulted with the nurses and doctors, paced the hallways, binged on whatever food we could find to calm our emotions, and provided regular updates to the family attending Bobby's funeral.

As Jerry's condition remained volatile, it was decided that he would be transferred yet again, this time to the Hospital of the University of Pennsylvania.

There, it was determined that Jerry, a kind, gentle, and loving man, needed a heart transplant. Despite him not meeting most of the criteria or the age limit, Jerry's doctors miraculously arranged for him to be put on the transplant list. He stayed in the ICU at HUP in critical condition as the family waited and prayed that a heart would arrive in time.

But our ten-day leave was up, and we had to return to Zambia, jolted and unsettled. It was hard to go back. Having witnessed the power of a top-notch health care system saving my father-in-law's life, I was newly outraged by the horrors Zambians faced in their collapsed hospital system. *All people on the planet should have access to the best possible medical care, regardless of whether you are living in Philadelphia or Lusaka!*

Two months later, Mindi got a call to come home. Her dad's damaged heart was failing, and he had just days or hours to live. We agreed that I would stay in Lusaka with the boys. Mindi packed her bags and booked the next flight home.

Stopping over in Johannesburg, Mindi was mentally preparing to say goodbye to her father and fretting about getting there on time. She called home and heard her mother's voice telling her a donor was matched. By the time Mindi arrived in Philadelphia, Jerry was being prepared for surgery to accept his new heart.

He had stepped to the brink of death, but modern medicine gave him a reprieve. Feeling the joy of Jerry's second chance, my mind was getting clearer and I was becoming more indignant. I refused to stand by silently while my Zambian friends and colleagues were dying like flies. I knew I could do better; that we could do better.

We humans had created a global system that allowed some people on the planet to have state-of-the-art heart transplant surgery and others to die of hunger. Global health was a sham. I could no longer stand by and be a cog in the wheel of this charade.

CHAPTER 33

The End of the Rope

A FEW months later, in July of 2000, I attended the International AIDS Conference in Durban, South Africa, representing UNAIDS to promote Debt for AIDS. Even though I had gone rogue against the policies of the U.S. government, my initiative was successfully gaining support.

I felt emboldened and started floating even bigger ideas. I was staying up late at night again, brainstorming strategies. I developed a concept note that proposed creating a Zambia AIDS trust fund that could manage the money from debt relief and additional donor funding in one central place.

It was becoming clear to me that we would need hundreds of millions—or even billions—of dollars every year to beat AIDS in Africa. As I saw other countries mobilizing for debt relief while the AIDS crisis marched forward unabated, I ballooned out this idea, writing a paper that proposed an audacious "global AIDS fund" that would leverage billions per year and support the rapid scaling up of programs to treat HIV and stop AIDS across the world.

I wasn't the only one starting to think in these terms. The few experts from UNAIDS, the U.S. Congress, and activists had found each other. We banded together to bring these ideas forward. We wanted to stop the dying. We had to find a way to bring this bold and transformational idea into reality.

I was keenly aware, however, that when you have all this money pouring into poor countries, you must deal with corruption. In Zambia, I had seen this corruption cancer feed on an already weak health system. I saw how government officials manipulated the procurement of essential medicines to benefit only themselves and their families. It sickened me to see this insidious grifting while people were needlessly dying. This was true in Zambia, and it was true around Africa.

Anticipating that pervasive corruption might prevent wealthy governments from supporting the idea of a Global AIDS Fund, I studied anti-corruption, consulted with experts, and wrote a short paper on concrete strategies to combat it. We had to hold governments accountable, especially if we were going to start pumping millions, or ultimately billions, of dollars into the programs.

At the conference in Durban, I slipped my paper into the UNAIDS delegates' packets for presentations that I would be giving.

When it was discovered, my UNAIDS supervisors told me I had to remove it—as my anti-corruption strategy was "not an approved UN policy." As I sat in the empty conference room where the delegates were soon arriving, removing the pieces of paper from each packet, I became more and more angry. My defiance gene clicked in once again.

My mind flashed to the avalanche of dying AIDS patients and orphaned children. It was incomprehensible to me that the UN wasn't interested in making sure the money for AIDS was used properly. Mentally, I went ballistic. I returned to my hotel and submitted my resignation letter to UNAIDS on that same day.

Later I contemplated what I had done.

Had I taken a stand for justice?

Was I breaking the silence?

Was the UN system broken beyond repair?

Had I lost my social navigational skills?

I decided that while I may have been abrupt in resigning from UNAIDS, my instincts were right. I was following my heart and my intuition. But there would be consequences for my radical choice to wage justice that day.

I returned to Zambia from Durban and broke the news to Mindi that I had quit my job with UNAIDS, and we had to leave Zambia. Fortunately, after an intense, winding legal journey through the Zambian court system, we were able to formally adopt Cletus in the late July 2000, right before we were scheduled to leave. Now we had four sons to pack up for an uncertain future. But Mindi was not happy. She and the boys loved our life and work in Lusaka. She resented that my "selfish" decision to resign was going to have a major impact on her and our sons.

A major wall rose up between us. She snapped at me whenever we had a conversation, or frequently avoided talking to me. At times, our bickering would erupt into loud, angry fights that scared all of us, including the boys. I responded by withdrawing from her and everyone around me to protect my own fearful heart.

But I had no regrets. I had become dismayed by the impact of the Washington Consensus that benefitted the powerful at the expense of the powerless. I was tired of our pampered neocolonial life. I could no longer enjoy having a cook, a nanny, a swimming pool, a driver, two guards, and a gardener—while the dying fields lay just beyond our whitewashed walls. I could no longer stand silently as Mindi was off to another afternoon tea.

I had reached the end of my rope. And now our marriage was facing its biggest test.

PART THREE
Demonstration

*Never doubt that a small group of thoughtful,
committed citizens can change the world;
indeed, it's the only thing that ever has.*

—Margaret Mead

Chapter 34

Returning Home

After nearly four years in Zambia, we were going home. Things remained tense between Mindi and me. But the complex packing process occupied us logistically. The U.S. government would cover all our moving costs. The problem was we had no idea where to go. We were a family of six: Cletus had just turned thirteen, Lian was seven, Yonah was five, and Emet was about to celebrate his fourth birthday. We had to consider carefully what was best for all of us and our very different needs.

There were heart-wrenching goodbyes to our close Zambian friends, including everyone I worked with at the Central Board of Health, the folks at Kabwata and Kasisi orphanages, and our expat friends and colleagues at the embassy, USAID, and the other U.S. agencies.

The most difficult was parting with household staff. Over the years, we applied our at-home version of waging economic justice by trying to improve opportunities for people who worked for us. They, in every sense, had become our family.

We invested in driving lessons for our guard Philip, so he could eventually move into a better-paying career. He was devastated by news of our departure—for days, he wept every time he spoke to us. We were able to secure a position for him at Kabwata orphanage. Mindi had taught our cook, Justone, to make bagels, which he turned into a start-up food enterprise. Mindi imported the special yeast he needed so he could keep up with demand from the U.S. Embassy food store and other customers. We believe that these were first bagels ever sold in Zambia, mainly to non-Zambians.

Mindi handed off the patients she was medically supporting at the Kasisi orphanage to other volunteers, but she was uneasy knowing that their continuity of care would likely suffer. We also knew that too many people in our circle would be dead by the time we were able to make a return visit. AIDS does not care who your friends are.

Cletus and I made a final visit to Kabwata orphanage. It was a perfect spring day in Lusaka, with a light wind and the smell of the jacaranda trees blowing in the air. Mrs. Miyanda planned a surprise farewell ceremony for Cletus, gathering all the children and caregivers in the front garden, now blossoming with lush plants and flowers.

Mrs. Miyanda gave a speech, challenging Cletus to make the best of this opportunity, then reminding him not to forget where he came from. Cletus quickly became overwhelmed. He visibly withdrew, his body hunching in on itself and his face becoming stone. He couldn't display any emotions about saying goodbye to the Kabwata family that had rescued him after losing his mom.

I was aware that everyone present had Hollywood images of how Cletus's life in America would unfold. Mrs. Miyanda said that Cletus was seen by his friends as the lucky one who was going to America. But I knew that we were leaping into a great unknown. Cletus would lose the comfort of his own people, their food, the beautiful smells of the winds of Lusaka, and the rich Zambian culture.

As we packed our bags, Mindi and I debated where to start the next phase of our family life. I was ready to explore all possibilities, including living in Jerusalem. I imagined I could work at the Hadassah University School of Public Health, and she could a find a clinical role as a family practitioner. I was briefly taken by the idea of fulfilling my father's Zionist dream, but Mindi nixed it. After living in Tel Aviv during college, she was not keen to repeat the experience.

My next idea was to move to Pemba, a small island in the Zanzibar archipelago off the coast of Tanzania. I had fallen in love with its remoteness and beauty during a visit there, and now I dreamed of helping out with local community-led development. I imagined the boys having formative learning experiences among families facing the realities of poverty, hunger, and disease.

I convinced Mindi to travel from Zambia through Dar es Salaam, with a side trip to Zanzibar and Pemba. Cletus had never flown on an airplane nor seen an ocean before, and we were thrilled to share his first experience of swimming and jumping in the waves with his brothers.

During our quick visit to Pemba, Mindi rejected it as a place to settle, as there were no good school options. And frankly, she was not going to embark on a new venture that was unfunded. She was fed up with the volatility of my career, and her top priority was the well-being and education of our children. I became more anxious and depressed as it began to hit me that we really were giving up our life in Africa.

Ultimately, we decided to go back to Philadelphia, even though Mindi and I had long ago agreed we would never live there again. Philadelphia was too connected with deep childhood tension and stress for me. The roots of my inner anger and self-loathing sprang from there. But at this point, we needed the support system of our extended families to provide a foundation for our rocky marriage.

We somehow expected to return to a time capsule that had been buried in December 1996—the previous century. While we did reconnect deeply with our families, everyone had busy, entrenched lives. The Cohen clan was focused on supporting Jerry, who was recovering from his heart transplant and adjusting to the debilitating side effects of the anti-rejection medicines. We, on the other hand, were unpredictable nomads.

We rented an old row house in West Philadelphia at 43rd and Osage Ave., at that time a barely gentrifying, almost exclusively African-American neighborhood. We chose the location in part because of Cletus, thinking he would feel more comfortable among people who looked like him. But he was surprised at how many African Americans he saw—most Americans he knew were white. He wasn't expecting that, and we weren't expecting his reaction. This was new territory for all of us.

West Philly was a huge step down from our swanky, neocolonial compound. The only daily reminder of our former life was the presence of Rebecca Chirwa, our sweet and savvy nanny, who joined us from Zambia once we got settled. We imagined that she could help Cletus with his cultural transition, cooking the foods we all loved, like *nshima* and its accompaniment of spinach, tomatoes, and chicken.

All the boys were attached to Rebecca, especially Emet. We were grateful for her sacrifice. She left behind her husband and young daughter so that she could join us in America.

As it turned out, Cletus only wanted to speak English, refusing to talk to Rebecca in their Nyanja language. He barely acknowledged her presence. He wouldn't eat the Zambian food she cooked, even though our other sons loved it. He wanted American food like Philly cheesesteaks, pizza, and soda.

But Mrs. Miyanda was right about Cletus. He proved to be extremely adaptable. Despite going to five schools in five years, he thrived in his new life in our big family. By the time he started high school a few years later, he wanted to be, and was, just like every other kid in school.

When Cletus joined our family, Mindi and I decided we would honor his religious origins, so we were going to be a family with Jews and a Christian. My own religious identity was shifting as I integrated new spiritual awareness gained from my meditation and spiritual practices. In my mind, underpinning all religions is the universal quest for love, justice, freedom, and peace.

I began experimenting with declaring my religious identity as "Peace." In our home we created a safe space where fluidity of religious identity was encouraged. On some days, I was pure Peace; on other days I practiced Jew-Peace. Mindi was a Jew-Buddhist, and the boys cycled through Jewish, Jew-Peace, or Christian-Peace. By experimenting with Peace as a religion, I felt our family culture was equalizing, and we were connecting more equitably, to ensure that Cletus never felt like a religious minority.

Still, Mindi and I weren't faring so well in our new life. Every day in Zambia had been an adventure. There, we were doing good and doing well. We were making a difference.

Now we were both unemployed and desperate to find work. We had no income, four growing boys, and a blank future staring at us. We also felt cut off from our friends. For years, we had seen things that most people we knew could never even imagine.

We had lived a daily family existence amid the devastation of poverty and a worsening AIDS holocaust. Now we were back in the American bubble. We didn't seem to fit in. Our experiences were too expansive; our perceptions of reality were intractably altered. We found ourselves having to regrow relationships with family and friends that no amount of emails could have nourished in our absence.

The beauty and trauma in Zambia left us wounded, but paradoxically, we felt even more compassionate and open-hearted. Months before, observing the dawn of the new millennium from Zambia, I reflected on the transition of centuries. We watched the global coverage of the transition to the 21st century on our satellite television as reporters from American TV networks stirred fears that the electrical grids would collapse when the date ticked over to '00. We were especially struck by their jingoistic descriptions of the U.S. as the greatest country in the history of the world, with the greatest people, and the greatest everything. Sitting in Lusaka, we laughed at the irony of extolling the goodness of America while arrogantly trumpeting its superiority above all others. *Why couldn't we honor the greatness of all cultures, seeing the American democratic experiment as part of the greater whole?*

Now here we were again, back inside the bubble experiencing reverse culture shock. I indulged in all my favorite Philly foods to alleviate the stress of all the transitions. I took the boys to a neighborhood park, where they quickly adapted to skateboarding and roller blading with local kids, as I sat there missing my life in Africa. I was feeling lost. And I was lonely.

Mindi and I were barely communicating. She was still upset about me quitting my job without consulting her, she was worried about my mental health, and she was stressed out about our lack of money. We felt displaced, on different paths, and our bond had thinned to supporting the logistical requirements of our sons, who were adjusting to their new schools and new life at different paces.

We sought help through marriage counseling. I was on the cusp of living my greatest fear: losing Mindi, a divorce, a fractured family—a replay of my own parents' failings.

Then just a month after our move, Mindi came to me holding a familiar object in her hand: a positive pregnancy test.

Chapter 35

Break the Silence

"**Y**ou have got to be kidding me." I am mortified to say, those were my first shocked words. Mindi was equally overwhelmed with the news of a fifth child. While we weren't talking much beyond logistics, we still shared a bed. Birth control hadn't been on our minds, just relief from the tensions of the past few months.

When we told family and friends, their immediate reaction was delight, and the second was the immediate assumption that we were "trying for a girl." In any case, Mindi and I had to get on with our lives and prepare for the next family expansion and our work in the world.

Now that I was back in Philadelphia, I reached out to Julie Davids from ACT UP Philadelphia (a chapter of the AIDS Coalition to Unleash Power), who wanted to learn more about Debt for AIDS and the idea of a global AIDS fund that I had been championing. In the 1980s, ACT UP launched a new generation of on-the-street activism. Their demands were to shatter the stigma and shame around AIDS ("Silence = Death") and to hold the FDA's and Big Pharma's feet to the fire. ACT UP's protests led directly to the acceleration and release of new AIDS drugs in the U.S and wealthy countries. They made the news regularly, with activists using theatrical civil disobedience tactics—chaining themselves to railings inside the New York Stock Exchange, shutting down the FDA for a day, and holding "die-ins" across the country. Building on their success, they were ready to combat the crisis globally. These were my kind of folks.

At that time, most African governments, including South Africa, were silent about the scourge of AIDS. South African President Thabo Mbeki infuriated the AIDS movement when he publicly questioned the effectiveness of the triple-drug cocktail of HIV treatment. In response, Congressman Ron Dellums called for a new, multi-billion-dollar American investment to combat AIDS in Africa—an AIDS Marshall Plan for Africa, modeled on the initiative that mobilized U.S. funding to rebuild Europe and Japan after World War II. Economist Jeffrey Sachs floated the idea of a multi-billion-dollar global fund to pay for treatment for every single person living with HIV and malaria. There was a strange confluence of cynicism and hope.

Three million people were dying of AIDS-related causes each year, but there was little in terms of a united, global effort to bring prevention and treatment to poorer countries. I knew this idea of a global fund was exactly what was needed. Of course, I'd thought of it back in Zambia!

To pay the rent on our modest row house and feed the family, I accepted a job with Family Health International (FHI), a leading nonprofit, to help write and edit an action guide for an "expanded and comprehensive response to the HIV/AIDS crisis in Africa." I was paid as a part-time consultant, which was a great relief.

I started traveling from Philadelphia to Washington frequently, and I immediately started connecting with the political scene. In Durban, I had met Congresswoman Barbara Lee of California in a hurried conversation in a hotel lobby. I had expressed my personal support for the idea of her predecessor, Rep. Dellums, for an AIDS Marshall Plan for Africa and she had introduced me to the leaders working behind the scenes to move this agenda.

Now back in Washington, I started having regular meetings with Rep. Dellums's former chief of staff, Charles Stephenson, a smart, middle-aged African-American political operative, and Michael T. Riggs, Rep. Lee's senior advisor on global AIDS, a young, tenacious force of nature who hailed from Tuba City on the Navajo reservation in Arizona.

Michael and Charles were pulling together Congressional support for combating AIDS in Africa, and they wanted a push from civil society. Their first priority was a bipartisan bill co-sponsored by Rep. Lee and Rep. Jim Leach, a Republican from Iowa. Their bill, the World Bank AIDS Marshall Plan Trust Fund Bill, was designed to mobilize U.S. government funding support for a new global AIDS fund.

A newly arrived doctor-turned-political-advocate in D.C., I was in my element. I had an inspiring meeting with members of the D.C. chapter of Jubilee 2000. By almost any measure, their global campaign had succeeded, and debt relief was working. One hundred billion dollars owed by 35 of the world's poorest countries had been cancelled, and these countries were using the savings to invest in the AIDS response, health, education, and poverty reduction. Buoyed by their victories and support from millions across the world, Bono and the Jubilee people were starting to look for ways to harness the political energy and momentum they had generated. To me, AIDS treatment seemed a perfect fit.

We were joined by Dan Driscoll-Shaw and Tim Atwater, the Christian leaders who were supported by a young communications expert named David Bryden. David was a behind-the-scenes brain from Jubilee 2000 with an inner fire for justice. With his guidance, I started networking with members of Congress and the faith-based justice movements. David connected me with Joel Segal, a senior staffer for Rep. John Conyers (Democrat from Michigan) who was leading a crusade for AIDS treatment for all Africans. He was supported by Chatinkha Nkhoma, a young Malawian activist woman living with HIV. I had met this vocal activist in Malawi earlier that year while working for UNAIDS. I'd seen her singlehandedly protest a Ministry of Health meeting, where she calmly and tenaciously defended the human right to lifesaving antiretroviral drugs.

Less than one month after I arrived home from Zambia, Michael, Joel, and I convened our first meeting to create a global AIDS advocacy movement. We brought together the Jubilee movement, along with congressional staffers from both parties, the Health Global Access Project (Health GAP), ACT UP Philadelphia, Physicians for Human Rights, and networks of African activists.

Now we had a full squad: U.S. policymakers, celebrities, faith communities, AIDS activists, and human rights campaigners—with an agenda to save millions in Africa from unnecessary death. We banded together that fall of 2000 to essentially give birth to the global AIDS movement under the mantra: Donate the Dollars, Drop the Debt, Treat the People!

By October, our coalition had a name: Global AIDS Alliance (GAA). We were ready to break the silence in D.C. and link our efforts to African activists. David and I were GAA's first D.C.–based staff volunteers. His domestic advocacy and communications expertise was a necessary complement to my raging activism, fresh from the dying fields of Zambia. I wasn't sure how far we'd go with this effort, but it was exciting and challenging.

After 15 years as a physician and a government suit, practicing in public and preventive medicine, suddenly I was in the mix with AIDS activists and Congressional staffers. And I was being asked to co-direct the new coalition with Chatinkha Nkhoma. I was unsure if I could transcend my familiar technocratic background and take on the leadership role. Joel Segal literally had to convince me that I could do it. He saw things in me that I could not see.

Joel would call me every day. He sent long emails telling me why I, a doctor just returned from the heart of the pandemic in Africa, could be a powerful voice for the suffering in Africa. Others started echoing Joel's call for me to serve, but my self-doubt lingered. I had never started up a new organization, I had never worked full-time in the rat's nest of D.C. politics. And GAA had no money. Whether Mindi and I resolved our differences or not, I still needed a salary to take care of my family.

Global AIDS Alliance was founded on love. In those first months, dozens of people worked to create this new organization, all without pay. Joel arranged our first biweekly meetings in unused conference rooms and the library of the Rayburn House Office Building on Capitol Hill.

I was on a learning curve that was practically vertical. As part of my informal job training, Joel arranged a lunch at the Monocle on Capitol Hill with civil rights leader Walter Fauntroy, former head of the D.C. office of the Southern Christian Leadership Conference—the organization created by Dr. Martin Luther King, Jr., to wage civil rights justice.

As we sat at a dark corner table eating Maryland crab cakes and French fries, Fauntroy shared lessons from the civil rights movement, particularly the role of public demonstrations to generate political pressure. He told stories of working with MLK on the March on Washington. I sat mesmerized as he explained how the activists stood up in civil disobedience against the police and their ferocious dogs, but only when the cameras were rolling. Street activism must be linked to media coverage to shape public perceptions. As a total novice, this was all new information to me. Fauntroy affirmed that he believed the burgeoning global AIDS movement was a step toward civil rights for all, across the planet, and he offered us his support.

At the same time my family was settling in Philadelphia, the country was in the final stages of the 2000 presidential election, Al Gore vs. George W. Bush. Living out of the country for the last four years, I didn't really have my pulse on domestic political dynamics anymore. Nevertheless, I'd been a big fan of Gore since hearing him speak in Moscow many years earlier. I had fallen in love with his vision for the environment, for health care, and for putting people before power.

On November 7, Mindi and I couldn't wait to get to the polls. We brought all five children, ranging in age from 13 to still gestating. As I corralled the preschoolers into the voting booth to pull the lever for Gore on behalf of our family, I felt myself part of a larger mission. I prayed that Gore was going to be the great president that would mobilize the world to finally fix the broken international institutions.

After the first World War, countries had joined to create the League of Nations. After WWII, the UN system was established. But I felt its era was waning. Over and over, from Niger to Mali to Zambia, I had become frustrated and disillusioned by the impotency of the UN. The Universal Declaration on Human Rights was not being realized through this massive, dysfunctional, nepotistic bureaucracy. I wanted to see its complete dismantling to make way for new institutions to rise—like a global fund to fight AIDS. I wondered to myself, *What type of global cataclysm would it take to shift humanity into a new approach during my lifetime?*

Reeling from my own tumultuous experience with UNAIDS earlier that year, I felt driven to destroy and rebuild. Channeling my inner Samson, I wanted to pull down the Philistines' temple at Dagon. It seemed plausible to me that the state of the world and its crises would awaken politicians to the opportunity right in front of them. Nearly 50 years later, it seemed to me that humanity could or should have enough imagination to replace the UN with new more effective institutions.

I wondered if Al Gore and I were on the same wavelength. If he became president, would he be the one to lead the transformation? During his two terms as vice president, he had created the National Partnership for Reinventing Government. A colleague of mine, Dr. Pamela Johnson, was its deputy director. At lunch one day, she cautioned: "Paul, don't try to take down the existing structures. Just work on building the next generation of new ones. Build the institutions of the future and the old ones will wither away."

I pondered this, but I wasn't sure I believed her. What I *did* know was that the approach to urgent health crises in Africa was completely failing. Even with UNAIDS, a partnership of eight different UN agencies, we were only putting a Band-Aid on a gaping wound—and no one seemed to care that human beings were dying by the millions each year.

But as GAA came online, my hopelessness rebounded into optimism. Finally, I was going to be part of an effort where people all over the planet were joining forces.

My plans greatly relied on putting a globally minded, innovation-focused progressive like Gore in the White House. I had become obsessed with the idea of this global fund that could mobilize billions of dollars, not just for AIDS, but to strengthen health systems, protect all children from preventable diseases, and expand sexual and reproductive health services for all women and girls. These are all issues that affect the spread of AIDS and other diseases as well as overall health and well-being. Only a bold and transformational approach could reboot the current failed responses that I witnessed and was part of in Africa.

Everyone knows what happened next.

Al Gore didn't survive my dream.

For the first time in modern history, the Supreme Court determined the outcome of a presidential election. I shouldn't have been surprised as Gore had distanced himself from President Clinton throughout the campaign and winning a third consecutive presidency from the same political party is never easy, even under the best of circumstances.

The night of the Supreme Court decision, I laid my head on Mindi's lap in our bed. She massaged my scalp, as we tried to process what happened. Another Bush presidency deeply concerned me. After all, his father, George H.W., who served as vice president and later president, had never shown any interest in AIDS. I was extremely skeptical that the son would do anything either. Our emerging global AIDS movement had a long, uphill battle.

I was surprised when just a few days later Tim Atwater, special projects coordinator for the Jubilee 2000 campaign, was able to broker in-person meetings with Jendayi Frazer of the Bush transition team. She was a world-class expert Africanist who had been head of the State Department's Africa Bureau under President Clinton. Tim Atwater, David Bryden, and a few other faith-based advocates gathered in the drab offices of Church World Services, behind the U.S. Capitol next to the Supreme Court. We were struck by how much Frazer genuinely cared about the AIDS crisis plaguing Africa. She left us with the unexpected impression that the incoming Bush administration was interested in responding.

I surged forward, putting every ounce of energy into launching GAA. And on January 20, 2001, as images of President Bush taking the Oath of Office flickered on a TV screen behind us, GAA held its first big planning meeting— essentially our launch—attended by more than 60 people representing a wide range of civil society organizations, including AIDS activists, students (the Student Global AIDS Campaign was launched by Rev. Adam Taylor at nearly the same time), faith leaders, civic groups, doctors, Africanists, the NAACP, and many others. Together, we tried to agree on what would be GAA's platform.

President Clinton's LIFE initiative was nowhere near the investment we wanted. We wanted not millions, but *billions* in funding each year. Nothing like that had ever been attempted for a single disease before, and people said we were crazy. But in my world, they were just waving a red flag at a bull. Of course, I was charging ahead.

On March 29, 2001, we held GAA's political coming-out party on Capitol Hill with Reps. Leach, Lee, Conyers, Nancy

Pelosi, Maxine Waters, Jan Schakowsky, Sheila Jackson Lee, and Senator Paul Wellstone. We rallied around our message: Donate the Dollars, Drop the Debt, Treat the People!

We called for $10 billion to combat AIDS in Africa, with the U.S. committing its fair share. We demanded rapid expansion of high-quality HIV drugs, including generically manufactured antiretrovirals, delivered at the lowest possible cost. And we called on the U.S. and other G7 governments to pressure the World Bank and the IMF to cancel all multilateral debt, using their own resources, for countries affected by HIV/AIDS. Tim Atwater called it "two global grassroots movements converging."

Bono gave his full endorsement to GAA, releasing a statement calling on President Bush and Treasury Secretary Paul O'Neill "to take leadership on this issue and direct the IMF and World Bank to cancel the debts which kill."

As well as my work life was going, my weekly commutes from Philadelphia to D.C. were taking a toll on the family. I would spend few days away most weeks, staying with different friends in Bethesda or in the Dupont Circle and Adams Morgan part of the city. Mindi was entering her third trimester with our fifth child. With her history of pre-term labor, she was put on bed rest and could not work. We agreed it was time to move inside the Beltway where the political action was going down.

CHAPTER 36

Angel of Light

In April 2001, our youngest son, Uriel Amani-Baruch, arrived. We gave him a Hebrew and Swahili name meaning "Angel of Light, Peace-Blessing" And that is what he was, and still is. He brought light into our lives at the time we needed it most. The pregnancy and Uriel's birth slowly started bringing Mindi and me back together.

We struggled to choose the right D.C. neighborhood to move our family of seven. While we had yearned to return to the more racially diverse Takoma Park, we were concerned the high schools were not the strongest. Our whole decision-making was focused on where Cletus could have the smoothest transition, and where the other boys would get the strongest possible education—all other considerations were secondary.

We decided on a contemporary home in the leafy, affluent, mostly white suburb of Potomac, Maryland. Winston Churchill High School was rated one of the best in the country. But Potomac was a tough pill to swallow for me. In my eyes, it was filled with corporate lobbyists and white-shoe lawyers. I feared it would be a trap where I would become normalized, complacent, and drained of my passion for action. We also had to pay for it: The pressure to bring in money was intense, as we had five boys to raise. Mindi returned to work as a family physician as soon as she could after Uriel's birth, and that—combined with my consulting and my modest new GAA salary—allowed us to start to thrive at last.

At the same time, the mostly white, rich-kid, self-interested culture of Potomac sparked culture shock for both Cletus and Lian. They missed their friends from West Philadelphia and Zambia.

I understood. I was deeply caught up in my own agenda after being traumatized by what we'd seen in Zambia. My angry activism made me rather self-righteous during those years. When I ran into peers with high-paying private sector jobs, I couldn't control myself, and I would aggressively and snarkily challenge their moral values, asking them outright about their commitment to solving the world's problems.

One day, I bumped into an old friend from college. He was living in the nearby upper-crust end of Potomac. He was a corporate lawyer defending chemical, oil, and gas companies against claims that they were harming their workers and the environment. I sarcastically asked him how he could live with himself. He just smirked back at me, chuckled, then turned his back and walked away. Mindi pulled me away to avoid any further confrontation. I grumbled as I imagined him driving his luxury car back to his huge mansion. It made me sad that such a smart person would be wasting his life in a greed-driven profession rather than advancing human rights.

Mindi and I learned it was best to avoid the country club crowd. Gradually we cultivated like-minded, big-hearted friends who were also struggling with the Potomac elitist culture.

After Uriel, we were certain our family was complete. Before his birth, Mindi had agreed to have her tubes tied, but in the flurry of his arrival, we forgot to remind the doctor to do the procedure at the time of delivery. Afterwards, she refused to schedule another operation—enough was enough! While I squeamishly hated the idea of having surgery on my private parts, I reluctantly agreed to a vasectomy. I'm sure Mindi would have performed the operation herself had she chosen surgery as a career. We were stretched beyond our limits, and were not going to risk any additional family expansion.

We were so happy that Uriel was healthy (and extremely cute), that I only had a brief flash of sadness knowing we would never have a daughter. I think this may have been a harder reality for Mindi to accept, but we assuaged our emotions by reminding each other that we would have lots of daughters-in-law and perhaps a granddaughter or two when our boys became parents.

Mindi returned to nearly full-time work within a few months and, as Rebecca had returned to Zambia, we hired a nanny named Patricia, who was a Rebecca's cousin and happened to be living in the area.

One morning I came down to the kitchen and found our ten-year-old fluffball Yote lying flaccid on the floor. Mindi and I rushed him to the vet. After an hour-long assessment, the vet said he needed emergency surgery to stop internal bleeding from multiple tumors, and we needed to rush him to a higher level veterinary facility. Mindi and I called around to find the best veterinary surgeon in the area, even though we started wondering how much this day was going to cost. It would cost several thousand dollars and Yote had less than a 50 percent chance of surviving.

The boys and all of us loved Yote so much. We found ourselves in a terrible position. We needed that money to pay the bills and keep the family afloat. As we hemmed and hawed, Yote passed away. I held his still body while sitting inside a large dog cage at the vet's. Mindi and I both cried. We took him home and buried him in the woods at the bottom of the hill behind our home.

CHAPTER 37

The Global Fund Is Real

Meanwhile, a global fund for HIV, malaria, and tuberculosis was finally taking shape, driven in large part by Kofi Annan, the UN secretary-general. The work of Jendayi Frazer, Bono, and the burgeoning global AIDS movement created the momentum that moved President Bush to seek some early big wins in his first few months in office. AIDS seemed like the right thing at the right time. On May 11, 2001, he held a Rose Garden event with Annan and President Obasanjo of Nigeria, a bold African leader who called for Africans to lead the battle against these three preventable, treatable diseases.

Few understand or remember that there was already legislation passed the year before to create the World Bank AIDS Trust Fund, led by Rep. Lee, the fiery California Democrat, and Rep. Leach, the Iowa Republican known for his compassionate conservatism. Funds were already set aside for global AIDS, thanks mainly to the bipartisan political mobilization led by Congressional staffer Michael Riggs. So President Bush basically inherited a legislative blueprint and initial seed funding that he used to express U.S. support for the establishment of a new institution, the Global Fund to Fight AIDS, Tuberculosis, and Malaria.

One of our key missions was accomplished. David Bryden and I stood outside the White House to greet the newly appointed global AIDS coordinator, Ambassador Randall Tobias. On this beautiful spring morning, I walked up and introduced myself to Tobias, congratulating him on his new appointment and handing him our press release.

We were calling for him to allow the government to use generic AIDS medicines from other countries, rather than the costly originals made by U.S. pharmaceutical industry—where he had recently served as a top executive. Our statement also called for multiple billions of dollars for the Global Fund. We didn't want this to be another empty American promise.

A few weeks later, in early June, I was invited to testify before Congress at the House International Relations Committee on ways to end AIDS in Africa. I never imagined that within a year of my tumultuous departure from Zambia I would have the opportunity to be the voice of Africa's voiceless. I joked with friends that I was in exile from Zambia, sent to the greed capital of the world, to try to bring some humanity to the American political identity.

In Africa, I had learned that some white South Africans called themselves reverse Oreos, white on the outside and black African on the inside. This resonated with me, because I felt more at home with the loving community spirit I experienced with Zambians than with the tight-wadded, ego-driven, white-male-controlled U.S. system.

The hearing began with Andrew Natsios, the newly appointed Greek-American head of USAID. Natsios categorically believed that AIDS money should only be used for prevention, and attempting to get the drugs to Africans at that point would be a waste of time. Africans, he rationalized in his testimony, "don't know what Western time is. You have to take these AIDS drugs a certain number of hours each day, or they don't work. Many people in Africa have never seen a clock or a watch their entire lives. And if you say, one o'clock in the afternoon, they do not know what you are talking about. They know morning, they know noon, they know evening, they know the darkness at night."

As Natsios made his racist argument, the room descended into an eerie silence, punctuated by a few gasps. We could hear the pencils of the reporters scribbling down every word. I and several African ambassadors were seated directly behind Mr. Natsios. Sitting to my left was the ambassador from Ghana. As his furor rose, he started to stand, attempting to stare Natsios down. I put my hand on the ambassador's forearm, gently easing him back into his seat.

We were in utter shock at what we had just heard. Reports of Natsios words rapidly hit the media even as the hearing continued.

When my turn finally came, I made the case for urgent American support to help the African people beat back the scourge of AIDS that was needlessly killing three million people each year. In contrast to Natsios's abominable dismissal of African capacity and their human right to access medicine that would save their lives, a clarity of justice arose within me. I confidently quoted American historian Arnold Toynbee: "The 20th century will be chiefly remembered in future centuries not as an age of political conflicts or technical inventions, but as an age in which human society dared to think of the welfare of the whole human race as a practical objective."

I told the committee that, as elected officials representing the American people and American values, they had the power and authority to cancel debt and provide sufficient resources for HIV/AIDS. That their actions could literally save millions of lives around the world. With the advent of globalization, the information age, the science and technology revolution, and America's unprecedented wealth and budget surplus, we could stop global AIDS now. "Can we miss this opportunity and responsibility to ensure that the 21st century will be recalled as one when human society—with a strong American partnership—stopped a global pandemic?"

Congressmen Henry Hyde, Tom Lantos, and other committee members nodded in affirmation at the justice-based approach I was espousing for American engagement. I left the room confused, with the anxious sweat drying on my shirt and my colleagues congratulating me on my words. I was glad I had done a good job but also completely shell-shocked. I realized that Natsios had articulated the policy position of President Bush. I didn't know if the Global Fund would be allowed to buy AIDS medicines, and we doubted that any further AIDS treatment programs were possible—meaning that millions of Africans would be left to die. We had our work cut out for us.

At the end of June 2001, the UN General Assembly held the first-ever Special Session on HIV/AIDS. GAA contributed our ideas to the Political Declaration that would be the much-lauded outcome document, but I was wary that it would have any impact on real people. I knew from experience that many of those UN declarations were just hot air on paper—words without action and accountability, the sign of a weak and failing institution.

We needed to do something public and three-dimensional to get the attention of President Bush and the other world leaders in New York that week. GAA had been working for months with ACT UP, Health GAP, and the African Services Committee to hold a large march and rally under the Donate the Dollars, Drop the Debt, Treat the People! mantra. On June 23, 5,000 people marched through the heart of Manhattan. People of every color, race, gender, sexual orientation, and economic class joined forces to wage justice for the people of Africa. We, the organizers, were ecstatic. I ran up and down the perimeter of the moving crowd, greeting everyone I knew and excitedly talking with total strangers as to find out why they were joining the march.

During the mass rally that followed in Bryant Park, a huge thunderstorm rolled up and the skies opened in a deluge. Soaked, many of us said out loud that we all felt that God was crying for all those who were dying unnecessarily.

From my place outside with the emotional crowd, I headed to the UN building for slightly more measured conversations with policymakers. I removed my wet ACT UP t-shirt emblazoned with "Silence=Death," put on my gray pinstriped suit, and made my first foray into my "inside-outside" advocacy. I walked steadily through the marbled halls with Abraham Lincoln's clear message in my head: "Have faith that right makes might." I felt centered and certain that I was on the right side of history.

From the deathbeds of my friends at the University Teaching Hospital, to those heartbreaking funerals at the Leopards Hill cemetery, to the streets of New York City, I had followed my heart and joined forces with the bravest activists I had ever met. We had taken the AIDS fight to the political centers of the U.S. and the world. I had risked my marriage by quitting a job that did not align with my moral compass. I had risked my professional reputation by calling for action that my peers thought was laughable. I had followed my heart. At times, I was deeply uncertain and fearful. But the real work was just beginning.

CHAPTER 38

Dublin

A COUPLE of months after the big march in New York, I found myself on flight to Dublin heading to my first meeting with Bono. I smiled to myself as I thought of my long-lost dream to become a *djembe* drummer—did Bono need a drummer? I wouldn't ask. My mission was to intensify Bono's engagement in the battle against AIDS in Africa.

I had been invited to a strategy session with Bono's key advisors. A minivan brought me to the semi-tropical coast of Ireland to the beautiful mansion where Bono lived with his wife Ali and family. The driver drove past a row of fans lined up on the road into his estate—I guess they knew the rock hero was in residence that day.

I walked into the dining room. There, seated around the massive dining table, was Bono, his music business management team, Bono's close advisor Jamie Drummond, and none other than Bobby Shriver, eldest son of Sargent and Eunice Kennedy Shriver (my Special Olympics heroine). It seemed so unbelievable.

Bono was designing a new organization to end poverty in Africa, building on the success of the Drop the Debt efforts. He and his team wanted to figure out how to align his goals with the Donate the Dollars, Drop the Debt, Treat the People! campaign plans that we'd hatched in New York. I was eagerly hoping Bono would invest in the work of GAA, as we were still in our early start-up phase and needed money to build our small team.

As the meeting began, I sat silently, trying to get the vibe of everyone's various perspectives and to see how Bono managed this kind of brainstorming session. He was good, making sure all voices were heard one at a time. Then it was my turn to share the perspective of a doctor just returned from the AIDS holocaust in Africa.

I pressed Bono to go beyond debt cancellation and to call for billions of dollars for AIDS treatment—a topic he had not publicly advocated for. I became really alarmed when some of music production folks in the room raised concerns about branding Bono and U2 with Africa and AIDS. In 2001, people were still worried about homophobic stigma. It was unreal to me. Thousands of African men, women, children, and babies were dying horrible deaths every single day! Now my patience was really being tested.

I tried to stay calm. But there was another visitor there: Scott Hatch, a Republican operative who was then working for ultra-conservative Rep. Tom DeLay of Texas. As I watched him across the table, I couldn't stop thinking, *What the hell? Why this guy?*

After the meetings ended at Bono's house, Jamie took Scott and me to eat at a local pub in the heart of Dublin. I knew it was a test of sorts. *Fine, I can be friendly, but I'm not going to buy a Republican view of reality if that's what he's selling.* I was clear in my mind that I wouldn't be co-opted to soften my demands for immediate, bold action. I was not going to appease the establishment, or the Republican orthodoxy that was always skeptical of foreign aid.

By now, Bono's position was becoming clear to me. He wanted to position himself as a centrist as his best chance to get American political support for ending poverty in Africa. His people wanted to create a "big-tent" bipartisan movement. This made me prickly and I felt unsure of my own positioning.

To his great credit, Bono had a moral clarity for justice. In the end, he forged forward to include AIDS as a central part of his work. But as it turned out, GAA wasn't the right fit as a partner in his immediate plans. Bono's coalition did invest in AIDS advocacy the next year, forming their own organization, Debt, AIDS, Trade, Africa (DATA), which later became the ONE Campaign. Bono and Bobby Shriver also led the formation of the (RED) campaign in 2006, which went on to raise a massive amount of public awareness and millions of dollars for the Global Fund to Fight AIDS, Tuberculosis, and Malaria. In the end, we were all aligned in efforts to end AIDS in Africa, even though our organizational efforts were independent.

And so my dreams of one day backing U2 on the *djembe* drum were crushed. But my brush with rock stardom was not over.

CHAPTER 39

What's Going On?

Leigh Blake is an unrelenting engine for activism in the arts. I first met this multi-talented British designer, filmmaker, journalist, and devoted music fan in Manhattan earlier in 2001. She had heard of Bono's interest in GAA and wanted to scope me out.

I walked into the chic cafe in my gray, official-looking suit. Leigh was dressed in a black chiffon dress under a studded black leather jacket. Her spiked blond hair, impressive heels, and beaming activist aura enveloped me, and our friendship began at that very moment. Like me, she had lost too many friends to AIDS. By the time I met her, Leigh had become a legend for marshaling top talent to donate their music and advocacy to global causes. "Everyone's a starfucker," she once remarked, "but I've never been afraid of celebrities."

Leigh first worked with Bono more than a decade before through her advocacy organization, Red Hot, and they have been good friends ever since. She makes him laugh, charming him with her wit and bold ideas for fixing the wrongs in the world.

Back in 1990, Leigh and Red Hot had recruited a collection of global pop and rock stars of the era—from David Byrne to k.d. lang to the Pogues to Les Négresses Vertes—to record an album of Cole Porter classics called *Red Hot + Blue.* Proceeds would go to fight AIDS globally. At a time when the AIDS movement was still pejoratively associated with homosexuality and far-off third-world countries, getting so many musicians on board—many in their earliest stages of success—was testament to her ferocious powers of persuasion.

The compilation album sold more than a million copies worldwide and is recognized as one of the first major AIDS benefits in the music business. The project continued with more albums and concerts, including the world's first televised AIDS benefit, seen in 60 countries. Ultimately attracting more than 400 artists, producers, and directors, Red Hot raised more than 10 million dollars for AIDS relief.

With money from *Red Hot + Blue,* Leigh built a clinic in Kenya in partnership with NYU Medical Center and Dr. Shaffiq Essajee. Outraged by the lack of action by the Kenyan government and the international community, Leigh was determined to expand services directly to more people on the ground in Africa.

Now in 2001, she was re-activating herself as a leader in the burgeoning global AIDS movement. At the café in SoHo, I shared the pain I witnessed in Zambia and how I was using my anger to fuel my activism for saving African lives. She generously offered us some of the Red Hot + Blue proceeds, and that's how we finally got GAA off the ground.

Leigh had the brilliant idea (she has about a million of those per day) of doing a remake of Marvin Gaye's "What's Going

On." She and Bono assembled a coterie of like-minded artists, calling them Artists Against AIDS Worldwide. They included Alicia Keys, Justin Timberlake and *NSync, Britney Spears, P. Diddy, Christina Aguilera, Gwen Stefani, Destiny's Child, Fred Durst, and many other superstars. The remake would be produced by Wyclef Jean, and revenues used for AIDS programs in affected countries and to fund AIDS advocacy campaigns worldwide, including GAA.

We had been constrained by the lack of financial support to drive GAA's signature campaign, Stop Global AIDS. The opportunity to raise money through a celebrity album was thrilling and unexpected.

On Labor Day weekend 2001, dozens of artists filed into a Manhattan recording studio on the Lower East Side one by one to sing a segment of "What's Going On." They had some basic information about the goal of ending AIDS in Africa, and most of them were satisfied with a superficial understanding of the crisis. I was the guy in the studio in the suit, a doctor expert on AIDS in Africa, and I felt awkward and self-conscious. I came from a different world. The truth was I had never heard of most of these music celebrities, so I was not as starstruck as I might have been. Still, the opportunity to engage these cultural icons was fun.

On our second day, a young African-American woman entered the studio. I accompanied her to the recording room where she would sing, and I was pleasantly surprised when she asked me about my experiences in Africa. She asked me how bad it was. I told her about seeing parents and children dying and about the many orphans being left behind. Her voice was hoarse, so I quickly ran out of the recording room to get her a cup of tea from the nearby kitchen.

As I heard her begin to sing her segment, my heart started to pound. It sounded like she was channeling God's pure love. With each clear, high note, she touched my soul. When she finished with her take, I scurried out of the room to find Leigh, telling her she had to connect me with this woman, Alicia Keys. She was the most curious and caring of anyone who I had spoken with that weekend.

When I returned home, my kids treated me like a celebrity, blown away that their dad had spent the weekend hanging out in recording sessions with Bono, Alicia, and the others. While I was jazzed by the experience, I chuckled at their wonder. I didn't know if the whole thing had been a waste of a weekend; I was still determining if my close encounters with these celebrities would have any impact on the people of Africa.

The following Tuesday, somewhat jazzed from my rock star immersion experience, I was to meet on Capitol Hill with Dr. Ken Bernard, who had been President Clinton's special advisor for international health affairs for the National Security Council. He was now working as Senate Majority Leader Bill Frist's lead staffer on global health. From there, I was heading to the White House to see Jendayi Frazer, now at the National Security Council. These were two huge meetings on the same day, and I was excited to brief them about the momentum of the global AIDS movement and to strategize on ways President Bush and Congress could dramatically affect the epidemic. Actually, this was more fun to me than sitting in a music studio.

I was in a conference room in Sen. Frist's office with just Ken, unpacking my ideas about ending AIDS in Africa, when a call came from Ken's wife. She was at home. Something was happening at the World Trade Center in New York. A plane crash.

We assumed it was a private commuter plane that had gone off course, so we went back to our discussion, but turned on the TV. When the second plane hit, Ken and I sat stunned. The phone rang again. We realized then that something crazy was going on.

The idea of a terrorist attack of that magnitude was so outside of the realm of reality. After taking the second call from his wife, Ken abruptly ended the meeting, and I found myself on the street outside the Capitol, dazed and dumbfounded. I couldn't think of where to go or what to do.

Absurdly, I was still determined to keep my meeting with Jendayi Frazer at the White House, one and a half miles away. I jumped into the nearest taxi. The excited announcer on the car radio was screaming that planes were heading toward us like cruise missiles. "The White House is being evacuated and there is fire reported!" the voice cried. The traffic around us was slowing down, and the taxi came to a dead stop. I craned my head out the open window to see if I could see smoke or fires.

"The State Department has been hit!" the radio announcer yelled. This was one of the most bizarre moments I had ever experienced in the city. Outside the taxi window, everything seemed to be moving in slow motion.

I thought I could see other commercial jets in the sky overhead. As traffic snarled, more and more sirens roared, coming from all directions across the city. Black limos carrying government officials crossed to the other side of the road and raced past the halted traffic. I fumbled for my cell phone to call Mindi. *Fuck, fuck, fuck.* I couldn't get a signal—the networks were overloaded.

The devastation I had chased around the world seemed to be hitting my own country—my own city—in that nightmarish moment. I felt small and defenseless, like an ant whose rock had been uncovered, and all my brothers and sisters and I were scurrying mindlessly in fear.

I've got to get out of here. I jumped out of the taxi as we neared a Metro station, throwing the driver a wad of cash. I boarded the Red Line subway towards home. The train was nearly empty, and the few of us onboard spoke to each other in stunned, halting, nonsensical sentences. Everyone was dazed, trying to figure out what was going on. We all had different tidbits of information but the puzzle was not fitting into place.

Thirty minutes later the federal government and all businesses and organizations closed, and the city was fully paralyzed. Some of my friends were trapped in an epic traffic jam in and around D.C. for over eight hours. I thanked my instinct to flee.

Uriel, who was six months old, was home with our babysitter. Mindi was at work in Rockville. The other boys were all still in school. I sat alone in my bedroom, riveted to the large TV, and watched in utter shock as the Twin Towers of the World Trade Center fell, one after the other, live and surreal, on the *Today Show*.

A few minutes later, my sister called from Philadelphia and wanted to know if I was okay. Marci asked if I had picked up the kids from school. Honestly, it hadn't occurred to me that the boys could be in harm's way. Maybe she was right. The moment Marci and I hung up, I got a call that the schools had started shutting down. I jumped into my car to get Emet at his preschool, then picked up Lian and Yonah at their elementary school. By then, Cletus had arrived home by bus.

I still couldn't grasp the full implications of what had happened that morning, but I knew it was bad. It was bad for the United States and it was bad for the world.

Mindi came home that afternoon. We fell into each other's arms in despair, rattled. Our own home didn't feel safe. We struggled to explain to the boys that this was a significant event in U.S. history, and that war was coming. I wanted to make sure they would never forget what evil looked like.

Four days later, on the Saturday afternoon after September 11, I drove the older four boys to a hill in Arlington that overlooked the Pentagon, which was still smoldering. As we gazed at the smoke rising from this icon of American power, I explained to my children that nothing was permanent. Life was fragile, and we needed to face the violent world we live in. A small group of men had waged war on America. Unimaginable.

My concepts of reality were altered, and I somehow needed my sons to join me in processing this crazy time. Permanence really was an illusion that we were experiencing in real time, not just an intellectual concept that I thought I understood. And safety and protection really were a privilege.

Weeks later, I was still in a kind of shock. Our Marvin Gaye "What's Going On" remake was due to be released in October, but now the date had to be shifted. All national emotion was hyper focused on patriotism, Islamophobia, war fever, and a thirst for revenge.

My heart hurt for all those killed, hurt, injured, and traumatized by the events of September 11. But at the same time, I struggled to accept that this tragedy was going to eclipse the ongoing devastation in Africa. I felt alone in my turmoil. The opportunity we were aiming for with "What's Going On" was slipping away. The dying fields, the holocaust of AIDS in Africa, would be obscured for months, even years, by the smoke of 9/11 and what now seemed like an imminent war in Afghanistan.

Bono was very thoughtful about this. As he told an international journalist: "At the moment, everyone is thinking about 9/11 and defending the country of America, and I'm with them on that. We also have to defend—as an outsider, as an Irishman, I can say this—the idea of America. This is what America is about. You read the Constitution, it is a poetic thing, standing with the weak and oppressed and guarding each man's sacred honor, or whatever the phrase is. That's the America I'm a fan of. There is a lot at stake [in Africa] lives, but there is also, back home, a sense of people wanting to believe in that again."

The record company, the producers, and the celebrities decided to repurpose "What's Going On" as a benefit album for both 9/11 and global AIDS, which was pragmatic and politically savvy. But, honestly, I felt a bit robbed, as our original plan for rapid action in Africa got diluted. In the end, some of the proceeds were donated to the American Red Cross 9/11 fund, and GAA ended up with much less than originally anticipated. While I shared the pain of 9/11, that didn't replace or cancel out the suffering that I still viscerally experienced on behalf of my African friends.

My team at GAA grappled over ways to ensure the AIDS crisis in Africa would not get lost in the shuffle of the War on Terror, which had quickly taken over the American psyche. "Not everyone else shared our priorities before 9/11, and now it will be even harder to persuade people to care," I told the staff. We knew we had to hunker down and never let up on the pressure to save as many lives as possible. We had to continue the fight for political attention—no matter what else was going on.

CHAPTER 40

Donate the Dollars

T IMES were changing. By 2002, Bono had become a political insider. People close to Bono told me that some of his friends were furious and had stopped speaking to him. They believed he was making a Faustian bargain by working with the Bush administration, which was now in a full-on war in Afghanistan. Bush was also signaling his intent to expand the War on Terror to Iraq. But Bono was an effective health champion, one who had become knowledgeable and mature enough in his advocacy to know that in the war on AIDS, you can't be too choosy about your bedfellows.

As activists, we struggled with how best to leverage President Bush to do more on AIDS, while at the same time opposing his war plans. I concluded that we had to seize the opportunity to make a deal with Bush for a bold initiative, even when our hearts were torn against his foreign policy. With help from his friend Bobby Shriver, Bono started pushing hard to mobilize Capitol Hill support.

Jendayi Frazer encouraged me to keep pushing for more action from Bush. Eventually, Bono got some high-level meetings inside the Bush White House, including with National Security Advisor Condoleezza Rice and Secretary of State Colin Powell. In May 2002, Bono and Treasury Secretary Paul O'Neill embarked on a trip through Africa, visiting political and nonprofit leaders, health clinics, and orphanages. They were trailed by a large, starstruck press corps that covered every stop and meeting like it was a global concert circuit. Bono handed out t-shirts branded "The Odd Couple Tour." It was a brilliant PR move.

For the first time, American eyes were finally on Africa and the devastation there. While it was thrilling that we had this breakthrough, I was chagrined that it took a celebrity advocate to get the media attention. I wanted to make sure that African voices were also being heard.

After returning from Africa, Bono joined President Bush to announce a major new initiative to prevent mother-to-child transmission of HIV in Africa. By then, scientists understood that giving women antiretroviral medicine during pregnancy and birth could prevent almost all cases of in utero transmission. This was a solid solution to the crisis of babies who were born HIV-positive not living past their second birthday.

Bono had somehow persuaded Republican Jesse Helms, the fearsomely right-wing, evangelical, America-first Christian senator from North Carolina, to join the AIDS movement. This was part of Bono's concerted approach to get support from unexpected leaders. We called this the "strange bedfellows" strategy. The combination of Irish rock star and conservative senator joining forces against AIDS in Africa was irresistible to the media, and global AIDS found the limelight once again. Helms controlled the Senate Foreign Affairs Committee, and he was notoriously dismissive of foreign assistance generally, and marginalized groups specifically. He once called gay Americans "weak, morally sick wretches," and endorsed a report blaming violence in America on Satan's involvement in the music industry. But Bono had charmed him into the fight against AIDS.

While I felt this announcement by Bush to prevent mother-to-child transmission was an important step forward, it was far too small of an effort to seriously diminish the impact of AIDS in Africa. I quickly concluded that if we didn't publicly criticize this step as inadequate, and if all Bush got was praise, then he would never feel the pressure to mobilize the billions of dollars necessary per year to get ahead of the epidemic.

Bush was also being nudged to do more by Secretary Powell, who had visited several African countries the year before and had been deeply affected by the suffering patients, frustrated aid workers, and medical personnel. Powell's concern transcended simple compassion. He saw the AIDS crisis in Africa as a serious national security issue.

Epidemiologists predicted that fully half the adult population on the African Continent could be wiped out in just a few years if nothing was done to slow the spread of AIDS. The breakdown of African economies and societies would allow terrorist forces to take control of collapsing countries. As I drove home one day from work, I heard Secretary Powell on the radio speaking at a UN meeting. "There is no enemy in war more insidious than AIDS," he declared.

There was a growing sense that the Bush administration was going to do something for Africa and had the money to do it. This was our opportunity. A gate was opening for GAA and the global AIDS movement. A new commitment from the U.S. government of at least $1 billion per year, or maybe even more, seemed plausible. Every part of civil society was mobilizing—and each one had different ideas for the money. The coalition of churches wanted the billion for Africa to deal with poverty, economic development, education, and health. The Global Health Council—the 30-year-old U.S. advocacy organization—wanted to carve up the billion five ways across child survival, clean water, family planning, food security, and AIDS.

The Global Health Council's intentions were great, but their request of only $200 million for AIDS wasn't going to have the kind of impact that would shut off the death spiral. My team at GAA wanted no less than $2.5 billion per year just for the AIDS epidemic. In my mind, that would cover the United States' 25 percent fair share of the annual $10 billion per year we estimated was needed to fight global AIDS. At that point, total expenditures were about $500 million per year, so we were demanding a major catapult of investment, and it needed to happen now.

I was determined that GAA was going to build the movement that would align all the civil society factions together under a single mission.

We would have that money.

This meant we needed a massive political crusade based on our demands. It was going to be truly transformational. After all, AIDS was an emergency. There was no time for half measures. There was no time for pragmatism and incrementalism.

Over the next 18 months, my team and our partners worked in a symphony of action. We collectively managed to corral 343 diverse organizations to align with us. The movement had the Congressional Black Caucus and the NAACP behind us, and we were in solidarity with African activists who came to Capitol Hill for testimony. We also had the Student Global

AIDS Campaign. We activated Washington's massive think tank system on Massachusetts Avenue to publish analyses and convene experts. We had the grassroots activists like ACT UP and Health GAP. We had the D.C. advocacy nonprofits like Jubilee USA, Africa Action, RESULTS, and many others. Then the churches came along and started to align with the rest of the coalition.

At first, everyone was focused on different things and sometimes polarized agendas. The Christian conservatives were brought in by the orphans' crisis but had no interest in halting or stopping sexual transmission or promoting evidence-based prevention methods like condoms. ACT UP wanted treatment for those living with HIV and action against LGBT discrimination. Orphans were not even on their radar. Ultimately, our movement would be joined by confederations of intravenous drug users and sex workers, who also needed a voice to protect their rights to be safe from AIDS and from being treated like criminals when they sought health services.

Strange bedfellows have always populated the AIDS movement around the world. Somehow it all worked. And that, to me, was the most consistently surprising aspect of over a decade of my AIDS work. I never imagined in a million years I would find common cause with the diversity of people who were now in my corner: rock stars, church leaders, LGBT activists, sex workers, anti-poverty groups, conservative politicians, and more. There has never been a cause quite like it.

CHAPTER 41

The President's
Emergency Plan

In 2003, with the GAA pushing hard on all fronts to mobilize American leadership in the global AIDS battle, our job was to build a broad-based movement and keep diverse interests on the same page long enough to make an impact. The most disappointing aspect of my advocacy at this time was how much effort I spent fighting other civil society organizations. I felt like Godzilla taking on the people who were protecting the status quo. About 60 percent of my effort was spent getting advocates to see eye to eye and convincing them we were fighting the same war. It was exhausting.

We had formed an aggressive, diverse coalition, but the Global Health Council, one of the biggest associations representing civil society, was holding their line at $200 million per year for global AIDS. They had their own coalition, the Global AIDS Roundtable, and they were unconvinced that we could induce the president and Congress to give us the multi-billion wedge of funding we were after.

Of course they were skeptical. Many of the members of the Global Health Council were card-carrying Beltway bandits of international development—organizations that are basically government contractors living off the largesse of the federal budget. I thought of them as "trough feeders" because of how they consistently suckled on the system, prioritizing their own survival over what was needed in the world. They were happy to overrun smaller, newer players in the development arena when it was to their advantage.

In 2002, the trough feeders weren't aiming for a big, bold transformation. They were cautious. They were pragmatists. And they thought we were crazy. Our plan was too unconventional for them to imperil their giant budgets.

More critically, they had a vastly different vision of how to do development. They were the "$200 million here, $200 million there" brokers, and tended to deal in massively scaled-up delivery of commodities that cost pennies. Cost-effectiveness was their guiding force: Two-cent packets of oral rehydration salts. Twenty-five-cent polio vaccines. Seventy-five-cent contraceptive injections.

This had been the paradigm for international development assistance from rich countries to poor countries for decades, and it was an approach the whole world agreed upon. Only invest in affordable interventions that can go to scale quickly. As for AIDS, they were thinking just as small. Condom distribution was the only intervention that was affordable based on their frame of reference.

But my GAA team wasn't talking about treatment and prevention only. We were talking about helping the orphans and vulnerable children left behind. We were talking about sexuality education for young people. We were talking about testing, care, and support for people living with HIV. We were talking about human rights for people who were being excluded, beaten, and jailed because of their sexual orientation or lifestyle.

Yes, we wanted to make condoms available to every sexually active adult. But we also wanted to make sure antiretroviral medication was easy to access, AIDS orphans could get the love that they needed, and human rights for all would be protected.

And critically, we wanted treatment for *everyone,* which added up to a lot of pennies. Antiretroviral treatment at that time cost $15,000 per person, per year, and there were an estimated 30 million Africans needing it. Just to treat those living with AIDS would cost $4.5 billion per year. The World Bank had come right out and said that treating HIV in Africa was not cost-effective. If we followed this logic, people who became infected with HIV could only expect to die.

In my mind, the idea that saving lives must be cost-effective based on a neoliberal philosophical paradigm had to be shattered. Every human life is as valuable as every other. And with enough money, we knew we could reach everyone in need, bring down costs, and give AIDS survivors the time they needed for pharmaceutical companies and the scientific community to catch up with cheaper, more effective drugs.

All I could think about was how baby David, how my secretary in Zambia, and how Cletus's mother would still be alive if they'd been given the AIDS medicines that were available to Americans and Europeans. Their lives mattered too. More to me than to the World Bank's orthodoxy.

Our message was to get the African people the help they needed now. We would advocate hard for what we needed, and to succeed we were asking for unfathomable amounts of money. More than any public health initiative in history. Now was not the time to be shy.

Our campaign went into full gear over the next year. We practically lived on Capitol Hill. Our diverse gang of activists held marches and rallied our constituencies. Churches wrote letters to Congress and students pushed universities to divest from pharmaceutical companies who refused to allow generic drugs to go to Africa. The tentacles of activism stretched far and deep into American life.

Then in January 2003, President Bush gave his State of the Union address and made a startling announcement. The government would be giving a massive $15 billion to fight global AIDS over five years. It was called the President's Emergency Plan for AIDS Relief—PEPFAR.

It was a stunning moment. The President had been given three funding options for the Plan: low, middle, and high. He chose the highest. Everyone was surprised by the amount. Our multi-pronged advocacy had paid off.

As I watched the speech, I grabbed the phone and called my friend David Bryden. As the announcement rolled off Bush's tongue, we gasped with joy. We were not expecting him to go big! We had created the political space for him to go all out on AIDS in Africa, and he filled it. We issued a press release that night saluting Bush's bold leadership.

This was President Bush's moonshot. He declared that within five years, the U.S. would support African countries to set time-bound targets to put 2 million people on treatment, prevent 7 million HIV infections, and care and support 10 million people, including orphans and vulnerable children.

Years later, I can say with certainty that setting these ambitious, accountable, 2-7-10 targets for the next five years were perhaps one of George W. Bush's greatest lifetime accomplishments.

President Bush devoted more than five paragraphs to PEPFAR in his speech, making it, at the time, the longest-ever State of the Union statement dedicated to global health. And then he changed the subject.

We would be going to war against Saddam Hussein.

Was this unexpected display of compassion for Africa just a tactic for President Bush?

Was PEPFAR a smokescreen?

I still don't know what motivated him to be so bold on combating AIDS in Africa. We had distilled the passion of 343 advocacy organizations and millions of Africans. Kofi Annan, Bono, Nelson Mandela, and Desmond Tutu were all on board. The movement to stop AIDS in Africa wasn't going away. At that time, no one knew if, or exactly how, those targets could be achieved. But our ambition, combined with the government's gigantic commitment of financial resources, unleashed a historic level of innovation in AIDS-affected countries. We were waging justice. And in my mind, we were waging justice to alter history and torque the world toward a more peaceful, sustainable community.

CHAPTER 42

Broken Promises

T HE juxtaposition of the historic AIDS announcement and Bush's march to war in Iraq was discombobulating. Later that night, Mindi and I sat glued to the TV and, while we cheered the AIDS announcement, we were scared about the prospect of another war and how that would ultimately lead to fanaticism and hate. We sighed with relief that our kids were too young to be drafted.

Then, by the middle of 2003, just six months after that State of the Union address, I was already on a collision course with the Bush administration.

The scope of PEPFAR was truly unprecedented, and breathtaking. Most people were completely surprised by the $15 billion windfall. I wasn't. Somehow, I had known that some president, some time, would do the right thing.

Still, the amount of money, expertise, and thought allocated by PEPFAR redefined the global AIDS response. The money would tackle not only HIV prevention and treatment, but also maternal and child health, TB, sexual and reproductive health for youth, harm reduction for drug users, services to empower and protect women and girls, and micro-financing to avert poverty and stop many more of the insidious tentacles of poor health and social inequity that creep into poor communities and fuel AIDS and other health epidemics.

On May 27, 2003, Bush signed P.L. 108-25, the U.S. Leadership Against HIV/AIDS, Tuberculosis, and Malaria Act of 2003, the legislative authorization for PEPFAR. All I could think was: *Dreams do come true!*

In the final stages of approving the bill, a staffer for Congressman Dana Rohrabacher, a somber Republican from California, approached my colleague Jennifer Delaney and asked her to propose specific language so that 10 percent of the global AIDS funding would be dedicated to orphaned and vulnerable children. Jennifer and I sat in a side room and drafted the language in a few minutes. The staffer hurriedly returned to the committee room, handed the language to the congressman, who then introduced the provision as an amendment. It unanimously passed and became part of the final legislation.

Congress planned to ask for funding for P.L. 108-25 in the next year's budget. Since it takes about a year for a federal budget to be approved, it would be calendar year 2005 before the "emergency" funds were available—two years after the big announcement. But PEPFAR's promise was to treat two million HIV-infected people in countries like Botswana, Mozambique, Rwanda, and Nigeria with state-of-the-art antiretroviral treatment over the next five years. While we waited, they died.

I was extremely frustrated at the slow pace. It made me wonder what qualified as an "emergency" to the Bush administration. We knew that funding could be made available immediately—political leaders can rapidly pump cash into the priorities they want to pursue. Emergency budgets had been passed for the wars in Afghanistan and Iraq and the War on Terror. AIDS was killing many times more people than all those wars put together.

In the proposed 2004 federal budget, only $1.6 billion of the promised $15 billion was earmarked for HIV/AIDS efforts in Africa. The bulk of the money would not be available for programs on the ground in Africa until 2007 or 2008. *Enough,* I said to myself, sickened by yet another exhibition of hedged federal commitment.

At that time, I was working part-time as GAA's executive director, eking out global advocacy from a budget of a few thousand dollars. I was incensed that Bush was regularly basking in praise for a political win that, so far, had changed nothing on the ground in Africa. The crisis would get worse for years until the U.S. money started to move.

In July of 2003, the President made plans for a trip to Africa—a victory lap for his grand AIDS initiative. My team at GAA decided to turn this trip into a protest opportunity.

Activists on the ground in Africa were anxiously waiting for the money, and they had no idea it would not be coming for at least two years. So, with Bush's itinerary in hand, we quickly mobilized them to plan protests and act as spokespeople at each stop of the five-day tour: Senegal, South Africa, Botswana, Uganda, Nigeria. They would demand immediate funds to meet urgent needs.

We worked with D.C. PR guru Jamie Shor to design and execute a media plan so that whenever President Bush stepped off a plane, the press had already talked to the activists before he uttered a word. We reached out to the White House press corps before and after each leg of the trip and made sure they put our spokespeople on TV.

Our campaign was called Broken Promises, and it was mightily effective. On every stop that week, the president was forced to answer tough questions from the media about the slow pace of implementation. In his press briefings with African leaders at each stop, Bush was put on the spot. By the third or fourth day, we were making headlines around the world, including a major feature in the *Chicago Tribune* that actually carried the headline "Broken Promises."

I was exhilarated to see local and global AIDS activists working together on this tight, strategic, advocacy blitz. Something was stirring inside me as I saw what a huge impact four people in a short-term rented D.C. office space could do.

By the time the Bush entourage arrived for the final leg in Nigeria, his people had ferreted us out. My colleagues on Capitol Hill were getting calls from the administration asking, "Who is this Zeitz guy? What is this Global AIDS Alliance?"

Although I was fairly well known among the organizations advocating in the Washington maelstrom, GAA was so small that we weren't on the White House's radar at all. It also wasn't paying my bills, so I had several complementary gigs going. One was serving as international coordinator for the Hope for African Children Initiative (HACI), funded by the Bill & Melinda Gates Foundation. In the convoluted world of international development partnerships, Gates was funding several large international nongovernmental organizations that gave money to HACI for orphans and vulnerable children— and that were paying my contract. HACI had in turn given start-up money to GAA, so they were sort of funding our Bush offensive. And offensive it *had* been, to some very influential people.

At the end of July, Mindi and I were on a road trip to the beach. We had just stopped at a gas station along the highway when my cellphone rang. It was my supervisor at HACI, Sam Worthington. He never called me on the weekend. I knew something was wrong by the sound of his voice.

Sam had gotten a pointed call from USAID administrator Andrew Natsios—he of "Africans can't tell time" fame. Natsios had told HACI, "You have to cut ties with Paul. Get him off the HACI payroll, stop funding the Global AIDS Alliance, delete all traces of him from the website." Sam called to tell me that I was being fired from HACI, effective immediately. HACI partners, dependent on federal funding, did Natsios's bidding. HACI had cut all its support for the GAA. And then page by page, they stripped its name and mine from the HACI website.

As we rolled away from the gas station, I was shaking in disbelief. I was under a direct attack by the Bush administration and I was about to lose half my income. The viability of GAA itself was in jeopardy. Mindi sat in a stunned silence, but quickly she rebounded with support and pride. She assured me that everything would be all right, we would make it work.

My elation from the success of the Broken Promises campaign turned to anger. This was a government power play at its finest, categorized by pettiness, a lack of vision, and the willingness to destroy our work because we weren't politically obedient.

And I was worried. I had five kids, and now only a part-time job from an organization that had rubbed the government the wrong way. My GAA staff and I went without pay for months afterwards. Mindi, working as a family medicine physician at a nearby clinic, struggled to pick up the slack. Our income was stretched thin as we worried each month about going into negative numbers in our bank account.

I had always thought of myself as an "inside guy." For years, my norm was to be the guy in a suit at the table, working within the walls and halls of power to get things done. And after two years as an outside guy with the nongovernmental GAA, part of me had been longing to go inside again, at the decision-making tables of government.

But this incident flipped a switch in me. I realized how susceptible I had been to abandoning my courageous positions and having my beliefs co-opted in order to fit in.

But far from sending me back to my corner, the administration's reaction energized me. I was keenly aware that I, the son of a Philadelphia hoagie maker, had gotten under the skin of the most powerful leader in the world and his people. I was ready to fight harder than I'd ever wanted to. So I took a mental step back and really evaluated my worth to the AIDS movement.

I had field experience. I was a medical doctor and an epidemiologist. I had an advocacy resume that was vastly different than the typical Beltway bandits—who, let's face it, don't do real paradigm-busting advocacy. Few were speaking truth to power; most were focused on maintaining their budgets and trough-feeding.

Almost all the development professionals I knew were themselves insiders, dependent on government funding, careful not to make waves. But I was becoming more and more fearless. I realized I brought unique talents to my work—my drive for bold action, my defiance, and my compulsion to take a stand for what's right.

Now, I decided, waging justice was going to come from a different direction. I was going to bring everyone I knew of influence into my work as I built an advocacy institution that would endure for years to come. I decided that GAA, which was intended to be a short-term mobilization campaign, was going to stay the course. We would be the gadflies of government and the conscience of compassionate Americans.

We would devote GAA to demanding faster action and more funding for the Global Fund and PEPFAR. We would focus on media attention using rhetoric that did not mince words. And we would keep attacking and holding Bush and Congress accountable. From the outside.

CHAPTER 43

Arrested

My friends from ACT UP, Health GAP, and Housing Works mentored me on street demonstrations. We were planning a protest for the fall of 2003 in front of the White House, demanding accountability from the president for the promises he made. The plan was for peaceful civil disobedience, but I wanted to push, and maybe cross, the line.

Asia Russell from Health GAP taught me how to get arrested. She explained that I had to stay calm and make the police drag me slowly into the paddy wagon so that journalists would have time to capture the moment. I wore a suit that day, as I wanted to look like Dr. Paul Zeitz.

Several dozen activists lay down in the pedestrian walkway in front of 1600 Pennsylvania Ave., illegally blocking traffic. As planned, I was quickly surrounded by a team of armed riot police. Cameras were snapping, and film was rolling. My arms were bound behind my back with a zip tie, and I went limp, forcing officers to heave me into the waiting van with a dozen other protestors.

About thirty of us were taken to a U.S. National Park Service police center and locked in a group cell. I had been brought up strictly to always obey the rules, and now I was breaking them. I was 41 years old and I had only ever gotten parking tickets and a couple of speeding tickets in my lifetime. I felt brave and righteous.

I remembered the lessons of Walter Fauntroy, who explained how critical media coverage was for demonstrations to have maximum political impact. National Public Radio, the *Washington Post*, and the *Boston Globe* all covered the protest, and we made our disgust with the White House known.

I walked into the house that night with a proud chip on my shoulder. Mindi and my boys—by now Cletus was 16, Lian was ten, Yonah was eight, Emet was seven, and Uriel was two—gathered around and hugged me hard. They sat entranced on the living room couch as I gave them a blow-by-blow account of my arrest in front of the White House. The younger boys danced in a circle sing-songing, "Daddy got arrested! Daddy got arrested!"

Anyone looking at us from the outside would have concluded that my sons had a happy, effective, motivated father who was working tirelessly to speak truth to power. They would have been right. But that was only part of the story. Soon I would start having disturbing flashbacks and recurring nightmares. An ugly sick secret about my childhood—and perhaps the main reason I spent my life enraged and indignant about children's rights—would begin to come to light.

Chapter 44

Soccer Dad

AN opinion piece I wrote for *Newsweek* in November 2003, "Africans Need More Than Our Sympathy," argued for an expanded response to the AIDS crisis, but started with soccer:

> *It was a beautiful fall afternoon when I arrived at the soccer game in which my 16-year-old son Cletus was playing. This was his first opportunity to play on the varsity team of Churchill High School. As the sun glittered, and the leaves fell from the trees, I watched proudly as Cletus led an offensive push toward the goal. I was amazed at his strength and determination.*

My role as a soccer dad was much more complicated than I let on. All my sons had a great affinity for soccer from their earliest days. Lian, Yonah, and Emet started lessons when they were small tots. Cletus learned to play soccer barefoot on the streets of the Kabwata neighborhood with improvised soccer balls made from tin cans. I was proud of him. He was a natural, and so unlike me.

I never played any team sports, and I always had an aversion to developing physical skills. I played basketball on a half-court behind my house with Barry, Kenny, and Ellen growing up, but never liked the pressure, shoving, and fierce competition. My disdain for organized sports made me feel like an outcast. I never knew why I felt this way.

During college, most of my friends were obsessed with playing and watching sports. I was not even interested. I cultivated a judgmental, self-righteous attitude about it, arguing to anyone who would listen that my friends were wasting their time just watching a ball go back and forth. I couldn't understand why people cared so much about such "pointless" games.

That changed in graduate school when my sociology professor had a heated discussion with me in front of the class, insisting that sport is the great social equalizer. It brings the community together to watch and play, including people of all economic levels, races, religions, political persuasions, and genders.

The professor's argument made sense. Even though I doubted I would ever dribble a ball competitively, that conversation started to shift my perspective and accept the value to society of our sports obsession. As an activist, I started talking to my friends about it. I wondered, *Could we somehow harness the energy and enthusiasm for sports into solving the world's problems?*

In any case, sports created plenty of tension at home with Mindi. All five sons played soccer in leagues. Mindi and I were a taxi service, shuttling them to practices and games. Weekends were often so busy that we would say goodbye to each other on

Saturday mornings and not see each other again until Sunday evening.

I would complain endlessly to Mindi, as this lifestyle aggravated me to the extreme. We fought about a balance between soccer and other activities—I wanted to make sure the boys had strong spiritual and religious awareness. Mindi wanted the boys to value spirituality as well as physical fitness. Battle lines were drawn between soccer and Hebrew school.

As a reluctant soccer dad, I was a constant source of frustration to my boys. I didn't fully understand the rules of the game. I would catch up on work calls and check email and Facebook instead of shouting, hooting, and clapping like the other dads. I showed up in person but not in spirit.

I did my best to support their interests, even though it went against my grain. Years later I would figure out the deep source of my sports aversion.

CHAPTER 45

Justice for Orphans

By the time George W. Bush delivered his second inaugural address in January 2005, my team at GAA could look back and see the arc of our labors and their true monetary value. Since 2001, Presidential budget requests for global AIDS had risen from less than $500 million to more than $3 billion. How many lives were saved with AIDS treatment and prevention? Hard to say. Saving just one life was worth it. And at the same time, with so many suffering, saving five million lives wasn't nearly enough.

My mind never strayed from the plight of children infected with HIV and those left behind—AIDS orphans. At that dark time in Africa, a child was being orphaned by the disease every 14 seconds. It was like a countdown clock in my heart. These children, many of them infected with HIV at birth, faced homelessness, illness, hunger, sexual exploitation.... I couldn't set up a Kabwata for all of them. I couldn't adopt all of them.

With the dedicated $1 million from PEPFAR, we started expanding orphan programs in Zambia, but that was only a drop in the bucket for what was needed there—never mind easing the injustices African children faced daily. It physically hurt to think of them.

The plight of the orphans in Zambia—and years before, the babies in our charge on that flight from Seoul—touched something deep in my soul. It was something I couldn't name or explain to anyone. For some mysterious reason, I connected with their struggle and felt their yearning to be heard and loved. I vowed to myself that I would never stop trying to create a better world for all of these children, although at the time I didn't understand why I was so deeply pulled to erase their pain.

GAA's next goal was a bill that would force funding and comprehensive programming into foreign assistance programs for orphans and vulnerable children. Rep. Barbara Lee was a powerful ally. So was the actress Angelina Jolie, who signed on as the spokesperson for Rep. Lee's bill. Jolie and her husband Brad Pitt were in the process of adopting a baby girl, Zahara, from Ethiopia to join her son Maddox, adopted from Cambodia in 2001.

Our work with Rep. Lee and other Congressional allies paid off: Congress passed the Assistance for Orphans and Other Vulnerable Children in Developing Countries Act of 2005 (P.L. 109-95). President Bush signed it into law on November 8, 2005. This act marked the first-ever comprehensive legislative response to the global orphans' crisis and highlighted the need for community-based care, food and nutrition programs, expanded educational and psychosocial services, and social protection systems. It was a historic milestone for global children's advocacy.

Jolie was interested in continuing this important work, so we invited her to be part of a new spinoff of GAA: Global

Action for Children (GAC). Jolie and Pitt welcomed their biological daughter, Shiloh, into the world on May 27, 2006 in Swakopmund, Namibia. Their plan was to sell her first photos to the media and donate 100 percent of the sales to children's charities.

One evening, I arrived home from work late. I grabbed the mail from the curbside mailbox and, standing with my briefcase over my left shoulder, leafed through the letters—a cable company offering the deal of a lifetime, a couple of credit card bills, and an inauspicious envelope from the Jolie-Pitt Foundation. I stood tall in that moment and slowly opened the envelope. Inside was a check made out to the Global AIDS Alliance to help launch GAC into an independent organization. For a million dollars! This was the largest one-time, upfront disbursement of a grant my organization had ever received.

I couldn't believe my eyes. Funding of nonprofit organizations can be so ethereal; the money hardly seems real most of the time. But this—it was cold cash, the most I had ever seen in one place. Shiloh's first photos had been sold to the media for almost $8 million—a record in celebrity photojournalism. After all the struggles, this was an affirmation that people believed in us. I ran into the house shouting with joy that our work for children in Africa could continue for years ahead.

CHAPTER 46

Visiting Home

In the summer of 2005, Cletus had completed his junior year at Churchill High School and made the decision to return to Kabwata Orphanage and Transit Centre to fulfill his high school community service requirement. Now 18 years old, Cletus was at the center of a strong group of interracial friends in a predominantly white school.

After five years in America, he was fully integrated into American youth culture with his trendy clothes, his rap and hip-hop music, a place on the varsity soccer team, and his fanatical love for the Philadelphia Eagles. He still had bittersweet memories of Zambia and Kabwata. He wasn't sure he wanted to go back. But Mindi and I encouraged him: We thought it was important for him to balance his Americanization with his roots in Lusaka. And so he decided he wanted to go.

We knew this would be a difficult trip into the past for our son, who had embraced his new life so completely. But we were also worried that ignoring his past could block him from healing from the grief of losing his mom and his family at such a young age.

We spent hours discussing the pros and cons of the visit with experts, including Sandi. All seemed to agree that Cletus was ready, and that he knew himself better than anyone. And even though we were concerned about how he would handle his emotions, and we would miss him, we sensed this was an important rite of passage.

I had traveled to Lusaka for work earlier in the year and used the opportunity to prearrange Cletus's visit. I desperately wanted to make sure that he returned as a Zeitz, with as little confusion as possible about his identity in our family and where he belonged. Although I didn't fully understand Zambia cultural norms, I feared that Cletus could be mistreated as a foreigner, and I wanted him treated with respect and dignity. We gave him the option to stay with family friends in the nicer part of town or at his old orphanage. He chose Kabwata, where Mrs. Miyanda was still working and several of his friends were still living.

That June, Cletus embarked alone for a month of service to the orphanage for which he would help care for the children, clean the chicken coops, collect eggs, and work in the garden. On arrival, he was given a small bunk in a tiny shared room with a couple of his peers. It was a far cry from our comfortable home in Potomac.

On Cletus's first day back, a small orphan girl died of AIDS. This wasn't as common an occurrence at Kabwata as it had been when we lived in Zambia, as many young parents who were HIV infected were now being enrolled into lifesaving AIDS treatment programs, so the number of sick HIV-infected orphans was dramatically smaller. This death put the whole orphanage into crisis mode as they prepared her funeral.

When Cletus called us that night, we could hear in his voice how rattled and upset he was. In America he was living a life completely untouched by disease and death, and one so different that it essentially barricaded him from the traumatic memories of his childhood.

Over the next month, we talked to him frequently. He said that it was hard to be back at Kabwata. As a six-foot-tall, physically fit soccer player, he towered over the rest of the kids who were shorter and thinner, stunted from deprivation and illness. He told us Kabwata had taken on many more children, and many very young ones. Some of the same children he had known as a preteen were still there, their hopes for adoption vanished.

Cletus returned home just in time for soccer tryouts at Churchill. Reflecting on the experience, he told us his appreciation had grown for his life in America and with a family and brothers that knew him and loved him. I told Cletus how glad I was that he had taken this journey to his home country, because I thought it was important to connect with his heritage and to process the grief that was buried inside himself. As a father, I was compelled to protect him from further harm, but because he was becoming an adult, I also had to let him go. He needed to navigate his own way to healing and happiness. I said:

"Cletus my son, I cannot know the level of grief and pain that you have endured, I see before me a strong man, and a loving man.

"I see your power!

"Sometimes it is O.K. to listen and consider the possible value of the divine wisdom of your parents, as collectively we have 80+ years of life experience, more than four times your life experience."

Cletus's journey back to Africa also made me aware that I had more work to do on my own healing path. Something inside me was burning me up. But, as I had always done, I focused first on my work. It was saving lives that gave me the strongest sense of purpose.

CHAPTER 47

Arch Tutu

Throughout 2006 and 2007, my team at GAA worked hard to maintain the political momentum to mobilize full funding from the U.S. Congress for the Global Fund to Fight AIDS, Tuberculosis, and Malaria and for PEPFAR. Both entities were now running large programs in countries all over the world. The pressure was on to make sure these funds were being used effectively and to keep the investments coming.

We needed fresh strategies to sustain the attention of political leaders, especially as the 2008 presidential election approached. We feared a change in political leadership could disrupt U.S. efforts to fight AIDS in Africa.

We needed allies. I enlisted the help of global moral luminaries: Holocaust survivor and author Elie Wiesel, the former president of Ireland, Mary Robinson, and South Africa's Archbishop Desmond Tutu.

Tutu was a mighty force of justice who fought apartheid from the pulpit and in the streets. Working with South African President Nelson Mandela, Tutu chaired the post-apartheid

Truth and Reconciliation Commission, which influenced the peaceful transition of power during the country's volatile period of transformation. Pauline Muchina, a dynamic Kenyan friend who was an expert on faith-based advocacy, introduced me to her friend and pastor Rev. Mpho Tutu, the Archbishop's youngest daughter. Rev. Tutu was completing her pastoral training at Christ Church, a small Anglican church—where George and Martha Washington had once prayed—in the heart of Old Town Alexandria, Virginia, directly across the Potomac River from Washington.

I arrived early at Christ Church for our meeting. But it took me awhile to find the back stairs to a small row of offices above the church. I was a little nervous, unsure exactly how this meeting would go. Mpho, a young woman in her 30s, welcomed me into her office with a big smile and a calming grace.

We began our meeting with a moment of silence so that we could settle into the present moment. Wow! This was my kind of meeting! I immediately felt safe and inspired.

I shared with Mpho my journey of fighting AIDS in Zambia, across Africa, in the halls of Congress, and in the White House. I told her that although we had made significant progress, we still had a long way to go to reach our goal of ensuring universal access to lifesaving AIDS treatment.

That meeting was followed by more conversations in the following weeks. Mpho agreed to become chair of GAA's Board of Directors. And, if he agreed, the archbishop would serve as honorary chair and act as a public spokesperson for our cause.

Several months later, Mpho invited me to her home. "Daddy" was in town and she had arranged for the three of us to meet. He shook my hand warmly, insisting I call him "Arch."

I was awe-inspired by Arch's wisdom and grace. He was a genuinely happy and generous man who made me feel at home in his presence. We spent an hour in deep conversation about how we would work together to support GAA's mission.

As we were wrapping up, the doorbell rang. In marched a group of about 18 parishioners from Mpho's nearby church. They had big smiles on their faces as they greeted Arch. Then more arrived, and everyone began gathering into a circle for the Eucharist.

As a Jew, I initially felt very awkward. I had no idea what was happening. Should I stay or go? Was I allowed to participate in this sacred ceremony? I knew that the Eucharist included a symbolic eating of Christ's body and drinking Christ's blood—which is not something I had ever done. I'm sure this seems quite natural to people raised in the Catholic and Anglican faiths, but the idea of eating and drinking Jesus Christ's body and blood was mysterious and a little scary to me. I checked in with Arch, asking if I could stay. He just smiled broadly, extended his right arm, and gestured for me to sit near him.

A minister from Christ Church welcomed the community in this sacred circle, and Arch then led the Eucharist prayers with a soft and steady voice. He smiled calmly and deliberately held eye contact with each participant as he connected with his or her soul. In my body I felt a spiritual transcendence. I was home—secure and blessed by the spiritual power of Arch as he awakened the healing and transformation in all of us. Far from feeling fear, I felt safe in receiving the wafer and drinking a sip of wine, understanding that I was honoring and respecting the community present.

After that, Arch became a reliable and committed advocacy partner. We communicated regularly, aligning our strategies in the battle against AIDS. He was one of the first people I knew with an iPhone, and he used it voraciously, messaging and emailing his contacts in never-ending, world-changing conversations. Until he retired, he answered my emails faster than my wife did.

We arranged media interviews for him and helped him publish editorials in the *New York Times*, the *Washington Post*, and *USA Today*. His strong moral leadership was just the authoritative voice to push the GAA agenda far and wide.

We were poised for success for the years ahead, and I felt great about the impact of my team at GAA and my own contributions. But inside me, I felt increasingly lost. While I still traveled to Africa for short trips, the deep connections I felt living in Zambia were unraveling bit by bit. I had been working hard in Washington to build programs for AIDS relief in Africa, but I had lost touch with whether they were having the impact I envisioned.

Anger and unhappiness arrived to fill in my empty spaces. I loved my wife and my five sons, but somehow, amid the busyness of our lives, I was losing my grip on what I was feeling within myself. When I did dare to look inside, all I could see was a dark caldron of despair. I yearned to be happy. I didn't know how.

CHAPTER 48

Pilgrimage

In February 2007, I left for a nine-day trip to South Africa and Rwanda to explore what was happening on the ground, where the programs being financed by PEPFAR and the Global Fund were expanding. Progress was underway, but I still despaired that our response was too slow. Millions of lives were being lost, and our collective response seemed totally inadequate.

South Africa's liberation from apartheid in 1994 had been a time of great hope. Paradoxically, it also became the catalyst for the rapid spread of HIV. The homelands travel bans had been abolished, and the newfound freedom of movement accelerated the movement of the virus as well. Racial segregation, entrenched gender inequality, and vast disparities in education and health had left South African society unprepared for the onslaught of AIDS. On top of that, President Thabo Mbeki's government denied that HIV causes AIDS, which dragged down the momentum of South Africa's response.

I visited one of the first antiretroviral treatment programs in Africa, which had opened in 2001 in Khayelitsha, a

30-square-mile shantytown along the Western Cape. By the time I visited, the clinic staff was getting medicine to 60 percent of the local population diagnosed with HIV and almost every HIV+ pregnant woman. They were making huge strides in reducing mother-to-child transmission of the virus.

But there were problems. A young doctor with a wide smile and sad eyes explained progress was slowed by a major shortage of both health care workers and affordable second-line drugs to treat people who develop resistance to first-line drugs. A lot more work—and money—was needed to break the trajectory of the epidemic.

After my visit to South Africa, I set off for Kigali, the capital of Rwanda and the center of the 1994 genocide. I was nervous, recalling my Metro-ride realization that my inaction made me complicit with the devastation. As my plane descended, I felt helpless, hopeless, and ashamed about my own behavior. Maybe by being at the devastation site, I could better understand: *How could this happen?*

For generations, Rwanda's two main ethnic groups, the Hutus and the Tutsis, had lived alongside each other in what everyone thought was a peaceful situation. However, the seeds of genocide had been sown in colonial days when the Belgians favored the Tutsis (15 percent of the population) over the majority Hutus. Although Hutus and Tutsis had intermarried for decades, animosities developed, fed by people hungry for power on both sides. Then during 100 days in 1994, 800,000 men, women, children, and babies were slaughtered, most hacked to death with machetes. So much for "never again" to genocide.

Kigali is a crowded city of some 500,000 people, situated in the rolling hills of central Rwanda. It was the rainy season. Each day began bright and sunny until afternoon, when clouds rolled in and intense, lightning-filled thunderstorms raged through the sky. I arrived at dusk, driving from the airport just as the rains stopped and a misty fog filled the air. A soccer match was letting out, and throngs of healthy-looking, dynamic Rwandans were walking the streets. I looked out the window with a huge grin on my face, feeling fascinated and optimistic by the normalcy of the urban chaos around me.

My reverie was shattered as our car passed the Hotel des Mille Collines, a beautiful building on top of a hill: the place dubbed Hotel Rwanda in the 2004 film about the genocide. Within those walls, manager Paul Rusesabagina sheltered more than 1,200 people. It was eerie to see it now, returned to a thriving four-star resort, as if the spring of 1994 had never happened.

The next day, I made a visit to an AIDS treatment clinic supported by a women's organization called WE ACTx. As I walked in, many of the women waiting wore expressions I could only describe as vacant. I talked with a young woman in her early 30s about her case. Her eyes were like empty windows. In a monotone, she described the rape and torture that she experienced during the genocide. She was thriving on her AIDS medicines, but her life would never be normal again.

I met with Agnes Binagwaho, the Rwandan government minister in charge of HIV/AIDS, to learn what was being done collectively to manage the post-traumatic stress affecting so many people. She explained that April, the month when the genocide began, is a particularly hard time for many survivors. It is the hottest month of the year, in the middle of the rainy season, and a time when genocide survivors sometimes become severely depressed.

Leaving Kigali for the next leg of my trip, I traveled by car with Vanessa Kerry, daughter of U.S. Senator John Kerry, who was doing work in Rwanda at that time. We traveled about two hours west toward Tanzania to visit Rwinkwavu Hospital, a small rural hospital with about 25 beds and several outpatient clinics. The hospital was being rehabilitated by Partners in Health, headed by two energetic medical doctors, Paul Farmer and Jim Yong Kim. Paul served on the board of GAA for many years, and Jim and I had worked together when he led the WHO's AIDS treatment program years before.

Partners in Health began operating in Rwinkwavu Hospital and its six referring health centers in May 2005, where they trained more than 700 paid community health workers to support and sustain more than 2,000 people on antiretroviral drugs. The organization set a gold standard for comprehensive health services for people living with AIDS, providing not only medicines, but food and jobs. The hand-to-hand partnerships between the Rwandans and Partners in Health was a powerful demonstration of an African Renaissance in action. It gave me great hope.

Taking a short walk away from the hospital, I came across a local genocide memorial, which are common throughout the country. A blue-and-white fence surrounded a small memorial wall in front of a large flat, concrete slab embedded in the earth. A mass burial site for unnamed hundreds. I closed my eyes and tried to absorb the paradox of the two stark realities that humans can create in one physical place. Thirteen years before, it was a senseless killing field, and now it was a hospital—a vortex of hope in a sea of illness and poverty. I prayed that the world would wake up and together make hope—not fear, anger, or despair—the premise for the way forward.

CHAPTER 49

Birkenau Boomerang

Several months after my South Africa and Rwanda trip, I arranged a private meeting with Elie Wiesel, the Nobel Prize–winning author and Holocaust survivor and one of my childhood heroes. He was a powerful moral leader and politically connected to the leaders of the Democratic Party. I wanted to recruit him to support the work of GAA as we prepared for the 2008 election season. I traveled to Boston University where he was a professor in the Department of Religion.

I climbed the dark, ancient stairs and arrived at a room on the top floor where several assistants were scurrying around. Piles of papers covered every surface and copies of his many books filled the shelves. A few minutes later, I was escorted into his serene office, filled with neater stacks of papers. It seemed he was preparing to publish many more tomes in the years ahead.

We sat face-to-face in two chairs in front of his desk. I thanked him and talked about the impact of his work on my life, telling him that reading his book *Night* in seventh grade had changed my life. We discussed the AIDS crisis in Africa. I asked him if it could be considered a modern holocaust. He cautioned me against using "holocaust" to describe the plagues affecting Africa, as he felt that word was uniquely attributable to what the Jews experienced under Nazi Germany, but granted that preventing the senseless death of millions of Africans was a moral responsibility for the world. He agreed to serve as the honorary co-chair of the GAA, bringing more moral gravitas to our cause.

Soon thereafter, I was off to Berlin to attend a major conference of global leaders in support of the Global Fund. I had also decided it was finally time to take a personal pilgrimage to Auschwitz-Birkenau—the place I had always feared yet yearned to visit.

I took a short flight from Berlin to Krakow, Poland, and from there, I hired a taxi to drive me west to Auschwitz.

There are actually three camps in the area: Monowitz, which was mainly a labor camp; Auschwitz I, the original; and Birkenau, the largest camp where the final solution was implemented.

Wearing all black, I spent the whole next day, Saturday—the Sabbath—walking to every corner of the vast death camps. From Auschwitz I crossed the train tracks and then entered the gated hell of Birkenau. It was a sunny and warm spring day. There was light breeze, the sky was a beautiful vivid blue, and the birds were chirping in an orchestra of song.

The beauty of the countryside shocked me. All I had ever seen were black-and-white silent films of cold wintry days and of Jews being mass-starved, enslaved, gassed, and cremated. I had never imagined that the sun could shine, soft winds could blow, and birds could sing in the midst of hell on earth.

I thought I knew a lot about the camps, but that day I learned much, much more. Firstly, there was a lot more resistance at the camp then I had understood. Many Jewish children were saved by Polish prisoners who would hoard food for them and help them escape. I also learned about a major resistance effort in 1944 led by women prisoners who destroyed one of the gas chambers and burned down the crematoria, using smuggled gunpowder from a munitions factory within the Auschwitz complex.

I was numbed by the experience. I could barely cry, although inside I felt a profound flood of weeping. The most jolting moments occurred inside the museum and its rooms full of Jews' clothes, shoes, and hair, some still tied in braids. The Nazis forced Jewish prisoners to shave the heads of corpses after they were gassed and before being burned. The hair was used to make socks. The image of Germans wearing the hair of murdered Jews still haunts me.

Birkenau is 24 square miles, and over one million people were killed there between 1942 and 1944. The Nazis were actually in the process of implementing a plan to radically increase the daily killing and cremation capacity when they were defeated. While walking the grounds, I felt a surge of compassion for all our Jewish ancestors, but also for the Poles, the gypsies, the Soviets, and the homosexuals who were also targeted by the Nazi extermination machine.

Adjacent to the fifth gas chamber and crematoria is a beautiful grove of tall, proud birch trees. Jews were held in these woods to wait when the crematoria were too full and backed up.

I was called into those woods.

I put on my prayer shawl (*tallit*), opened my prayer book (*Chumash*), and sat under a birch. I conducted an entire prayer service, and I read from the Torah. Each week on the Sabbath, Jews, no matter where they are worshipping, read the same passage, or *parashah*. As I chanted every word of that week's reading, I felt a sense of powerful transformation and victory. Those who were slaughtered in that place could not have imagined that 65 years in the future, a Jew would be chanting the Torah in freedom, with an open, yet weeping heart.

Here under the beautiful birches, my ancestors lived in limbo for days as they waited their turn to be gassed and then burned. I tried to imagine their fear. It was in that moment that I realized that my own inner fears were helping me and hindering me simultaneously. I spoke a phrase from Torah out loud: *And may you bring a blessing upon me also!*

After my solo prayer service, I continued to walk to the distant edges of Birkenau—chanting in a soft, grieving voice, "Justice, justice, you shall pursue."

I had borne witness to so many devastations that humans created for each other—in Hiroshima, in Rwanda, in AIDS-ravaged Africa, and now at Birkenau—I had a revelation:

I will boomerang myself toward justice and peace;

I will transform and redirect the evils of the Holocaust;

My intensity for justice will outmatch the evil-doers to create peace within myself and around all of us.

This visit to Birkenau stirred up my psyche irreparably. I knew that somehow, I needed to finally face my inner demons.

CHAPTER 50

What About the Boys?

ONE afternoon during the winter of 2008, I was sitting in a meeting in New York City with members of the global women's movement talking about violence against women and girls. Girls are highly vulnerable to HIV infection and other sexually transmitted diseases because of the prevalence of rape, sexual abuse, early marriage, and other manifestations of gender inequity.

Sexual abuse is a cycle that is passed down through families, my colleague from the women's movement was saying. The group was planning a major advocacy campaign to roll out in Africa. For our part, GAA was advocating for a multi-billion-dollar, whole-of-society response to fight gender violence. We wanted to bridge the divide between groups that focused only on violence against women and those that focused on children's issues by creating a combined campaign addressing violence against woman *and* children. It seemed logical to me.

I was the only male in the crowded conference room among more than 25 women passionately railing against sexual violence against women and girls. But as they talked, it became clear that no one in the room was at all interested in violence against *all children.*

They never were. They were looking at it from one perspective only. As if women and adolescent girls were the *only* victims of sexual abuse.

As I sat there, I felt my hands balling into fists. My body started to shake all over. I felt a rage rising from a deep, mysterious place within me. Inside my head, I heard my own voice screaming.

I tried to calm my trembling hand as I raised it. I challenged the group in a steady voice that I felt was coming from someone else:

"What about the boys who are victims?

"How can we interrupt the cycle of violence if we don't address their needs?

"What about the *BOYS?*"

One of the experts replied, "Don't worry. We'll deal with that."

I became so furious at that inadequate answer that I rose and walked out of the room, wobbly on my feet and trembling.

Where did that *come from?*

What was going on with me?

Why was I was being triggered into rage?

Why was this affecting me so emotionally?

Later that spring, Mindi and I learned that a young male we knew had been sexually abused, the assault happening when

Mindi was nearby with our sons. I was heartbroken. This was hitting too close to home, perhaps even right under our noses. My mind descended into a frenzy of panic.

Was I doing enough to protect my own boys from abuse?

What if something had already happened to them and we didn't know?

Was I too busy fighting to protect children in Africa, while my own children were left exposed?

These thoughts kept me up at night and terrified me. I would wake Mindi up at 2:00 in the morning and ask her again and again if anything had happened to our boys, and had we done enough to protect them. Cletus was 21, Lian was 15, Yonah was 13, Emet was 11, and Uriel was seven. They went to overnight camps, played sports, had male teachers, and were often left alone with family. We had always taught our sons to let us know if somebody made them feel unsafe, but Mindi and I had never been overly neurotic about the risk that they could be sexually abused.

That spring, I had my first experience with some strange flashbacks—dreamlike fragments of a memory—a crack in a veil of amnesia. With each episode, a vague cloudy image became a little clearer, until one day I saw what my mind wanted to hide from me. I was small, maybe six or seven years old, and I was sitting on the floor of a gray-tiled shower between a pair of long hairy legs. I was shyly staring up, but I could not see his face. I only could look up and see his long hairy legs. I felt a six-year-old's sense of confusion and shame.

I shared this bizarre memory with Mindi. She listened. I started trembling. "Stay calm," she told me gently. "We'll figure this out together."

I had never been more grateful for the woman I married. Knowing she would be at my side no matter what gave me strength to open my mind to whatever lay hidden beyond my consciousness.

As soon as I acknowledged this memory, more vivid ones began to take shape. But they stayed just beyond the view of my mind's eye, like shadows, jagged fragments, and mists dissipating, preparing to reveal their true form.

Then in July, my stepfather, Joe Smaul, Mom's second husband, died suddenly of a massive heart attack at age 75. He and Mom had married 20 years earlier when I was in medical school. Joe had been a wonderful grandfather to our children, and he was my first parental figure to pass away. I felt rattled by the fragility of life.

After his burial, we returned to their home, a three-story townhouse in the suburbs of Philadelphia for the Jewish rite of mourning called *shiva*. People from my Philadelphia past came and went all day—some I hadn't seen in 30 years. I was overwhelmed and lightheaded from past and present clashing and colliding.

After the visitors left, I sat in the living room, while Mom, Marci, and a few close friends ate dinner in the dining room. I could just overhear my mother talking about the shocking news about a man who we knew who had experienced sexual abuse growing up. She turned her attention to Marci, my sister, and asked worriedly, "Did anything ever happen to you? Are you sure? Are you really sure?"

Suddenly, I found myself on the floor. I was startled. My mind was racing to try to figure out what was going on:

I don't know how I got here, but my body is rigid.

I feel literally physically paralyzed.

I can't move my arms or my legs.

Nothing like this has ever happened to me before.

I had lapsed into a state of primal grief. I could not move. I could hardly breath. All this time my mind was silently screaming.

What about the boys?

What about the BOYS!?

A man close to us had been sexually abused, but Mom never thought to ask *me* if I had been hurt. Only Marci.

After a few minutes of lying unnoticed and unmoving on my mother's living room floor, the feeling came back into my hands and feet. I got up slowly, head spinning, and went into the upstairs bedroom to call Mindi, who was back in D.C. tending to our kids. "I just had the weirdest experience of my life," I told her.

I was frightened. I couldn't understand what had just happened. My mind could not grasp what it had done to my body.

Mindi reassured me that everything would be okay, and that I would have to figure out a way to explore the flashbacks and now this unexplained "startle response" experience.

I returned home and went back to my work routine, but something was cracking open in my psyche. I needed a break. I needed help.

Chapter 51

Yes, We Can

In the midst of all this, the 2008 presidential election was underway. Political transitions were the super fuel of our advocacy efforts because new leaders bring new agendas. We wanted to make sure that the next president would build on the positive aspects of Bush's leadership on PEPFAR and the Global Fund.

We had two major tasks in front of us: first, to ensure that President Bush and Congress would recommit to these programs for the next five years, because the 2003 legislation was set to expire just as the president's second term was expiring. Second, we wanted to put candidates on the record for their support these programs and challenge them to do even more if they won the presidency.

The main Democratic challengers were Senators Hillary Clinton, Joe Biden, and Barack Obama, all of whom we felt would be strong allies in the global battle against AIDS. I had worked directly with Biden's and Clinton's senior staffs on legislation efforts and had spoken directly to both in recent months. I felt confident in their commitment to Africa. But Senator Obama, still in his first term, had less of a track record. We hoped his intelligence and Kenyan heritage would compel him to stay the course of global AIDS as well. John McCain was the leading Republican candidate and he never spoke about this crisis as far as I knew.

We mounted a campaign to get candidates to sign GAA's Presidential Pledge for Leadership on Global AIDS and Poverty, which called for at least $50 billion in global AIDS spending by 2013—more than three times what we demanded in 2003—and included a fair-share contribution to the Global Fund. With this level of investment, we could dramatically expand the size of programs in Africa, accelerate prevention programs, and ensure that nearly every person who needed lifesaving AIDS medicines would receive them. We had proven over the prior five years that money was the oxygen for bold and transformative action. Now we were aiming high for the next phase.

Candidate Obama had already announced his commitment to increase AIDS spending by a whopping $1 billion per year, making a public statement at a high-profile faith-based event hosted at Saddleback Church in California by Rev. Rick Warren and his wife Kay, two purpose-driven religious leaders. That was as far as he would go. Denis McDonough, lead policy advisor for Obama, told me Obama was not willing to sign anything—he had already committed publicly to doing more.

Then, while on the campaign trail in New Hampshire, Biden was cornered by a group of AIDS activists from the Health GAP coalition. Before the encounter was over, he became the first presidential candidate to agree to sign the pledge. Clinton signed next after ACT UP Philadelphia threated a major protest at a Clinton campaign event on Halloween. Her policy lead, Brian Deese, got her okay after a fast-track review.

After that, we went back to McDonough. He convinced the reluctant candidate to finally agree to the pledge, but explained that Obama was extremely cautious about being forced to make commitments from outside pressure.

Senator McCain never signed the pledge.

Using the momentum from the pledge signings, the Democratic-controlled Congress signaled to President Bush that they would go along with a $50 billion reauthorization bill if the president acted fast. To secure his legacy, President Bush used his political leadership to ensure that PEPFAR would continue after he left office, pushing Congress to act immediately. That summer of 2008, Congress approved $48 billion for the next five years of U.S.–funded HIV/AIDS programming in Africa.

I was thrilled. My Global AIDS Alliance team and other AIDS activists showed once again that a small group of organized people can wage justice and have a global impact.

Now, we had to ensure that the next president of the United States would keep his or her word. Political momentum was leaning toward a Democratic victory, so we decided to host a side event at the Democratic National Convention to maintain political support from the nominee, Sen. Obama. We celebrated strong Congressional leaders at an awards event, honoring Sen. Barbara Boxer, Reps. Donald Payne and Barbara Lee, and others.

Later that week, as Sen. Obama delivered his acceptance speech in Denver's giant Invesco Stadium, I could feel the energy of the crowd surge the longer he spoke. I had never felt anything like it before. Each phrase he uttered sent waves of emotion through the crowd. It was a physical feeling. Everyone was standing tall, connected, and aligned with the same vision.

"At this moment, in this election, we must pledge once more to march into the future!" he challenged us. Then he quoted Hebrews 10:23: "Hold firmly, without wavering, to the hope that we confess."

Yes, we can, I thought. Finally, someone was saying to the crowd of 80,000 what I had been saying to myself, my family, and my colleagues for years. That we can transform the trajectory of our country and the world. We can join forces to build a nation that stands for hope, freedom, and peace. We can defeat pessimism.

Obama was elected handily on his platform of hope and change, and we had our marching orders. My team and I at GAA were firing on all cylinders. It was another political opportunity—our best yet, I thought.

But just a month later, by end of the summer, I was in a messed-up state, and my spirit failing. I was 46 years old and somehow had completely burned out. GAA was strong and moving forward, but I had destroyed my body. I weighed 272 pounds—90 pounds too heavy. My relationships were fraying—both at home and work. I wasn't offering my best self to my family or anyone else. I continued to have flashbacks whenever the topic of sexual abuse arose. I finally slowed down enough to hear the insistent inner voice that had been telling me all year to get some help.

I successfully negotiated a sabbatical from GAA that coincided with the presidential election and transition. I had no idea what "help" and fate had in store, but I knew I needed a break.

PART FOUR
Revelation

As human beings, our greatness lies not so much in being able to remake the World—that is the myth of the atomic age—as in being able to remake ourselves.

—Mahatma Gandhi

CHAPTER 52

Breaking Point

Over the prior couple of years, I excessively overate comfort food as a way of soothing my inner turmoil. My daily transition from the cauldron of D.C. advocacy warfare to my tumultuous seven-person household was always a challenge.

I like things in order, and I usually walked into a house of chaos. Desperate for solace, I would walk into the empty kitchen, open the refrigerator, and clear out the leftovers. I knew it was wrong, and that I was being unhealthy, but I couldn't stop myself. This self-medicating was wholly ineffective. It fueled my self-hatred and poor body image. But I felt trapped, unable to fill my inner hollowness and emptiness despite my loving and tolerant wife, five sons, and successful, productive work life.

For two years, I had been taking Rabbi Shefa Gold's intensive Kol Zimra chant leadership training program. The chanting helped. Sometimes I could break through the veils of self-hatred in flashes, getting more and more tastes of self-love and compassion.

Chanting is a powerful spiritual technology. Sacred words become "the lanterns" that enable us to heal and bless ourselves and others. Chanting in community has both personal and communal benefits—deepening one's center and being part of a group enhances the energy in the experience. It is often in the silence after the chant that one's soul experiences divine insight.

But now, a shadow of perpetual dissatisfaction with everything and everyone engulfed me. Despite meditation, yoga, chanting, therapy, and all my other attempts to get on a healthy track, I couldn't shake a persistent self-loathing. I was angry at the world, at my family, and, mostly, at myself. I was drained.

For most of my life, I had clung to the idea that deep down, I was "normal." I assumed that everyone else struggled daily to control themselves, just like me. Now I realized I was more tortured than other people. I learned from Mindi that other people—especially those who pursue the level of self-scrutiny and training that I did—actually *did* achieve a life filled with inner joy and happiness. But somehow, I couldn't break through.

I was my own demon, and I was enslaving myself.

My mind was a nonstop, horror-filled film factory. Scene by scene, I rolled through images of my future degradation, divorce, loss, and world destruction.

I watched these mind-films and saw the patterns of my self-destruction and my bleak future play out—I was trapped in the booth, both projectionist and audience. As hard as I tried, there was nothing I could do to shut off the self-hatred.

It was a difficult way to live. I *needed* to be "normal." I needed to view myself that way. On paper, I was. Normal childhood, normal family, normal existence. I also knew I was lucky. I was surrounded with unconditional love from a lot of people. I had a good brain and the drive to go to college, finish medical school, and then become a doctor. I followed my dream of working in global public health and carved out a career where I could actually help the most helpless. People living with HIV. People dying of AIDS. Children who were suffering from poverty and homelessness and preventable diseases. People who had no rights.

So why did I feel so miserable and unworthy?

Why did I eat so much when I wasn't even hungry?

The pain within me was erupting like a volcano and I didn't know why.

As my sabbatical from GAA began, I enrolled in a comprehensive weight management program at George Washington University. I was drawn to the program because it used an integrated approach that included medical care, nutrition advice, exercise, and behavioral and psychological therapy.

One evening in class the therapist, Bill, discussed something called "fat dependency syndrome." He explained that women who have been sexually assaulted often overeat, gaining weight as a means of protection—an armor to feel safe. They enclose themselves in fat as a shield.

My mind whirled. Always the student, I had become fascinated by the concept of emotional eating, but I had never contemplated that some of the heavy women in the program and in the world may have been sexually abused. I began viewing overweight women very differently, shifting from judgment into profound empathy. Without fully understanding why, I became intensely curious about fat dependency syndrome and began a deeply personal inquiry into my own past.

At the same time, under the mentorship of Rabbi Gold, I studied the Song of Songs, one of the scrolls of the last section of the Tanakh, or Hebrew Bible. It is also the fifth book of Wisdom in the Old Testament of the Christian Bible. The Song of Songs is read on the Sabbath during Passover, marking the beginning of the grain harvest and commemorating the Exodus from Egypt and the liberation of the Israelites from slavery.

A famous Rabbi named Akiva, who lived 2,000 years ago, proclaimed: "The entire Bible is holy. But the Song of Songs is the Holy of Holies." While the passages describe the relationship between two intoxicated lovers, scholars believe they are a metaphor for one's potential relationship with the divine. For me, the Song of Songs words became the remedy for my broken relationship with myself.

I read, studied, and chanted the Song of Songs throughout my three-month sabbatical, with the aim of opening my heart to my own song, which I knew resided in buried memories of the past.

CHAPTER 53

Kaleidoscope

DID I have fat dependency syndrome as a buffer to protect myself from abuse? That was impossible! I had no overt memory of sexual abuse from my childhood. That could not be my problem.

But the strange flashbacks were happening more and more, and at random times. Over the next few months I started to think that maybe I had been sexually abused. But how or when, I had no idea. More questions weighed on me. *Was it real? Was it my fault? Was I a willing partner?* A little boy in me felt dirty and bad. The adult in me anguished: *Why did no one protect me?*

As I faced the possibility that I had been violated as a young boy, a kaleidoscope of emotions ravaged and entangled me. Words barked inside my head: *sacrifice, powerlessness, anger, alienation, isolation, worthlessness, confusion, disconnection from my body, loss of control, pleasure vs. pain, anxiety, grief, depression, shattering, fear, sadness, bereavement, exploitation, disregard, guilt, betrayal.*

I was 46 years old. My sense of self was in jeopardy. Was it possible that everything I thought I knew about my childhood wrong? Now I had investigative work to do to gather facts and sort through the questions: *Who am I? What kind of messed-up place did I come from?*

It was very hard for me to admit that the flashbacks were real. I decided I had to share my memories with each of my parents, one on one. I didn't think about the consequences. I felt driven to dig into the past to try to find out the truth.

Mom, still mourning the recent death of her husband, came for a weekend visit to Potomac. I needed her to know that I was deeply struggling. On Saturday morning after I heard her wake up, I knocked on her bedroom door and said I had something serious to talk to her about.

As she sat up in bed, her eyes wide, I shared details of my flashbacks—a little boy sitting before the long, hairy legs of a faceless man in a gray tiled bathroom. I felt sure at that time I'd been molested by an unknown adult male. I couldn't remember who it was or what, exactly, had happened. But the little boy was overwhelmed by feelings of confusion and danger.

This is what I explained to Mom and then I asked her if she had any idea who it might be, or what actually happened.

Mom became almost hysterical. "No! This couldn't have happened!" She screamed. But in the next sentence she was shrieking apologies. And then excuses. She did not know! She couldn't have known! It wasn't her fault! Then she was in shock and started to cry, hugging me and trying to give me words of comfort, as she had always done throughout my life. She said she had no idea who the man could have been. But though she become more and more upset, after that first denial, never for a second did she doubt that I was sharing truth.

A few weeks later, I drove to Philadelphia to talk to Dad. In his dining room, he sat at the opposite end of the table as I talked, his hands gripping the edge, eyes bulging like a deer frozen in headlights. He looked like he wanted to be anywhere but in that room. Like he might run. In a grim tone, he said he "was sorry to hear" that something had happened to me. But he did not seem at all surprised, which was in fact, very surprising and confusing to me.

Talking to my parents was the opposite of cathartic. It catapulted me into a profound state of grief. It *must* be true that something happened to me. I was grieving the loss of my self-image of "normal." I was grieving the years I wasted in deep-rooted self-loathing and the loss of the sense of safety my parents were supposed to provide for me. I grieved the loss of my innocent childhood.

I took long daily walks on the trails of the C&O Canal along the Potomac River, feeling lost and alone. A deep-felt shame that was enlivening my inner demons was finally being excavated.

I wept and wept. To cope with the pain and grief, I anchored myself to chanting the Song of Songs. I repeated prayers of comfort over and over, untangling the knots of despair that were ravaging my mind. I felt like I was walking through the desert and I was searching for the promised land of liberation and freedom.

I repeated my favorite mantra in my mind over and over again: *Justice! Justice! You shall pursue!*

I shared everything with Mindi, who was deeply saddened, but also not surprised. I checked in with Sandi, Mindi's mom, who never had any suspicion that I had been abused during our therapeutic work many years earlier. She told me it was not uncommon for abused children's memories to emerge during middle age. Mindi was my steadfast rock of support. After returning from my long walks, I cooked dinner and helped the kids with their homework. Some evenings we watched a movie. Enjoying my family was the only solid thing in my life.

One day, I came from my walk in a panicked state. I told Mindi I needed to talk to her privately. We went up to our bedroom, shut the door, and I told her I was agitated by the thought that I could have done something to harm or abuse my sons. Jarred by unexpected flashbacks over the past six months, I was terrified that I may also have blocked memories of myself being a perpetrator. If there were memories about my childhood that I had repressed, were there things about the way I acted as a father that I had also hidden from myself?

After a deep exploration with Mindi, I became certain that I was never an abuser. Like me, most survivors of sexual abuse would find it abhorrent to commit a similar act toward another vulnerable victim. Research shows that only a very small percentage who have suffered sexual trauma will go on to become abusers.

CHAPTER 54

Shattered

In early 2009, I was ready to go back to work, but I didn't want to go back to GAA. The inner anger that fueled my activism over the past eight years had dissipated, and I yearned to work on a broader agenda of creating a just, peaceful, and sustainable global community.

I was under 200 pounds now, having lost over 80, and was feeling healthy and rejuvenated. I felt as if the demons from my past had been at least partially exorcised from inside my heart. I wanted to pursue peace and justice full-time from a new place. On the frigid afternoon of January 20, as I stood on the National Mall to celebrate President Barack Obama's inauguration, I imagined that the adversarial stance GAA had taken during the Bush era would no longer be needed. I felt free to pursue my dreams for a better world.

But my colleagues and the board lobbied for me to stay. It wasn't the right time to leave, and I returned to my job as executive director. GAA was on the brink of obtaining our largest million-dollar grant ever for a global campaign to end pediatric HIV/AIDS. I had worked on the proposal for this campaign for more than two years, and I wanted to see that vision fulfilled. The board agreed to explore the transformation of GAA into a new organization that would continue AIDS advocacy, but also take on a broader range of peace and justice issues around the world.

Although I had finally gained some acceptance about my confusing memories, I was still struggling to accept the reality of my sexual abuse as a young boy. It was as if I had lived two childhoods at the same time: the one I remembered and the one I had forgotten. The anger, the internal turmoil, the weight gain—it was all explained by events from a blanked-out past. I was sure sexual abuse had happened, but I still didn't remember who or what it was.

In April 2009, Dad came down for a weekend to celebrate Passover. Even though it wasn't my favorite activity, Mindi arranged for the Zeitz men to go on a half-day fishing trip on the Chesapeake Bay in a private charter. My father, the expert, taught my kids how to set up the rods with bait and how to lure the rockfish in and hook them when they bit. It was a cool but very sunny day, with three generations of Zeitz boys happy together at sea. I beamed as I watched my sons enjoying this precious time with my father. It had been four months since I had shared my flashback, and Dad's gentle treatment of me over the weekend showed a palpable empathy for what I had been going through.

On Sunday, as we drove to Union Station for the train back to Philadelphia, Dad was uncharacteristically emotional. As we neared the station, he softly said to me—seemingly out of nowhere, "Paul, I understand how you feel about what happened to you."

My heart started pounding hard, and I gave him a questioning look. I was surprised that he brought this topic up so directly, and only in the last three minutes of his visit, after spending the last four days together.

"*What?*" I asked, unsure of what he was saying.

"Stuff happened to me when I was a kid," my father blurted out. Then he shared a few quick stories about abuse he had suffered as a young boy. His father and older brother both abused him.

"And that was just the tip of the iceberg," he stated quietly.

By then, we had arrived at the train station. With a quick goodbye, he jumped out of the car to get on his train. I drove home in a stunned silence. My mind was racing with questions, but I had to focus on getting back to work.

GAA had convened an April 30 kick-off meeting for the Campaign to End Pediatric HIV/AIDS (CEPA) that would roll out in six African countries. I went to bed the night before the meeting feeling excited and revitalized. I had reached the peak of my professional success. I was beginning to understand myself, and my life seemed to be getting back on track.

A few hours before dawn, I woke up startled from a deep sleep. I gasped loudly, and the words exploded out of me before I could fully comprehend them.

It WAS him!

It was Dad!

A lurid memory had broken through, searing and raw. I felt sick.

When I had begun working with my therapist Bill on memory retrieval during my sabbatical, he had gently inquired a few different ways about whether my father could have abused me. But I had denied it vociferously. It couldn't be my dad—it couldn't be anyone in my family. That would kill me. *I loved my Dad.*

That morning I lay in bed, nauseous and shattered. My own story was a lie. My family's story was a lie. My father's story was a lie. My entire life was a lie.

I was utterly devastated by this revelation. My identity and sense of myself was totally and completely splintered—I had never experienced anything like this feeling before.

I grabbed the journal I keep by my side of the bed and wrote until my hand went numb. My entire life had been an invention. I have never felt safe. Now I had to ask the most profound question I had ever faced: *How do I know what the truth is?*

I was facing the naked source of my hatred for my father. I hated his voice, his actions, his smell, his way of being. I hated the gifts he bought me. I hated going fishing with him and I hated all his powerboats. And now I knew why.

Dad used to say to me as a child, "If it feels good, do it." I hated that too. He was so devastatingly wrong.

For nearly 40 years, I had lived with a profoundly effective amnesic barrier that prevented me from remembering the sordid details of my past—but that barrier also allowed me to become a doctor, husband, and father. Now, I finally understood why I hated gym class, and particularly hated being in a locker room shower in middle school and high school—I was terrified. I finally understood why I never played or liked team sports or even working out in a gym. I finally understood why I was always suspicious of adult male authority figures—I didn't trust them. I finally knew why I hated myself and my body so voraciously throughout my whole life. I finally understood why I had such a hard time opening my heart and trusting others.

I also understood why I had been shaking with fury at that meeting in New York City when I seemed to be the only one who realized that boys, too, could be victims. And now I understood why as a child I would scream to myself as I pounded my bed with forceful punches, *I will never be like HIM! I will never be like HIM!*

I didn't know how I was going to go to work that day, but I had no choice. I had to put on my suit and my smile and be Dr. Paul Zeitz, executive director of the Global AIDS Alliance. But who the hell was *he*? With Mindi's hugs and love, I was able to get out of bed and get dressed.

I called Carol Bergman, my deputy, and told her something was going on and I might not make it through the whole work day. I gave her Mindi's contact numbers in case I ... well, I didn't know how I was going to cope that day, or if I would be able to ask for help myself. I didn't trust myself to stay sane.

For a few hours, I was able to put the 40-year-old amnesic barrier back in place. I made it through the day, and then went straight afterwards to see Bill for an emergency appointment. I told him about my memories of Dad sexually abusing me. He was not surprised at all.

I wanted to know why this earthquake of a memory would surface that night, of all nights? By any outward measure, I was succeeding in life. By my own inward measure, I was healing spiritually and emotionally from a chaotic childhood. Perhaps my unconscious mind felt that I was now strong enough to handle the fact that I was a survivor of incest—that my own father had shattered a sacred trust with his son and raped me when I was seven years old.

Any time earlier in my life, when I was feeling weaker and more vulnerable, the amnesic barrier could never have been breached. I couldn't have coped with this truth. My mind had protected me all those years until I was ready. I realized, with Bill's help, that I had been living with post-traumatic stress since childhood—the root cause of decades of deeply ingrained self-hatred and self-destruction.

A few weeks later, my mother came down for another weekend visit. Once again, we sat quietly together, just the two of us, and I shared with her that I had uncovered another layer of memories. I was a nervous wreck, as this was going to be a nuclear bomb. I knew she was fragile, still grieving Joe's death, but I trudged forward—courageously and bull-headedly—to share my truth.

When I told her what Dad had done to me, she was utterly crushed. She had had no awareness of what was happening at the time. As we both cried, we went over all the ways our family home was a cauldron of dysfunction and blind spots. As devastating as it was to lay this burden on Mom, I was left with a sense of inner calm, as if freeing myself from bondage.

On June 2, I took Dad to dinner in Philadelphia at my favorite Chinese restaurant in Chestnut Hill. It was his 73rd birthday. I was reeling with both clarity and anxiety. It was the first time I had seen him since my memory of his assault surfaced, and we had a very strange dinner.

Without saying anything about my new memories of him as my perpetrator, I shared my feelings on the impact the sexual abuse memories were having on me and how it helped me understand why I had been so tortured with self-hatred and deeply held inner rage. Without confronting him, I believe I had struck a chord. I sensed that he knew that I knew the truth.

Over the next two weeks, my father went into a full psychological and physical meltdown. I heard from others that immediately after our dinner, his health deteriorated rapidly. He developed irritable bowel syndrome and couldn't control his physical functions. He couldn't eat or sleep normally. For two weeks, his condition worsened until I suggested that he should go to a psychiatrist. He was having a nervous breakdown, yet he refused to go for help.

My father's dramatic reaction was the last layer of validation I needed to confirm the truth. *Why else would he become physically sick over it?* At last, everything was making sense.

Part of me felt a venomous rage and hatred but, paradoxically, I also felt a deep wellspring of empathy and love for him. He was my father. He had also been abused as a child. I held these truths in my heart at the same time.

A couple of Sundays later it was Father's Day, and I knew I couldn't have another fake, strained encounter with him. I didn't feel safe with him, but I needed to confront him directly with my memory of his sexual abuse of me. I called him on his cellphone.

I reached him in the car as he was on his way to my sister's house, and I asked him to pull over, which he did. I told him I was not going through another Father's Day pretending that things did not happen. Dad kept saying in a hushed, yet firm, voice, "We need to meet—we need to do this in person." I said I wasn't doing that. I said that I did not feel safe meeting with him in person and that I could not wait a second longer to reveal the truth of my memories.

My father denied everything. He cut me off, saying he never wanted to speak to me again, and hung up.

CHAPTER 55

Standing for Peace

T HE fact that Dad stopped talking to me made me furious, but I did not want him to suffer. I wanted him to get better, and perhaps I wanted him to admit to someone, anyone, what had happened to him, and what he had done to me. I wanted this for my own healing, for his healing, and for the healing of our relationship.

I cautiously started sharing incest memories with a few people—those who had been around me during the early years of my life when the abuse happened. Everything was matching up.

My father had to groom me to create the dynamic where the sexual abuse could occur. I remembered the pervasive presence of pornography in his bedroom and around the house. In the closet where he stored his fishing gear was a stack of dirty magazines over three feet high.

I had a long overdue talk with Marci, my sister. As we took a long walk in a park by her home near Philadelphia, she recalled our family flying to Florida when I was seven years old; Dad and I sat together in one row, and Mom and Marci sat a couple of rows in front of us. She remembered seeing Dad showing me a pornographic magazine on the airplane. I had no memory of this incident, but it corroborated the bizarre environment of my childhood. By distorting the boundaries of normal sexual behavior, Dad must have created an aura of deformed sexual norms that enabled the abuse.

It took me about 18 months to piece together the emergent fragments of memories with the facts I could find. They were like the thousand pieces of a puzzle coming together in fragments, which, only after much time and effort, became mental images. And some of them were so vivid, remembering them was like a punch in the gut.

Ultimately, I was able to recall 14 separate episodes of abuse in detail. I journaled prolifically, explicitly, about each episode, until I had five full notebooks. As there was no forensic evidence or video documentation of these events, I only had my now crystal-clear memories.

Over the next year, I made many attempts to reconcile with my father. I called him and even showed up on his doorstep in Philadelphia a few times. I got my cousin involved as a go-between when I wanted him to come to Emet's Bar Mitzvah in November 2009.

Each time, I was rebuffed. When I tried to talk to him, he would tell me I was crazy. He would tell me how disappointed he was in me and in Mindi for supporting me. After Emet's Bar Mitzvah, I sent him a handwritten letter:

22 November 2009

Dear Dad,

I'm sure that this is a very hard time for you, as the dynamics between you and me have changed dramatically in the past several months from what they had been in the last 40 years. I also understand that Marci has stopped talking to you since Rosh Hashanah.

As I'm coming to terms with the terrible memories of childhood sexual abuse by you and the damage it did to me over my life, I want you to know that I have reached a place of relative compassion and forgiveness—at least most of the time. I am also working hard so this doesn't happen to other children. I don't think what happened to you or me as a child should ever happen to other children.

Honestly, I do have periods of intense rage, mourning, and despair. But I decided not to get trapped in those places. Having been trapped for decades of my life in an extensive defense mechanism within myself for so long, I can certainly understand how trapped you may be feeling.

As I've worked to release myself, I've come to experience freedom where I don't hate myself so intensely, and with that, I've been able to become a happier person and a healthier person. I am also a better son, brother, husband, father, and co-worker. It has been very hard work to get to this place, and it is hard work to sustain this freedom, but it has also been worth it.

I wanted to let you know that you were missed at Emet's Bar Mitzvah. Many people asked how you were. Our response was that you were sick with *something chronic and you couldn't make it. This is all that your grandchildren know about your past.*

At the Friday night Kabbalat Shabbat service, I brought the Kiddush cup you had given to Emet at his bris on his eighth day of life. I shined it with silver polish and I shared with the 40 or so people attending that we were using the cup that Emet's Pop-Pop had given to him. Emet sipped some wine as he said the blessing from that cup. Also, during the healing song, I sent prayers of healing to you.

During the Torah service, you were called up to Torah for an Aliyah in absentia. You were called as Moshe Ben Freda v' Benyamin. I brought you into my heart as I stood next to my son Emet during this part of the service, and I prayed again for your healing.

This has been a hard time for me, as I wanted so much to share in Emet's Bar Mitzvah with you. I really can't understand how you've chosen to say "good-bye, good-bye, good-bye" to me, to Mindi, and to our children—your grandchildren.

Dad, you are 73 years old. You are not getting any younger, and I hope that you won't spend the final years or decades of your life in an isolated and separate place from your children and grandchildren. This is a decision only you can make.

I will only interact with you if you accept that I am approaching you from a place of my truth, my honesty, and an authentic desire to rebuild our family and our new, healthier way, and if you will approach me in the same way.

Thanks for considering my perspectives.

Paul

It crushed me not to have a relationship with Dad. He was getting old and his health was poor. I could not feel whole and healed as long as there was this fracture between us. The past was the past and I was choosing not to live in it any more. I was taking a stand for peace, reconciliation, and healing. If only my father could too.

My relationship with Mindi deepened and transformed during this time. Through a series of human growth workshops that we attended during 2009, we reached new levels of healing and commitment. We sat together on a park bench, we looked into each other's eyes, and we agreed to stay together in our sacred union, forever, no matter what! There would be no more time or energy wasted on internal stories or fights between us about the possibility of getting a divorce. We were going to be together forever! My soul soared with joy that we had reached this moment.

PART FIVE
Liberation

*I am only one; but still I am one. I cannot do everything; but
still I can do something; and because I cannot do everything,
I will not refuse to do the something that I can do.*

—Edward Everett Hale (American author,
historian, and clergyman, 1822–1909)

CHAPTER 56

Speak Truth

THE revelations that I was a survivor of incest were life-altering. I committed myself to the hard work it would take to accept my new understanding of my past, and emerge as healthier, thriving man. I was learning to shift and gain control over the deeply embedded negative mind patterns that had tortured me for most of my life. An incest survivor, I finally understood why I was so drawn to waging justice and to fighting for those marginalized because of race, gender, sexuality, economic status, and other human differences. I still had more work to do, but I was trying my best to be more honest with myself and live more authentically.

Instead of shaming myself, I committed to being comfortable with my true self and to recognizing my full power and self-love. Maybe this sounds a little metaphysical for a practical-minded activist, but I was rebooting my internal operating systems. I was intent on transforming every aspect of myself from self-hatred to self-love. I was more and more able to choose to live with a sense of joyful and humble self-liberation.

When looking in the mirror, instead of saying to myself, *You're fat and ugly,* I would say, *You look pretty good for someone your age!* I had tastes of inner happiness and I was striving to live without shame.

My work was going well. With the $1 billion promised from President Obama, my activist friends and I were dizzy with optimism. The Campaign to End Pediatric HIV/AIDS (CEPA) was up and running in six African countries. A vibrant network of African activists was partnering with me and my team to accelerate programs for children with AIDS, so that they would receive lifesaving medicines as quickly as possible. These kids had been left behind for too long, and now we were aggressively tackling this major gap. AIDS was going to be history.

But in May 2009, we received crushing news from the White House. President Obama was launching a global health initiative that proposed cutting funding for AIDS. His team had decided that universal health care around the world was the greater priority than the focused effort to end AIDS. But my team wasn't going to let him get away with it. It was time to join forces with our African activist friends again.

Soon after the news hit, I was on my way to Nairobi to meet up with James Kamau. James, with his brightly colored *dashiki* shirts and salt and pepper hair, had led Kenya's advocacy for access to lifesaving AIDS medicines for years. He was HIV positive, politically astute, and fearless. James and I had been friends and colleagues for many years and he grabbed my hands enthusiastically, grinning from ear to ear when I arrived. Philip Thigo, a 20-something technology whiz who was pioneering the use of Kenya's national SMS texting system to allow people to track government spending and stop corruption by local political leaders, joined us. The three of us sat together for a couple of hours, figuring out a strategic response to Obama's misstep.

James mobilized a press conference led by a pan-African cohort of activists in a central Nairobi hotel. Local and international media showed up: the *New York Times*, AFP, the Voice of America, and many others. We demanded that Obama not cut AIDS funding to Africa.

It was a brazen rebuke to a popular new president, and I knew our press conference and the subsequent media attention surrounding our demands embarrassed the administration, which was paradoxically trying to downplay Obama's Kenyan roots. As I was boarding the airplane to fly from Nairobi back to Washington, I got a text from a senior administration official. "You need to stand down. Now is not the time for more AIDS funding" was the gist of the message. "Never!" I texted back, then turned off my Blackberry and shoved it in my pocket.

My refusal was not well received in Washington. Returning to the United States, I quickly found out that my team at the Global AIDS Alliance was blackballed by White House officials. We were no longer invited to meetings, my phone calls and emails were ignored.

As frustrating as this was, it was also a challenge. When doors are slammed in my face, I don't turn tail. I fight back. So my team, our allies, and I mobilized all of our resources to respond. *The New York Times* published an impassioned, personal, and cutting op-ed from Archbishop Tutu: "Having met President Obama, I'm confident that he's a man of conscience who shares my commitment to bringing hope and care to the world's poor. But I am saddened by his decision to spend less than he promised to treat AIDS patients in Africa." Tutu then reminded the president that the Global Fund has become "the premier model" for results-driven international aid, since financing for projects is supplied in increments only when programs show tangible progress. That a message like this was coming from a moral leader of Tutu's stature reportedly upset President Obama. A high-level administrator told me in a whispered side conversation that Obama had been disturbed. But it didn't matter. The Obama administration still made cuts to AIDS relief, which forced the Emergency Plan launched by President Bush to stop enrolling new patients who urgently needed lifesaving treatment. It was awful. The day I got the news I felt numb and betrayed. I felt like banging my head against a wall. My hopes and dreams for President Obama's steady leadership on ending AIDS were gone. He had other priorities. I understood that a president has tremendous responsibilities, but this was outrageous—we were only asking that President Obama keep his word.

As frustrated and disappointed as my team felt about Obama, America's betrayal brought powerful alliances into my life. Mrs. Graça Machel, Nelson Mandela's wife and a powerful justice activist in her own right, became a collaborator after we met and she agreed to serve as the chair of CEPA.

At a meeting held in September 2009, Mrs. Machel chaired a two-day strategy meeting with African pediatric AIDS experts and my Global AIDS Alliance team. Mandela's health was failing, and I could see the toll his decline was having on her. Nevertheless, softly and gracefully she told the group, "We must stand together for our children, for our African children." As she spoke, all I could think was that I was listening to the wisdom of a modern African heroine for justice. I was humbled and blessed to be in her presence.

It was a strange time for me. Ostracized by the staff of our new African-American president in Washington, I was collaborating more closely than ever with my fellow African civil society activists and with African moral icons like Arch and Mrs. Machel. We would work around the president's shortsightedness. AIDS wasn't going away. And neither were we.

CHAPTER 57

Justice Experiments

Our AIDS advocacy work continued into 2010. I was committed to it, but I was also restless. I felt driven to take on new and bigger justice issues. I felt a moral obligation to be part of applying the highly effective strategies and tactics that the AIDS movement was using to address other challenges, here in the U.S. and around the world. So I began working intensively on a new plan to launch a global peace action network. During a long hike on the Billy Goat Trail along the C&O Canal near the Potomac River, I decided to extend my commitment beyond global health to embrace the ultimate goal of realizing global peace in our time. I didn't know exactly what role to play in this agenda, but I was compelled to contribute.

Initially, I convened a few small brainstorming sessions in my office at the Global AIDS Alliance with thought leaders on global justice. These were noisy, impassioned, messy problem-solving meetings where every idea was welcome and considered. Carol Bergman, my deputy; Daniella Ballou-Aares, a young and brilliant strategist from Dalberg Global

Development Advisors; and Harvard University's effervescent Professor Sanjeev Khagram attended. Sanjeev was a passionate and brilliant advocate for justice. He came to the United States as a child refugee, fleeing Idi Amin, the wretched Uganda dictator who expelled over 60,000 people of South Asian descent, including Sanjeev's family. Carol asked tough questions about what could practically be done, Sanjeev was the most connected with global advocacy networks, and imagined them working together more strategically, Daniella paced and furiously drew diagrams on the white board. The meetings of this "peace-action" brain trust held in my office were the highlights of my week.

The global peace action network I envisioned started coming together, and I became more confidant in convening larger design meetings with a larger circle of like-minded leaders to develop an actual strategy for accelerating advocacy for justice and peace—globally! Our discussions were extraordinary, free-flowing and mind-blowing as we imagined catalyzing efforts to create a more just world. As each person spoke, the others would riff and expand one strategic idea to the next, over and over in a swirl of possibility. We synthesized the tsunami of ideas that were waving through the room. I experienced our minds melding, as concrete transformational plans of action for waging peace and justice emerged.

One Thursday afternoon in September 2010, I was closing up the office. It had been a long day, the weather was turning cold, the leaves were turning colorful and starting to fall, and I was trying to calculate if I could pick up Chinese food for dinner on my drive home. The phone rang just as I was pulling the door shut. I debated answering it. "Zeitz here." On the other end of the line was Professor Jim Sherry, from the Department of Global Health at George Washington University (GWU).

He told me I had been chosen to receive a Global Health and Development Achievement Award. I was utterly surprised.

The ceremony was held on December 10, 2010, the Day of Human Rights, in a party room on the top floor of Tonic at Quigley's pub near the GWU campus. I was deeply touched by this award because I had been selected by the public health students. I was looking around a room packed with over a hundred people, including fresh-faced students, like I had once been. Also attending were my mom, Mindi, and Carol from GAA.

With a sense of confidence, humility, and pride, I decided to say what was really on my mind! I was eager to share my true, unfiltered vision for peace and global justice. I walked to the podium. My voice didn't waver:

> Speak truth, be bold, and serve justice for all. I have dedicated my life to these principles.
>
> I am gravely alarmed at the utter collapse of the American dream for the vast majority of Americans. We have become cynical, apathetic, rejectionist, and resigned....
>
> Our political system is broken and our leaders— dependent on corporate largesse—can no longer effectively serve the interests of the American people. The time for resignation and hopelessness is over.
>
> The status quo of political inaction and backroom deals must end today and every day going forward. Together we can stand for justice. Together we can insist on integrity in our political leaders. Together we can create a new patriotic movement to transform our

country and once again make it "by the people, for the people," rooted in the realization of rights for all.

Together we can wage justice for America. We can reclaim our pride, our hope and re-emerge as a beacon for the world.

I proposed to launch a Justice Movement by holding a March for Justice on Martin Luther King Jr. Day, 40 days later, on January 20, 2011, nearly 48 years after Martin Luther King's "I Have a Dream" speech. The crowd happily applauded and many people thanked me for my inspiring words.

The next weeks were a frenzy of activity as I mobilized support for the March for Justice. My team at the Global AIDS Alliance was not sure why they were working on this global peace initiative instead of advocacy for ending AIDS and protecting children in Africa, and I felt the first waves of resistance. I knew my staff was grumbling to each other. And then they brought their complaints to me directly. Honestly, I was not the best listener, as I was totally focused and driven to make the March for Justice succeed. I didn't have time to assuage any nay-sayers.

The permitting came through: We had a permit from the U.S. Park Police to march and to hold a post-march rally on the very spot Dr. King delivered his stirring "I Have a Dream" speech. I felt like a miracle occurred, and that the ease with which the March for Justice was coming together meant I was on a just and righteous path. I spent 16 hours a day reaching out to justice activists working on labor rights, economic opportunity and jobs, and climate justice in the U.S. I was working to find allies and was rallying disparate groups to join forces for jobs and justice.

The morning of the January 20 was sunny and bitterly cold. Though I had been organizing a public event, I started the day with a dear friend from the sacred Hebrew chanting community, Susan Windle. I needed some time with a spirit buddy to be in the present moment, think about where I had come from, and reflect on where I was going. We went that morning to Arlington Cemetery and visited the gravesites of Robert F. Kennedy and John F. Kennedy. As I stood there, I felt a solemn moment of possibility. I was honoring their legacy by keeping the torch for justice alive in our time. I was also healing my own wounds of injustice by rejecting my father's abuse and connecting to the righteous values that my mom had inspired me to develop since I was a young kid.

We then walked to the Martin Luther King, Jr. Memorial, where we joined the group of activists, including Mindi, my sons, my sister-in-law Nina, old friends, new friends from the U.S. domestic justice movement, my AIDS activist comrades, and even some of my reluctant co-workers at the Global AIDS Alliance. We all came together to march along the Tidal Basin to view the MLK memorial under construction, and then marched to the Lincoln Memorial.

The air was so cold it stung our throats. My buddy Matt Kavanaugh from the Health GAP coalition had frost on his beard. But there was much warmth, excitement, and momentum in our small band of about 40 patriots, walking together to keep warm and to ignite a torch for justice in our country.

During the march, I led the chanting:

What do we want? Justice!

When do we want it? Now!

What do we want? Justice!

302

When do we want it? Now! Now!

Mindi, only 5 feet, 2 inches in her warm boots, walked close by my side, her hand in mine. I was so proud to have her and the boys by my side: Yonah, a burgeoning 15 year old; Emet, who had just had his Bar Mitzvah, and, at 13, was starting to shoot up; and 9-year-old Uriel, running in circles around us and proud to hold a sign that read "Jobs and Justice, Now-Now!" (but quick to complain it was too heavy and pass it to his older brother). Only Cletus and Lian, away at college and boarding school, weren't there.

The marchers and many others gathered on the steps of the Lincoln Memorial, near the spot where MLK spoke, for a small rally of about 50 people. David Newman's sweet song of "Love, Peace, and Freedom" welcomed us as we marched up the steps toward Lincoln. Regular Americans from all walks of life—a student, a doctor, and a musician—each gave a short speech. When it was my turn, I spoke with the confidence and optimism I was feeling that day:

> *I am inviting you to commit today to build a 21st century "Era of Justice," where liberty and justice for all becomes a way of life for all.*
>
> *Last week's tragic explosion of violence in Arizona shocked my soul and mobilized my sense that our country is ailing, when six everyday Americans, including a nine-year-old child, are needlessly killed, and more than a dozen others are seriously wounded, including Congresswoman Gabrielle Giffords. We send all of our prayers of healing and strength to all those affected and we pray for the full recovery of all those wounded.*

These events remind us that the American dream is extremely fragile and affirm my belief that we are at the cusp of an historic crossroads. As so many Americans are caught in a cycle of hopelessness and cynicism, our political process is now broken and government is failing to solve ever-worsening domestic and global challenges.

Just then I was interrupted by a large and very impatient Park Police officer. Our time was up, he insisted. The other speakers had gone on too long. The next rally had to be set up. The officer loomed over me, demanding I halt the rally. Now I had to decide whether to go into peaceful civil disobedience mode and get arrested, or end the rally and disperse.

My kids were there. My wife. As much as I didn't like getting shut down in the middle of my speech, standing up to this burly Park Police didn't feel like an option. Fear won out. I chose to comply. But I was immediately crushed and depressed beyond belief. I felt I embarrassed myself in front of my sons. I balled my hands into fists. Though we had to pack up the rally before it was finished, I decided then that my deep desire, my gnawing need, to share my vision for global justice would not be relegated to the shadows.

That same day, the Pulitzer prize–winning reporter Alex Raksin wrote an article about the event for the *Huffington Post*. He emphasized that we were demanding an end to America's economic disparity through comprehensive tax reform, significant jobs and housing bills, justice for workers, and fair treatment of seniors, veterans, and others whose resources are at risk, as well as a health initiative to ensure that life-saving treatments are available to the sick both at home and abroad:

The movement, Zeitz hopes, will be a coalition of people united not by their orientation to the left or right but by their conviction that America should be something more than a mere servant of amoral corporations—companies that even after receiving hundreds of billions of dollars in taxpayer bailouts now hoard $1.5 trillion in cash reserves.

As the crowd disbursed, my kids ran to the nearest vendor and bought cups of hot chocolate to warm their frozen fingers. I was so cold, I could literally feel the warm cocoa rolling down through my body. At home, it took me several more hours to warm up. As I thawed, my deep frustration at not completing my speech shifted into a sense of pride:

A march for justice had actually happened!

The people who thought it would never happen were proved wrong!

I felt confident that I could successfully birth a justice movement and simultaneously continue my AIDS advocacy responsibilities.

But a few weeks after the March for Justice, most of the Global AIDS Alliance team, some of the organizational funders, and the board of directors thought I had gone too far, too fast. Caught up in my own fervor for justice, I had ignored the signals of resistance and opposition. I was forced to resign. The goodbyes were awkward. Some of my staff were not entirely sorry to see me go.

Everything I had worked on over a decade was suddenly and unexpectedly gone. Mindi and the boys helped packed my things from my GAA office on a Saturday morning: I took my books, all my newspaper clippings from the prior decade, my published papers and reports, and one by one I removed the pictures from the walls of my office. A chaos of emotions flooded my heart.

What came next for me was a deep feeling of grief, and a very familiar sense of shame. I had already been grieving the collapse of the Campaign to End Pediatric HIV/AIDS and now I was also deeply grieving the loss of my leadership role of the Global AIDS Alliance. I was a walking contradiction: utterly determined to fight for economic and social justice for every American and every citizen of the world, and utterly defeated by this setback.

In the weeks that followed, I tried to meditate, do my chanting, and remind myself to breathe. I kept myself busy running the kids to school and soccer practice, taking long walks in Cabin John Park, and staying connected with close colleagues. I probably looked fine from the outside, but the truth was that my mind was caught in a cycle of regret and shame for months. I couldn't stop subjecting myself to relentless criticism and self-loathing:

> I had disappointed my activist colleagues in Africa and all of the people who may have benefitted from our work.

> I had worked so hard for so long, and now it was gone.

> I had followed my own heart and I had been rejected by people I loved and respected.

I wondered:

> Had I gone too far?

Would I always fail when I followed my heart?

What could I learn from this failure?

Mindi was distraught that I had given up my career with the Global AIDS Alliance, and she wasn't convinced that I could translate my passion for global justice into a paying job. Within a couple of months, my self-confidence returned after I landed some interesting consulting gigs, and I reconnected with my closest allies from the AIDS movement as we plotted the next phases of our advocacy. Ultimately, I decided that I had to honor my heart in any way that I could, even if I wasn't certain that my experiments for justice would succeed.

Chapter 58

Occupy Justice

Out of the blue, on September 17, 2011, a thousand protesters gathered in downtown Manhattan, walking up and down Wall Street. Nearly 200 people camped overnight in Zuccotti Park, two blocks north of Wall Street, in what became known as Occupy Wall Street. By October 9, Occupy protests had taken place or were ongoing in over 951 cities across 82 countries, including over 600 communities in the United States.

I was totally enthralled by the potential of this spontaneous movement. The global movement for justice was being born! The Occupy movement stood for advancing social and economic justice and new forms of democracy. I started hanging out at the Occupy encampments in D.C., reconnecting with some of the justice activists that I had met during the planning for the March for Justice.

After many discussions in the encampments and on conference calls with activists across the country, I joined a small group of activists who felt that it was perfect timing to launch a new political party, the Justice Party USA. I was introduced to Rocky Anderson, former mayor of Salt Lake City, who emerged as the political leader of the Justice Party. Anderson is tall, with a full head of gray hair, very smart and confidant. Hailing from the fiercely independent state of Utah, he felt both political parties were corrupt, and that President Obama was a sellout. After leaving the mayor's office, Anderson formed the nonprofit High Road for Human Rights to address economic fairness, civil rights, and environmental issues. Rocky Anderson and I were justice soulmates. We wanted to create a revolution in the political party system, we wanted to win elections, and we wanted to give our fellow citizens a choice to go beyond the entrenched Democratic and Republican duopoly and create a more just America and a peaceful world.

My passion for the nascent Justice Party USA was fueled by my renewed sense of self-worth. I knew now what I needed to do: align my inner compass with my outer work in the world. I published a detailed prospectus calling for the formation of the Justice Party USA—a political manifesto. Mindi and I invested thousands of dollars to launch the Justice Party National Committee, which I registered with the Federal Election Commission. I was to serve as the interim chair.

The Justice Party platform focused on four objectives: Economic and jobs justice to close the economic gaps that divide Americans; electoral justice by advancing reforms that promote direct democracy; U.S. and global health justice, including heath care reform and support for full funding of the Global Fund; and environmental justice, ensuring that climate change is a priority and economic development and food production are enabled in a sustainable manner. We were a revolutionary party. We were "Justicrats"!

With high hopes, we rushed to launch the party at an event at the historic Daughters of the American Revolution headquarters in D.C. in early December, to coincide with the Day of Human Rights. We rented 200 chairs and arranged a podium surrounded by American flags.

Sadly, only about 25 people showed up, including my ever-faithful family: Mom, Mindi, and the boys. Unfortunately, the event was very poorly planned and poorly attended, and the kick-off of the new Justice Party USA was a dud. I had messed up by pushing for a fast kick-off event, and we all had taken on more that we could handle. We held a meeting with the organizing group immediately afterwards, and Anderson went ballistic. I left as quickly as I could, as I didn't want to have a public fight with anyone, and I felt we were all responsible for this setback.

Over the next several days, I continued to work to support the effort by catalyzing state committees of the Justice Party. Like-minded activists in California, Texas, Illinois, Utah, West Virginia, and other states were mobilizing. But Anderson and others were still extremely angry about the failure of the launch event. Rocky and I met for lunch in a quiet restaurant near Dupont Circle, and he told me that he wanted me to serve as the policy director for the newly forming Justice Party, rather than the interim chair. I was outraged, as I felt like I was the fall guy for what I saw as a collective failure. There seemed no way around it. I left the party I had co-founded after months of intensive work.

I was truly sad that I was not able to stay engaged with this effort, as I believed that a justice movement in the U.S. was urgently needed to protect the American dream so that it would be alive for my kids and future generations. While I felt that I had somehow failed, I didn't feel any shame. My strong sense of self surprised and elated me. Something had changed in my internal operating system. For the first time in my adult life, I was no longer operating from an anger-driven, self-hatred internal system, but rather was living and making choices based on my own sense of integrity from a place of self-love. I took a mental inventory: I was grateful for taking risks, being bold, challenging the status quo; I was at peace with my own mistakes; I was looking forward to the next opportunities; and, despite all the turmoil, Mindi and I were hanging in this together.

Several months later I re-engaged with the Justice Party when the founder of the Texas branch asked me to represent him before the Federal Election Commission as he was fighting to ensure that Rocky Anderson, presidential candidate of the Justice Party, would be listed on the 2012 Presidential election ballot. I had no legal training nor expertise on election law, but I prepared and confidently testified in defense of the Texas Justice Party's claim for ballot access. As I sat before the election commissioners in a courtroom-like hearing room, I was laughing hysterically on the inside. I could never have imagined myself officially fighting for electoral justice for the people of Texas. I loved that I was challenging myself and crossing into this new zone of advocacy.

I didn't have to be just the AIDS doctor, the Africa expert, or the public health policy wonk. I was able to prove to myself that from a place of integrity I could take on a wide range of justice issues in America and around the world. I was also realizing that the medley of justice issues that I was fighting for were all inter-related and inseparable. What I wanted was a holistic movement for social, economic, and environment justice—including our planetary health—that was transformational and revolutionary. That's what I had to create.

CHAPTER 59

Purification

I_N late 2011, Jerry's health was declining rapidly. My father-in-law was battling leukemia that had been triggered by the anti-rejection medication he had been taking since his heart transplant 11 years earlier. From September to early November, Jerry was in and out of the hospital nearly every week, until finally he said he had enough.

The entire family gathered at his home. Sandi was holding his right hand. Mindi his left. I crouched by his feet, resting my head on the foot of the bed. Jerry took his final breath. Sandi, Mindi, and everyone present wailed with grief.

A few hours after Jerry died, Sandi gently asked me if I would be willing to serve as the family representative at the *Tahara*—the ritual Jewish purification ceremony that involves washing the body and dressing it in its white shroud. The same kind of shroud Sandi and Jerry had procured for me all those years ago.

The night before the burial, four of us descended into the basement of the funeral parlor. Jerry's body lay under a white sheet in a dark windowless room. We poured water over his body in silence. I silently chanted blessings of healing for his soul. I remembered how Jerry looked at Mindi when we got married, his heart bursting with love for his daughter. I thought of how he sat telling jokes with my kids. How he laughed with three-year-old Lian. "What did the 0 say to the 8?" Jerry boomed. Lian's eyes went wide with curiosity. "Nice belt!"

As the waters flowed over his body, I imagined the full arc of his life from birth to death. I thought of how after his heart transplant, Jerry had made peace with death, living with an appreciation for each extra day of life. Washing the body of the man I had loved and who had loved me for so long, I felt a profound sense of gratitude. Jerry had been a generous and righteous father figure to me for most of my adult life.

Over the three years since my own father had stopped speaking to me, my murderous rage over my early childhood sexual abuse had cooled to regular rage. But even this residual anger was hurting me and my family. I knew I had to get rid of it. My persistent inner anger was a toxic fuel that was still poisoning me.

In October of 2012, I decided to drive 12 hours to Ohio by myself to attend a "Weekend of Recovery" hosted by an organization called Male Survivor. In the car, I tried to chant, but couldn't. I tried to calm my mind, but couldn't. I tried to crowd out the thoughts and self-doubt, but every time I cleared my mind, they returned. Finally, I just let myself brood and doubt. *Was it true?* Even after three years, I still struggled with this question. I didn't want it to be true.

Maybe I had never been abused?

Maybe I had made all of it up?

*Why as a young boy did I playfully sing a song,
"Incest is best! Incest is best!"*

That was a weird song!

Where did I learn that song?

Why did I sing it?

About halfway to Ohio, I made the choice to shut down these doubts forever. My father had admitted to me that he had been physically and sexually abused as a child. The images and memories I had were real. There was no reason on earth I would ever have invented what had happened to me. There was no reason on earth I even could have made it up. It was too gross. It was too disturbing.

During the weekend, within a small group of other male survivors of childhood sexual abuse, we were invited to share our stories. I read my explicit and detailed memories from my journal out loud. It was the only time, before or since, that anyone saw or heard what I had written. I had never even shared the memories with Mindi. As I read from my journal, I felt strangely self-possessed, an awkward sense of pride. Saying my story out loud, no matter how sickening and disgusting it sounded, was a key step in removing my shroud of shame. I became friends with one of the guys, a successful corporate leader, a tall middle-aged man my age from the Midwest who also survived paternal incest. We shared the trials and tribulations of our lives and our struggles to find happiness. Talking to him made me feel less alone in the world.

I learned from my fellow survivors that weekend that incest and rape is personal violence against one's bodily integrity. From an early age, I instinctively knew that my body belonged to me and to no one else. When my body was violated, it shattered my trust in my dad, but also in everything. My trust in society, in justice, and in my relationship with the world around me was destroyed. Since my body was wired to feel pleasure, the incest caused me terrible pain but also unwanted and confusing pleasure. Since the abuse was perpetrated by someone I loved and relied on for survival—my father—it was even more devastating. Because I had experienced male-to-male rapes, I had bouts of confusion about my sexual preferences as I became an adult.

But I was not alone. All the other male survivors were going through similar internal chaos.

I learned that some of those behind the Weekends of Recovery had come from the AIDS movement. They had been doing community organizing for people living with HIV/AIDS before treatment became widely available, and they had developed several models for helping people cope with the trauma of living with a likely terminal illness with a difficult end. The instructors of the program learned that some of their clients had been sexually assaulted as children, so once the AIDS hospice program was no longer needed, once lifesaving AIDS medicines were available, the program pivoted to a focus on male survivors of childhood sexual trauma.

This made me question my innate passion to work on political advocacy on HIV/AIDS. I wondered, *Why had I picked a cause that was in so many ways about sexuality?* At first, I was all about child survival. But in the dying fields of Zambia, I was constantly meeting young adults whose lives would be cut short because of the elemental human act of procreation, bonding, and pleasure. In the world of HIV/AIDS, you get deep into the underbelly of life. You get to talk about sex. But you also get to talk about sexual rights and sexual identity and to wage justice for the right to good health and safe sex. One of the fundamentals of the AIDS movement is that no matter what your sexual practices, it is your right to be treated equally and with dignity, sexual dignity. That weekend helped me understand that my commitment to ending AIDS may also have been my unconscious fight to reclaim my own dignity, which had been stolen from me decades before.

I came home from the survivor weekend a much more grounded man. Not long afterwards, Dad's health began declining. He kept falling and was in and out of the hospital. And he started to return my phone calls. I was still struggling with bouts of anger, but I wanted to re-connect with him. I wanted him to spend time with his grandchildren, and felt it was important that we forgive each other, in whatever way that was possible, before he passed away.

CHAPTER 60

Endless Possibilities

By the end of 2012, my father and I were talking for just a minute at a time, about nothing. Months would go by before we talked again. Then we started talking every couple of weeks. He was in and out of the hospital. He took a bad fall at home, he was unstable walking and was now chair-bound and seemed depressed. One day I stopped by to visit him. He had been home alone all day and he sat stone-faced and fixated on a dreary black and white TV documentary about World War II. He barely looked at me when I walked in. My volatile, lively, violent father was reduced to a wizened old man, sitting all alone, stuck in the past. This made me feel very sad.

I brought him dinner from a local deli: brisket, green beans, and kasha and bowtie pasta. As we sat quietly eating together, he looked up at me. In a hushed voice he blurted out that his mother had tried to abort her pregnancy multiple times with a hanger because she hated her husband so much, and she didn't want to bear any more of his children. "They never stopped fighting," he whispered. "They screamed at each other all the time. Neither of them wanted me. So much screaming. He verbally tortured her for risking my life."

Had I heard him correctly?

He was never supposed to be born?

I sat silently trying to digest this horrid story, one I had never heard before. I realized that, 77 years old and full of regrets, Dad was trying to tell me that he came from a very dysfunctional family. He had suffered so much abuse and trauma as a child, and he had passed that trauma on to me.

Several months later, Dad needed to be hospitalized. He was now in hospice care after a bout of sepsis nearly destroyed his kidneys. I took my family to visit him. Our sons were young men now, ranging in age from 12 to 26. Mindi came too. We all crowded into his hospital room being our noisy selves. Dad told us how beautiful it was to see all of us and how much he appreciated us being together. He squeezed Emet by the hand and told him he loved him. He hugged all the boys for the last time.

Dad was dying. Over the course of the next few days, I drove back and forth from the hospital to the seaside town of Brigantine, New Jersey, where we rented a house with large porches to catch the ocean breezes. I took long walks on the beach, sorting out my swirling and paradoxical emotions, a mixture of grief and loss juxtaposed with growing sense of inner freedom. Mindi and our sons were around to provide support. The seven of us would lie together in a king-sized bed, something we had done throughout the years we had all lived under one roof, we hugged, laughed, and shared our feelings. We passed a talking stick around a circle, giving everyone an equal chance to speak, be heard, and be listened to. We went around the circle three or four times, until everyone had said their piece: sharing their feelings about my dad's dying process and updates on their plans for the months ahead.

I felt so deeply loved and supported by the nuclear family that Mindi and I had created. My revelation in 2009 about my history of incest with my dad had hit us all—along with my mom, my sister, and the rest of the family—like a tsunami. Four years earlier our lives were flooded with shock, shame, and, fury. I was feeling vulnerable on the cusp of my father's death. Mindi and my sons seemed to know instinctively that I needed deep love from each of them to sustain my inner balance.

A few days later Dad took his last breath. I was back in Potomac when I got the call. Instead of facing my kids with the news, I ran into the woods behind my home and I wailed in grief, feeling safe among the tall trees. Two days later, on a warm August morning, we gathered together for the graveside funeral—Mindi's family, my family, my childhood friends, and many other friends and relatives. As we approached Dad's burial spot, Mindi and I were shocked to see that the gravesite was only two rows behind the grave of her father, Jerry. Mindi and I looked at each other deeply and we shared a moment of awe that our families were so intertwined in life, and now also in death.

As the rabbi chanted the burial prayers, my sister stood by my side holding my hand firmly. Others spoke in honor of Dad, as did I. As part of my eulogy, I quoted Sri Swami Satchidananda:

Death can come at any minute, in any way.

We do not know what is in store tomorrow, or whether there is a tomorrow, or even a tonight!

But still, we have the golden present.

Now we are alive and kicking.

What should we do now?

Love all, serve all.

As we buried Dad that day, I felt a surprising wellspring of inner peace. When it was my turn to throw dirt onto his casket, I purposefully imagined the burial of incest, the cancer that had infected our family. The evil parts of my family and the anger within me were finally dead and gone. I forgave Dad and I forgave myself too for how hard I had been on myself. I relieved myself of any sense of shame, as I was not to blame. Finally, I was able breathe easier, without any buried feelings of anger or hate.

After his death, I thought about my dad a lot: while I was brushing my teeth in the morning, stuck in traffic on the Beltway, even, sometimes, in long meetings at work. When I looked into the mirror, I laughed at how much I was looking more and more like him. I continued to deepen my inner forgiveness of his crimes against me.

During these daydreams, I imagined how hard it had been for him to be an unwanted, unloved little boy. He had never asked to be born into abuse and chaos—as I knew so well. It is not easy for anyone. I reflected on my own life and those of others, and I imagined others forgiving me for all of my mistakes. I imagined that more and more people could live with a deep commitment to forgiveness towards others and themselves. I imagined that each of us could deepen our daily experience, our sense of our own inner spirit, driven by possibility and hope. I imagined that all people, everywhere, could join forces, each waging justice in their own unique way, co-creating peace.

Epilogue

Serve Justice for All

AT the end of 2013, the year my father died, my family gathered for a camping expedition in Tofino, British Colombia. Lian was attending Quest University in nearby Squamish, British Colombia. We spent the days hiking lush trails, scrambling up steep hills that were covered with slick moss, and hearing the seagulls calling to each other overhead. As the family sat for dinner in a local fish restaurant after a long day in the woods, we each discussed our plans for our life going forward.

Mindi was working to grow her medical practice and hiring another doctor. Cletus was studying at an institute to become a personal trainer. Lian was committing his life to global mental health. Yonah was just starting college at St. Mary's College of Maryland, interested in politics, economics, and criminal justice reform. Emet, a high school junior, was deep into his science and math studies and preparing to apply to college. Uriel, in middle school, was keen on becoming a professional soccer player. I spoke last:

I am committing my life to sustainable development, to the Sustainable Development Goals (SDGs) being developed by the United Nations. That's what I want to do now. Now is my big chance to put every ounce of my energy to support the design and implementation of the SDGs. This is something I can really get behind—a new global agenda aligned with my justice values.

Since we always talk politics at the dinner table, my kids and Mindi already knew that a global agreement was being negotiated by the United Nations and the international community that would be finalized in two years—in September 2015—when an assembly of heads of state from all governments of the world convened.

I know some of my sons were rolling their eyes—Dad and his never-ending social justice dreams. But I also felt my family lifting me up, knowing that I was constantly seeking to fulfill on my life's work. Mindi looked across the table deeply into my eyes and nodded her support.

In June 2014, I joined the Obama administration. When I first got back to government work, I felt like a vegan eating dinner at a pig farm. But I also knew I was in the right place: making changes from the inside out in an office with the Department of State by working on global AIDS and harnessing the data revolution for sustainable development. In my own small way, I was supporting President Obama's mobilization of the entire U.S. government, the UN, and countries from around the world to support the most ambitious global agreement ever developed. The Sustainable Development Goals and the Paris Agreement on climate change were unique in focusing on time-bound, measurable goals and targets to measure progress in the global action plan for achieving social, economic, and environmental justice. The SDGs plan included ending poverty, hunger, gender inequality, and combating violence against children—all of which resonated deeply in my soul.

The idea behind the SDGs and the Paris Agreement was to move humanity to the cusp of creating the ability to respond to each of the existential threats facing the survival of the human species. Leaders of every government on the planet would commit themselves to not just one, but *two* major agreements that will shape the future of our people and planet over the next decades—a convergence of justice and hope. I was going to do everything in my power to ensure that the timebound and measurable SDGs were going to have a beneficial impact in every city, town, and hamlet on Earth.

The big day finally came, the September 2015 UN General Assembly in New York City. After taking the train from Washington to New York, I made my way through the gauntlet of security and walked into the UN headquarters surrounded by a melting pot of humanity. The world was joining forces to end poverty, end hunger, achieve gender and racial equality, protect the planet and oceans, and ensure peace and security. On my way into the hall, I greeted Mrs. Machel, who was part of the South Africa delegation. As I sat in the heart of UN headquarters, I eagerly awaited the final vote by the world's leaders, assembled in the General Assembly Hall. My soul soared with hope. I was witnessing history. People all over the planet were joining forces to transform the world.

I had the agreement for the Sustainable Development Goals in hand and as I scanned the final text I was struck by Section 53. I kept reading it, over and over again, as if it were a sacred chant:

The future of humanity and of our planet lies in our hands. It lies also in the hands of today's younger generation who will pass the torch to future generations. We have mapped the road to sustainable development; it will be for all of us to ensure that the journey is successful and its gains irreversible.

I felt like my life had come full circle. The outer world was aligning with my inner pursuit of justice. The vote was taken. All 193 nations approved the sustainable development goals.

Victory!

The world is finally coming together!

How can we capture the magic of this moment, like lightening in a bottle?

I wept a few soft tears. I felt happy and excited, and I was overwhelmed with a sense of responsibility, because now I felt like I was also personally responsible for doing everything I could to achieve these ambitious goals. I wiped my eyes dry, closed them, and tried to calm my breath and reflect. My whole life raced through my mind from birth to this moment: all of the events, struggles, feelings, and dreams, my battles against the status quo, my despair over my own self-hatred, my commitment to save lives, my healing:

I only have a short time to live my life;

I take a stand for a world where children don't experience violence, sexual assault, or incest;

I commit to waging justice so that all people can have winning lives and can live in healthy balance with Earth;

I serve others by waging justice for the entire world, one step at a time.

For me, justice is the path to peace.

Reading Group Guide

*T*HIS *guide for* **Waging Justice** *includes an introduction, discussion questions, and ideas for enhancing your group's reading experience and discussion. The suggested questions are intended to deepen group members' understanding of the book, as well as inspire them to turn the book's lessons into their own experiments for waging justice within themselves, their relationships, their community, and our world. Taking action together, we can co-create a healthier, more peaceful, and more just world. It is Dr. Zeitz's hope, as a doctor, activist, and impassioned voice for justice, that this guide will spark curiosity, enrich conversations, increase enjoyment of the book, and motivate all readers to wage justice in ways that work for them.*

Introduction

AFTER a tumultuous childhood in Philadelphia, Paul Zeitz, the son of a Jewish hoagie maker, lands at Muhlenberg College in Allentown. Being away from his family "opens something up" in him. A lifelong introvert, Paul starts making friends, pledges a fraternity, and enjoys being popular. He becomes a student organizer, runs for student office, and sets his sights on becoming a doctor.

In medical school, life gets even more interesting. Paul is fascinated by the complex information he is learning. He travels to Moscow to champion an end to nuclear proliferation and gets a glimpse of life behind the Iron Curtain. Both abroad and at home, Paul feels a deep connection to his peers and mentors who all share an interest in healing.

On the outside he looks like a young man at the top of his game. But on the inside, Paul is struggling and unhappy. He finds intimacy difficult. As hard as he tries, he does not know how to open his heart to a partner. He is color-blind and this presents unexpected obstacles—he realizes he cannot become a surgeon because he cannot distinguish between the greenish-brown bile duct and blueish veins. Perhaps most irksome, he starts to question if modern medicine is the right way to make a lasting impact. When a patient in severe liver failure comes into the ER and is stabilized, the doctors don't seem to care that their patient will binge drink again as soon as he is released and end up right back in the hospital. *Where is the healing in that?* Paul wonders. *What about addressing the underlying causes of disease?*

Then Paul meets the woman of his dreams—a fellow doctor-in-training who also happens to be the daughter of his former therapist. He is instantly attracted to her. They share a similar commitment to changing the world, spend countless hours imagining a future together, and even take a heartwarming trip to Korea to escort four orphans home to their American families.

To truly fight for justice, as well as for the relationships that matter most to him, Paul must first come to terms with the dark secret that threatens everything he believes about his past. With bold and courageous truth-telling, Paul finds a path to forgiveness and healing for himself and his family. Driven by the quest to serve justice for all, Paul devises an ambitious program to achieve truly sustainable development. *Waging Justice* is an honest, raw, searing memoir that lays bare everything, from the killing fields in Zambia, to political battles in Washington, D.C., to the fragility of the human heart.

An Antidote to Hopelessness

F<small>ROM</small> devastating hurricanes to calls to impeach the president, we are being reminded daily that we are living in a time of huge social and geopolitical upheaval. The amount of injustice in the world right now feels overwhelming to many of us. How can we respond when we feel overwhelmed by the latest random act of gun violence, the increasing threat of war, the worsening of the climate crisis, the rise of white supremacy, and the distortion of truth? Many of us feel trapped in a state of confusion, and at times hopelessness.

Enter *Waging Justice*. Waging justice, as Paul Zeitz shows throughout this book, is a way of living life grounded in a personal commitment to speak truth, be bold, and take action. We can turn our fear into action that matters, for ourselves and for our world. We can act quickly and we can act now! We can each, in our own way, help make progress towards gender equality, racial justice, and a robust response to climate change. Each action or good deed by each of us creates a ripple of justice. Ripples turn into waves, and waves of justice can become a sweeping transformation that takes us closer to living in a global, peaceful, and sustainable world.

Topics and Questions
for Discussion

1. In the first paragraph of *Waging Justice,* Paul Zeitz writes that he was "eager to be part of this world," and was born about a month before his due date. Discuss how Paul is intense, active, and socially engaged, even as a small child. What factors, in your mind, lead him to being such a sensitive, determined, and sometimes angry young person?

2. When he is in first grade, Paul comes to a startling realization: The way the world looks to him is not the way it looks to other children and grown-ups around him. How does being red-green color-blind affect his life? Do you have a moment from your early childhood when you realized there was something different about you?

3. Why do you think Paul wants to become a doctor? As he studies and practices medicine, in what ways does modern medicine appeal to his determination to wage justice, and in what ways does he find that modern medicine falls short?

4. From the Holocaust to children orphaned in the HIV/AIDS epidemic, death is a subject that plays an important role in this story. How does the death of his friends and colleagues in Zambia affect Paul? What do you think of his death shroud meditation practice? How do your feelings and thoughts about your own death and the death of your loved ones affect your life and your activism?

5. As an activist fighting the spread of HIV/AIDS and in favor of children's lasting good health, Paul insists that funding to African countries include an anti-corruption strategy. However, his supervisors at UNAIDS (the Joint United Nations Programme on HIV/AIDS) insist that anti-corruption is not an approved United Nations policy. Infuriated, he quits his job. What do you think of his decision to stand by his principles even though his integrity cost him his livelihood? Have you ever found yourself in a similar situation?

6. Throughout the book, Paul explores how different spiritual and emotional practices help him through difficulties. Discuss what therapy, meditation, chanting, and the Male Survivor weekend teach him. The book implies that to do outer work—and help save the world—you must also do inner healing. Do you agree or disagree?

7. There are many pivotal scenes in this book—times when Paul feels he has made a breakthrough in his thinking or has learned something that he cannot unlearn—that makes him recommit to waging justice. Perhaps the most dramatic is when he comes to realize that he is the victim of early childhood sexual abuse. What scene do you think was the most pivotal? What discovery or

change point resonated most with you? What discovery or change point surprised you most? Has anyone in your family been affected by incest?

8. What do you think of Paul's father? Do you feel sorry for him, as a victim of a long history of incest and child abuse, or do you feel furious at him for perpetuating sexual violence by assaulting his son?

9. Paul has worked both outside government, trying to hold it more accountable, and inside the system, trying to change it from the inside out. Which kind of activism do you think is most effective? Is one better than the other?

10. Throughout the book we learn what waging justice means to Paul: helping the poor, providing life-saving medicine to those who need it most, keeping children safe from sexual violence and disease, providing homes for orphans, holding countries accountable for the preventable deaths of their citizens. Do you agree or disagree that these are the most urgent ways to wage justice? What does waging justice mean to you?

11. If you are already an activist, how will this book inspire you to move forward in your own activism? If you have never been socially engaged before, what kind of activism would you like to do in the future? Where do you think it is most important to wage justice in the world?

Enhance Your Reading Experience

1. Throughout *Waging Justice,* Paul Zeitz makes an argument in favor of social activism. One of the prime messages of the book is that *we are all* responsible for social injustice. Together as a group, choose a cause that matters to you; then spend an afternoon waging justice together. You could clean a public space, volunteer at a local food bank or library, sign up to be Big Brothers or Big Sisters, write letters on behalf of the causes that mean the most to you, or take another justice-driven action. After your time waging justice, discuss the experience as a group. What else can you do to address injustice? What do you think needs to happen to create a more just and peaceful world?

2. *Waging Justice* is a brave book. It exposes male on male violence and incest, which both continue to be taboo subjects. What is a secret you have never shared before? What are you most ashamed of? What secrets do you think are buried in your family? Ask everyone in the group to spend a half hour writing a story or memory they have never admitted to anyone. Members can then

choose to share their story with the group or keep it private.

3. We live in a time where activists are increasingly taking to social media (Twitter, Facebook, SnapChat, Instagram, even Pinterest and sometimes LinkedIn) to get their message of social justice across. Choose a hashtag inspired by the book (e.g., #SpeakTruth #BeBold, #WageJustice, #BreakTheSilence #ServeJustice4All) and have each member of the group write a post on social media in favor of waging justice. Take some time to comment on and share each other's posts. Then discuss the role social media plays for today's activists.

4. *Waging Justice* tackles many controversial topics, including what constitutes effective policy to combat HIV/AIDS, international adoption, combating poverty and disease, preventing child abuse, climate crisis, and even circumcision. Choose one or two of these topics and host a Lincoln-Douglas type debate. Let each speaker make an argument in favor of their side for a prescribed amount of time (two or three minutes is usually enough), then give each speaker a chance to rebut the other speaker's argument, after which each makes closing arguments. Make it even more interesting by requiring the debaters to choose the side they disagree with. After the formal debate, discuss the topic together as a group.

5. Form a *Waging Justice* "Circle" or "Community" with your family, community, faith organization, employers, or anywhere. Consider bringing together different groups or networks of people who don't normally connect. Consider bringing together people across the political spectrum and create a culture of transpartisan

community. Consider including people who are working on different aspects of justice, so that we can break down the walls and silos and build towards a unified justice movement. Join others who are waging justice in whatever ways you can, wherever you are.

Build the Movement

For more information and join me in waging justice:
www.drpaulzeitz.org
Twitter: @paulzeitz
Facebook: https://www.facebook.com/DrPaulZeitz/

Disclaimer

Author's Note: In writing this memoir, I have recreated events, locales and conversations from my own memory. In order to maintain their anonymity, I have in certain circumstances left out names and identifying characteristics of individuals or places. I may have also changed certain nonessential details, compressed timelines and left things out in service of the reading experience.

Acknowledgements

S PECIAL thanks to Martha Frase who first sat down for long writing weekends that shaped the contours of this memoir and gave me the confidence to keep going. To my editor extraordinaire, Jennifer Margulis, I am deeply grateful for your amazing effort to help me find my literary voice, for your stellar editorial skills, love, and spirited guidance. Gratitude to the reviewers who provided valuable insights, including Deri Reed, Andy Golden, Tim Rockwood, Jirair Ratesovian, Innocent Kateba, Susan Windle, Emet Zeitz, Mindi Cohen, Marci Valen, Cheryl Siskin, and Sandi Cohen. Finally, profound thanks to the whole team at Balboa Press, especially Marsha Minion, Pia Jameson, Heather Carter, Mary Oxley, and Kelly Martin, for partnering with me to produce this memoir. Thanks to Karen Phillips for your beautiful art design of the *Waging Justice* icon. Thanks for the guidance and support of Lisa Weinert and Jennifer Kurdyla for getting this book into your hands. Bryan Stevenson's memoir, *Just Mercy,* deeply touched me and inspired me to share my story.

In writing a memoir that covers 53 years of life, there are so many people that have been part of my journey, and I am incredibly thankful to *everyone* in my life for your love, support, and guidance. Special love to Jill Cott, all of my cousins, aunts and uncles, and my late grandparents Rose and Sam Landsburg and Freda Zeitz who all helped raise me. Gratitude to my lifelong friends Barry Schiller, Ken and Nina Kitnick, and Ellen Fine and their partners and children for bringing me great love, laughter, and support.

During college, thank you to my ZBT brothers for the fun, and to my dear friends David Weber, Marty Duvall, Brett Macaluso, Phil Halper, Mark Pressman, Celeste Moretti, Lisa Aulfinger Kessler, Jill Michelman Pappas, Diane Pedicini Duvall, Debbie Friedberg Nachlis, and so many others, for our shared journey.

My medical training years were enriched through my close camaraderie with Laura Robin, Josh Rabinowitz, Kathy Campanella Lambert, Donna Ruzicka Farrell, Betsy Fitzgerald Voye, Thomas Biggs, J. Preston Reynolds, and professors Zenia Chernyk, Ken Veit, Joe Dieterle, and the late Dan Wisely, J. Peter Tilley, and Milton and Lillian Terris.

I am deeply grateful for the support of my professors during my public health training years, including the late D.A. Henderson, Carl Taylor, Ciro de Quadros, and Richard Morrow; professors Robert Black, Carl Kendall, Gilbert Burnham, and Stella Goings; my friends and colleagues Nosa Orobaton, Virginia Ward, Howard Strickler, Cynthia Whitman, Mary Yarborough, Deborah Helizer, Brazey de Zalduondo, and Paul Seaton. Grateful thanks to all for enriching my John Hopkins learning experience.

Over the decades of my professional career, I am grateful for the opportunities to work closely with inspiring colleagues from around the world. My day-to-day work was inspired by the late Michael Taylor Riggs, Jo Cox, and Jonathon Stern and by my friends and colleagues Al Bartlett, Murray Trostle,

Ron Waldman, Paul Hartenberger, Ann Pettifor, Brad Lucas, Susan Gilbert, Lisa Baldwin, Dieter Fischer, Hope Sukin, Mary Harvey, Peter Henriot, Katele Kalumba, Nkandu Luo, Ben Chirwa, Rosemary Kumwenda Phiri, Elizabeth and Yiannis Serlimitsos, Joel Segal, Chatinkha Nkhoma, Pauline Muchina, Rev. Mpho Tutu, Charles Stephenson, David Bryden, David Gartner, Joanne Carter, Heather Nolan, Susan Cohen, Carol Bergman, Heather Boonstra, Jodi Jacobson, Eric Friedman, Leonard Rubenstein, Mel Foote, Christos Tsentas, Jennifer Delaney, Leila Nimatallah, Leigh Blake, Jamie Drummond, Lisa Schechtman, Deborah Bickel, Masauso Nzima, Sam Worthington, Rolake Odetoyinbo, Peter McDermott, Theo Sowa, Michel Sidibé, Bience Gawanas, Adam Taylor, Naina Dhingra, Kim Nichols, Amanda Lugg, Paul Farmer, Jim Kim, Ngozi Okonjo-Iweala, Charles King, Irũngũ Houghton, Andrew Stern, Ruth Messinger, James Kamau, Peter Van Roojen, Gorik Ooms, Paul Davis, Matt Kavanaugh, Chris Collins, Emily Gibbons, Neil Boothby, Chewe Luo, Lorrie McHugh, Christine Lubinski, Tom Hart, Mark Dybul, Christoph Benn, Eric Goosby, Stephen Lewis, Peter Piot, Sandra Thurman, Michael Iskowitz, Gillian Huebner, Deborah Birx, Daniela Ligero, Asia Russell, James Kamau, David Chipanta, Sharonann Lynch, and so many others.

I am indebted to the support I've received during my adult spiritual journey from my teachers Shefa Gold and my Kol Zimra family, Marcia Prager, Rachel Hersh Epstein, Fred Scherlinder Dobb, Arthur Waskow, Phyllis Berman, David Cooper, Shoshana Cooper, Sara Schley, Suresh Schlanger, Laura Lippman, Prahaladan Mandelkorn, Betsy Jameson, Swami Vidyananda, and the late Rabbi Zalman Schacter-Shalomi. My personal healing journey was immensely supported by

Rachmiel O'Regan, Donna Mousley, Gloria Haws, Bill Picon, Howard Fradkin, and my Weekend of Recovery brothers.

I'm grateful for my global colleagues who share my passion for sustainable development, including Amina Mohammed, Joe Colombano, Daniella Ballou-Aares, Sanjeev Khagram, Philip Thigo, Alice Gugelev, Marina Kaneti, Claire Melamed, David McNair, Bruce Preville, Michele Ehlers, Aditya Agarwal, Larry Sperling, Paige Munger, Jenny Ottenhoff, Christalyn Steers-McCrum, Jeanne Holm, Kat Townsend, Cindy Huang, Agnieszka Rawa, Kemy Monahan, and so many others around the world.

I deeply acknowledge my gratitude to Mom and my sister Marci and her family for providing me unconditional love and for riding this journey of life together, always. To my late Dad, Mark Zeitz, I am deeply grateful for the love we shared. To Mindi's mom, late father, brothers, sisters, and their families, I am so grateful and honored that we are family. To my beloved sons, Cletus, Lian, Yonah, Emet, and Uriel—you have no idea how much joy and inspiration you bring to me each and every day as your proud father. To my wife, Mindi Eve Cohen, I am eternally grateful for your ever-present unconditional love and support through all the chapters of our shared journey.

About the Author

D R. Paul Zeitz is a physician, epidemiologist, and tenacious, energetic, award-winning advocate for global justice and human rights. He has dedicated his career to catalyzing large-scale global impact. Dr. Zeitz is currently waging justice in the U.S. and globally to mobilize community-wide action to achieve the Sustainable Development Goals (SDGs) and Paris Agreement compliance by 2030. He serves as the co-founder of SDG Compacts and the Sustainable Development Games at the Global Development Incubator (GDI) and the U.S.A. Focal Point for Action for Sustainable Development, a global social movement. He has been happily married to Dr. Mindi Cohen for 27 years and they are the proud parents of Cletus, Lian, Yonah, Emet, and Uriel.